MW00791312

SHATTERING
THE TRUTH MIRAGE

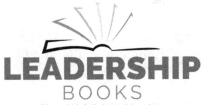

LEADERSHIP
BOOKS
Thoughtful, Relevant Leaders
From Around The World

The Truth Mirage Series:

- *The Truth Mirage*: An Introduction to Worldview for Biblical Christians

- *Shattering The Truth Mirage:* How to Share A Witness Across Worldview Barriers

- *Assaulting the Truth Mirage:* Incursion Apologetics - Apologetics on the Offense

- *Understanding the Truth Mirage:* A Worldview Encyclopedia of Religions, Cults, and Philosophies *(Coming soon)*

- *Dispersing the Truth Mirage:* An Explanation of a Biblical Worldview *(Coming soon)*

Shattering the Truth Mirage:
How To Share A Witness Across
Worldview Barriers

By

Freddy Davis and Tal Davis

Shattering the Truth Mirage
Copyright © 2023 Freddy Davis & Tal Davis

Publisher:
Leadership Books, Inc., Las Vegas, Nevada and
New York, New York

Printed in USA.
For Worldwide Distribution.

ISBN: 978-1-951648-11-4

Table of Contents

PREFACE

Who Are We To Be Writing This To You?

• • •

And Why Should You Be Reading It?

First of all, we found that producing the necessary breadth of perspective to adequately help you witness in today's societal environment, required the collaboration of the two of us. While either one of us could have written a book on witnessing that would have provided you with great value as a Christian, together we have created a resource that goes far beyond what either of us could have produced alone.

Probably like you, the importance of sharing our faith has been a personal conviction of ours since the time we became Christians … for us, from our teens. In our experience, we have, no doubt, run into most of the same obstacles to witnessing that you have. Our hope is that with the information in this book, your Christian witness can leap ahead based on our experience and study.

So, who are we? We are Freddy Davis and Tal Davis.

Even though we share the same last name, we are not related—at least in any family way that we have been able to determine. But we both did grow up in Tallahassee, Florida, and originally met at various Christian events during our high school years. We also attended the same university and seminary—at the same time.

Then, we both went to work for Christian missions organizations—Tal working for a domestic missions agency and Freddy for an international one.-And so today, we are associates in
MarketFaith Ministries, a Florida nonprofit ministry dedicated to the study of worldview and how its understanding is so important to the spread of the gospel in America.

http://www.marketfaith.org

Thus, we share both similar and different backgrounds, but our experiences are quite complementary. It is these complementary elements that have resulted in our collaboration in ministry and on this book, and that have blessed our working together.

This background allows us to provide you with information, knowledge, and the strategies and tactics about how to share the gospel message in a way that goes well beyond the traditional approaches—information that will provide you with the tools you will need to be a confident and effective witness for Christ in our increasingly pluralistic society. To begin, please allow us to introduce ourselves to you.

Freddy Davis:

I was raised in a very active evangelical Christian home that had me participating in church from before I can even remember. As such, I grew up immersed in the teachings of the Bible. When I was eight years old, my parents took me to a Billy Graham crusade. When the invitation was given at the end of that service, they encouraged me to "go down front and accept Christ." Being the obedient eight year old that I was, I did it. And, because of my church upbringing, when my church pastor talked with me about accepting Christ, I knew how to respond properly to him, too.

However, as it turned out, I really didn't know what I was doing. I was just following the encouragement of my parents and our church tradition. It wasn't until I was a young teenager that I had an actual encounter with Christ and came to know Him in a personal relationship. From that moment forward, my life changed.

Soon thereafter, I felt God's calling to enter vocational Christian ministry. So after finishing college, getting married, and completing seminary, I became a church pastor. Two years after that, my wife, Deborah, and I felt called to overseas missionary service. We served as missionaries in Japan for nearly twelve years, then, after the Iron Curtain collapsed, transferred to the former Soviet Republic of Latvia, serving there for five years. It was during my years as a missionary that worldview concepts became important for me.

I quickly found that aside from the language barrier, when there is a desire to share Christ with people who hold very different worldview beliefs, one can't just assume that the listener will understand the gospel message when you share it. It is necessary to somehow bridge the concept gap into their worldview before the gospel is even understandable to them. Serving in two different countries expanded my knowledge and experience in doing just that.

When we returned to the states, it did not take me long to discern that American society had radically changed while we were away. Whereas it had been dominated by Christian Theism during my growing up years, I soon recognized that a naturalistic worldview had taken over. I also recognized that most of the American Christians with whom I interacted didn't understand what was happening in our society, nor how to express the Christian message across the barrier created by this now-predominant worldview.

So, I started writing about the topic and began **MarketFaith Ministries**—a worldview discipleship ministry. Over the years, I have had the opportunity to share worldview knowledge with scores of people in dozens of churches and other Christian organizations in order to help them become more effective witnesses for Jesus Christ.
It is my deepest desire that the principles you learn in this book will put you in a position to acquire the skills and develop the confidence to share the message of Christ with anyone you know—even those who have entirely different worldview belief backgrounds.

ix

Tal Davis:

My background has some similarities to Freddy's but also differs in some respects. As a child, while I did not attend an evangelical-oriented church, I did get a basic knowledge of the Bible. When I got into my teen years, I was not sure of what I believed … or why. I knew my relationship with God was not good but had no understanding what to do about it.

In my junior year of high school, a close friend became involved in a campus Christian ministry. I immediately noticed some dramatic changes in his life. Over the course of about four months, he shared with me how he came to know Jesus personally, and how I could do so too. Finally, I realized that my relationship with God was based on grace through faith in Christ alone and I accepted Him as my Lord and Savior.

In the last part of high school and into college, I studied the Bible and learned how to share my faith in Christ using several methods. After college, I married Barbara (my wife of now almost fifty years) and-soon after that headed off to seminary. For ten years I served several churches, either in youth ministry or pastoral ministry. In 1988, I was called to work for a major denominational missions agency in the area of interfaith witness. For twenty-three years I traveled throughout the United States and various foreign nations to teach Christians how to recognize and evangelize people in non-Christian cults, sects, and world religions.

Since 2011, I have worked with my friend, Freddy, at **MarketFaith Ministries** to equip believers to share Christ with those holding non-theistic worldviews and non-Christian religious beliefs.

It is our hope that this book will aid you, our readers, to:

- ✓ understand the important differences in the various worldviews, and

- ✓ better prepare you to share the gospel with those who do not know a personal relationship with Jesus Christ.

- ➤ Thus, it is our desire that you may become equipped to share the living hope that is only found in Jesus Christ with the non-believers you encounter.

See www.marketfaith.org for more worldview resources.

INTRODUCTION

Why Read ... and How To Read This Book To Best Get Its Message

"Dr. Davis:

> We both know you god has been dead for around 2 thousand years. He was a con-artist of his day, along with his 12 friends. They took ideas from different religions of the day and turned it into a religion that would worship. Christianity is just another name for a dictatorship.
>
> jesus and his 12 friends were not only con-artist of the day, but were thieves, liars, murderers and rapist of small children. The christian religion was invented for the purpose to control people, judge people, find fault with people, get people in trouble with the law of the land, gossip about people, among other things, all in the name of a god.
>
> --Alfred"

Sounds pretty harsh, huh? Well, if you ever interact with non-Christians, in person or on social media (as in this example), you come across folks with a wide variety of attitudes. Many, like Alfred here, are bitterly antagonistic toward the Christian faith.

But make no mistake about it, people like Alfred are not in your face by random chance. God has brought them to you for you to share His gospel message with them. When you meet people like him, at the very least, you want to help them get past their bitterness and be able to share with them calmly how they can acquire peace and meaning in their lives.

Now obviously, most people are not as bitter and angry as Alfred. Nonetheless, as Christians, we need to be able to share hope in Christ with all people, no matter their disposition toward Christianity— positive, negative, indifferent, or unknowing. Of course, the objective is to help them understand why Jesus Christ is the only solution for their lives, and to invite them to receive Him as their personal Lord and Savior.

Sad to say, after engaging Alfred over about a two-week period, he did not, by that point, come to faith in Christ. What he did though, was receive a meaningful understanding of the gospel message. Not only were his wrong assertions about Christianity corrected, but we were also able to speak specifically to the pain and anger he was expressing. Alfred was left in a position to personally receive Christ if and when he would decide to do it.

As believers in Christ, we are commissioned by God to be messengers of the gospel. We are not responsible for the way people respond to the message, but we are commanded to communicate it in ways that are understandable so that those who don't know Christ can receive Him if they are willing.

This is not easy, especially when dealing with people who hold very different beliefs from Christians or are antagonistic to Christianity. In fact, in many ways it is more difficult now—right here at home—than at any time in American history. America used to be relatively homogeneous when it came to religious beliefs—with the Christian faith dominating the culture. Not so anymore, as MANY extremely diverse beliefs are now openly expressed in America's public square. In fact, the faith system now increasingly dominant in this country's public institutions is Secular Humanism—a belief system that is actually quite antagonistic to Christianity.

Obviously, no single individual can turn the cultural tide alone. Nonetheless, every believer, at the very least, ought to be able to clearly (i.e., accurately, effectively, and efficiently) communicate the basic gospel message of Jesus Christ. And this book will show you, in detail, how to accomplish that goal.

We, the authors of this book, have lived this out in our professional and personal lives—both in the United States and in other countries around the world where the Christian faith is relatively unknown. With more than 100 combined years of experience sharing the gospel message, even in settings where Christianity barely exists, we have taken this path because of a God-breathed passion to bring people to Christ, and to build up His church.

In many of these different settings, we have interacted not only with people holding different attitudes, but also with people coming from a wide variety of worldview and religious traditions. The expertise represented in the pages of this book about how to share Christ in America's increasingly pluralistic society is based on extensive study, as well as equally extensive experience across a wide range of worldview and belief system environments.

It is our contention that the key to dealing with such a wide variety of humanity's worldviews and religions in our diverse, twenty-first century society is found in learning and strategically employing the principles of worldview. It gives us the ability to both analyze and bridge the gaps between ours and these others. This paradigm not only makes understanding other beliefs very simple, but also provides a way to make the truth of the gospel message comprehensible to anyone.

Using the worldview principles in this book, you will learn to perceive and analyze the basic belief assumptions of those with whom you interact. Knowing these, you will be able to express the gospel message in ways that make sense to people in the contexts of their belief backgrounds. What this means, in simple terms, is that the principles explained in this book will equip you to share the gospel message effectively … with anyone you come across, no matter what their belief background may be.

Our conviction is that you can't approach sharing the gospel with someone who is an Atheist in the same way you would with someone claiming to be a Wiccan. You can't use the same method of gospel presentation to a Buddhist that you would with a Muslim. However, regardless of the non-believer's belief system, there is a way to engage that person with the gospel message that at least makes sense to them. The evangelistic strategy and tactics outlined in this book have been used to share Christ effectively with people from many different backgrounds. Let's face it, many, if not most, Christians don't share their faith with others at all. The reasons they don't share vary. Some just don't have a heart to do it. That is a spiritual problem that needs to be dealt with between the individual and God. For others, it is simply a matter of anxiety or lack of confidence in talking about faith matters—

especially with people from other religious backgrounds. That fear can be successfully overcome, and in this book we will show you how.

What you have in this volume is a step-by-step approach that will give you the knowledge, skills, and confidence to share the gospel with ANYONE!

If you learn these principles, you will gain the ability to be a faithful witness for Jesus Christ in ANY situation: your workplace, your college campus, your home, on mission trips, or wherever you meet people.

For a more systematic approach to learning and applying this material, we have also provided, in the back section of the book, a study guide that includes key questions and teaching notes. Using this study guide in a small group environment will enable you not only to learn the material as presented in the book, but also to get feedback from your peers that will expand your and their insights.

So, what are you waiting for?

- ✓ Read this book to see that today's world *actually can* hear and understand the gospel message from you, and

- ✓ Read this book to learn to unravel worldview differences, and

- ✓ Read this book to equip and prepare yourself to witness … to each lost person God brings to you in today's pluralistic religious environment.

The key to being a faithful and effective witness of the gospel message lies only pages away. You may never encounter someone as unfriendly to Christians as Alfred. But if you do, why not be equipped to respond to him, or anyone else, with loving, reasonable explanations for your faith in Christ—explanations they can understand, accept, and act upon?

Turn the page and start reading now, to take a bold first step towards accomplishing His goal for you.

Freddy Davis
Tal Davis

PREAMBLE

Expressing Your Faith in The New Societal Environment

A particular church identified an unreached people group in Senegal, West Africa, in order to share with them the gospel of Jesus Christ. The church began interacting with this tribe by sending over a group of volunteers whose goal was to communicate the gospel message to them for the first time. Before they went, these sincere individuals went through special training for the project. They studied the customs of the people, their religion, and, of course, how to share the gospel message. When they made their first journey, they used a translator to speak with individuals in the people group in order to explain the message of Christ. Later, when the church volunteers returned from their trip, they were given the opportunity to share their experience with the church.

At that point, these short-term missionaries were still very excited about what they had experienced. But when the church listened to them share, it was easy to detect a bit of confusion. One young woman in particular, we will call her Mary, illustrated this perplexity. She told about a special connection she made with a particular Senegalese young lady. The relationship led to a private conversation using a translator and gave Mary an opportunity to share her faith. Seemingly, this young Senegalese woman was interested in hearing what this missionary volunteer had to say, so Mary shared with her the Romans Road gospel presentation. But even though Mary shared the presentation just as she was trained, the young African woman had a difficult time grasping the meaning of the message. In sharing her experience with the church, Mary expressed a profound frustration that she was not able to communicate the gospel to her new friend in an understandable way.

Listening to her testimony, it was easy to tell why Mary's problem happened. This volunteer was explaining theological beliefs based on a theistic worldview to someone who was an Animist. These are two entirely different ways of understanding the actual structure of reality. Without first building a bridge across this very basic belief gap, mutual understanding is virtually impossible.

Missionaries who work in overseas environments have almost always had to use a more complex approach to sharing a Christian witness than has the average Christian in America. Throughout most of the history of our country, the vast majority of people believed in Christian Theism. This is not to say that everyone was a Christian, but the worldview foundation that American society was built upon was Christian Theism, and those who lived in America, at the very least, understood its concepts.

Thus, when Americans shared the gospel message with other Americans, they didn't have to take the differences between worldview beliefs into account. All they had to do was preach or explain the gospel content itself as taught in the Bible. Of course, not everyone who heard the message accepted it, but at least they understood it.

That, however, is virtually never the case in countries where societies are established upon entirely different worldview beliefs.

Now while American society used to be dominated by a biblical worldview, in contemporary times that has all changed. As recently as the 1960s, the vast majority of Americans still operated from a Christian worldview foundation. Even those who were not believers, or who were not active in church, for the most part, believed in the God of the Bible. That is just not the case anymore. Several significant historical factors account for the change.

First, over the past century or so, Naturalism has gradually surpassed Christian Theism in its dominance of virtually every part of American culture. Our educational institutions now have a naturalistic base, and every child going through that system is taught curriculum based on naturalistic worldview presuppositions. Obviously not all teachers are Naturalists. In fact, many are strong Christians. But the system itself oozes a naturalistic worldview, and the kids get it almost by osmosis.

- While students are not necessarily taught that God does not exist, they are taught "as if" God does not exist.

- Virtually no mention of God is allowed (lest "the system" be guilty of endorsing a specific religion), so Naturalism's atheistic beliefs have become the default faith environment.

- Naturalistic assumptions underlie what is taught in the natural sciences, social sciences, business, the arts, and virtually every other subject area.

Ironically, this is also true regarding the teaching of religion itself— even in many historically Christian universities and seminaries.

But not just America's educational institutions are affected. So is virtually every element of the culture:

- The entertainment industry is dominated by naturalistic beliefs. The rampant immorality and anti-God themes so prominently portrayed in the movies, on television, in music, and on the stage are simply artistic expressions of naturalistic assumptions.

- The news media is dominated by naturalistic beliefs. The liberal bias of the mainstream media has been well documented, and that secular mindset is based on naturalistic presuppositions.

- We also see naturalistic dominance in government, business, and even in many self-identified Christian churches.

Even modern communications networks, print media, social media, billboards and signage, unsolicited telephone calls, and broadcast text messaging are increasingly dominated by naturalistic influences.

But while Naturalism dominates these contemporary American cultural institutions and communications media, they are not the only competition to the Christian faith.

- Because of modern information and transportation technology, beliefs from all the other worldview systems have flooded into American culture over the last half-century or so, as well.

- Adding to that, massive numbers of immigrants continue to come into the country, bringing their worldviews and religions with them.

- As a result, many Americans have been brought up in or have converted to other religions, having been influenced through contact with adherents of these other beliefs.

Yes, it used to be much easier to share a Christian witness in America than it is now. And the reason is not that the message has changed. Rather, it is because the people to whom we must deliver the message come from more diverse worldview and religious backgrounds.

It used to be that one could simply read the Four Spiritual Laws booklet, explain the Romans Road from the book of Romans, or elucidate some other step-by-step witnessing presentation to a non-believer. The Four Spiritual Laws, for instance, starts out, "God LOVES you and offers a wonderful PLAN for your life." In the past when Americans heard that statement, they knew exactly what was meant. They understood that the message concerned the God of the Bible.

But now, things are very different. What if you read that statement to a Naturalist? They don't even believe God exists—and would stop you right there.

What if you read it to an Animist? They believe in many gods and/or spirits. They would ask you to explain which one you were talking about. What if you read it to a Far Eastern Thought believer? They don't believe in any kind of personal God. These words would make no sense to them at all.

What if you read it to a non-Christian Theist? They do believe in God, but in a different one than the Bible reveals. They would totally misunderstand or misinterpret what you were saying.

It used to be in America that to share the gospel message, we only needed to build one conceptual bridge—the gospel bridge—in order to tell an individual how they could invite Christ into their life. But now we need to build another bridge *first*—a more basic, worldview bridge—so that the gospel message will even make sense to them. When it comes to sharing the gospel in America today, every believer must now have skills that only missionaries to foreign lands used to need.

The purpose of this book is to equip you, your study group, or your church, with an understanding of today's complex witnessing environment, and provide you with the skills necessary to operate successfully within it. This will then allow you to share your faith with anyone you encounter, regardless of their worldview background. This is now necessary in order to shatter the many belief mirages that exist in the world.

In this book, you will learn to build both bridges—a worldview bridge and a gospel bridge. These will prepare you to:

- effectively shatter the untruths of false beliefs and
- deliver the gospel message in a way that people holding any worldview will understand.

Building these bridges upfront will allow a non-believer with whom you talk to make an informed decision on your gospel presentation.

This kind of knowledge is obviously valuable for those who plan missionary careers in places with different cultures or dominant religions—or even for those who participate in short term missionary opportunities.

But it is now just as critical for you—the average Christian in America—wanting to be an effective witness to their lost friends and other lost persons ... on the job, in school, or in the myriad of other places in our twenty-first century society.

We pray that this book will give you the tools you need to be a confident and faithful witness as you live your life for Christ in this lost and lonely world.

PART I

Introduction to Christian Witness

Most Christians believe that it is important to share their faith with people who don't know Christ. At the same time, there is a great deal of ignorance, confusion, reluctance, and even fear when it comes to this task. Because of this, it is prudent to begin by introducing some of the key concepts that we find in the Bible concerning evangelism. There are several important matters that we need to address as we look at the topic of Christian witness.

First of all, what is it? It helps to define our terms at the very beginning so that there will not be any confusion as to what, exactly, we are dealing with. We also need to understand what the Bible says about: why it is important, and who has the responsibility to do it—when, where, and with whom.

Since this book is about sharing a witness across worldview barriers, we also need to know something about the very concept of worldview: what is worldview, exactly, and why it is important that we understand its concepts and implications?

Finally, if we are going to take this task seriously, it is essential to prepare ourselves for the task: what exactly do we need to learn, and what skills do we need to master in order to become effective in sharing our faith?

CHAPTER 1

Starting with the Basics

"I object!" cried the defense lawyer. "The prosecution is badgering the witness!"

—or—

"I object! That question is not germane to the case."

If you ever watch a TV courtroom drama, you will doubtless hear these statements, or other similar ones. What you have is some person on the witness stand giving testimony about something, usually a crime he saw happen or has knowledge about, questioned by two lawyers—one wishing to establish the testimony as true, and the other trying to discredit it. As that happens, the judge must decide whether the lawyer's objections are proper ... or not. Obviously, the court's goal is to get to the truth, and the judge is the arbiter of the process in that environment.

But the judge is not the one who is responsible for expressing the truth to the court. He is merely a referee.

Neither is it the lawyers' job to share the truth. They are simply partisan representatives of one side of the dispute or the other.

Rather, the ones who are responsible for expressing the facts underlying the truth are the witnesses. They are the ones who have the information from which the truth may be uncovered.

What Is *Witness*?

The word *witness* is used widely in various settings, secular as well as religious. For instance, one common place it is used is in a courtroom, as we saw in the illustration above. But while that is a legitimate and important context for the word, it is not the only one. Our purpose here is to look at the word, specifically in a Christian context. We are particularly interested in how it applies to the responsibilities of our Christian faith and the activities related to living out our faith.

Witness: As a Noun and as a Verb

The Christian's use of the word witness is expressed in two different forms, or parts of speech, each with several meanings. For the purposes of this book, we need to understand both these forms and their meanings in order to get at how it plays out in our faith life.

---

wit·ness
noun
> 1. one who has personal knowledge of something
> 2. one who gives evidence

verb
> 1. to bear witness: testify
> 2. to bear witness to one's religious convictions (share a witness)

> —Merriam Webster

Witness in its Noun Form

The first form of this word is a noun: *i.e.*, the name of something we *are*. In this form, the word refers to a person, like the one in a courtroom, who has firsthand experience with, or knowledge of, a fact or event.

In our Christian context and our emphasis in this book, our focus is on the fact that since we know Christ, we have a personal relationship with Him. As a result, we have firsthand knowledge of what He has done in, with, and for us.

We have that knowledge because we have directly experienced how He generated change in us, and how that change is now expressed in the way we live our life. As witnesses of that change, we are in a position to *tell* and to *show* other people *what* has happened to us and *why* it happened … and to convey how they could have it, as well. Sharing both our personal experience of Him and His work in our lives makes us a witness in the noun form of this word.

This noun usage is from the Greek term, *martus*, which is found in many places in the New Testament. In most cases, it refers to those who give testimony to some fact or statement. In some instances, it can also refer to those who have given their lives for Christ as martyrs. (See Acts 1:8, 22:20; Revelation 2:13; and 17:6.)

So, how is this noun-form of witness used in Scripture?

In the first chapter of Acts, Luke records Jesus giving His final command to His disciples.

> But you will receive power when the Holy Spirit has
> come upon you; and you shall be My *witnesses* both
> in Jerusalem, and in all Judea and Samaria, and even
> to the remotest part of the earth. (*emphasis* added)
>
> —Acts 1:8

But perhaps the best-known passage that expresses the call of Jesus to be witnesses, or messengers of the Good News of the gospel to the world, is in Matthew's Gospel:

> And Jesus came up and spoke to them, saying, "All
> authority has been given to Me in heaven and on
> earth. Go therefore and make disciples of all the
> nations, baptizing them in the name of the Father and
> the Son and the Holy Spirit, teaching them to observe

5

> all that I commanded you; and lo, I am with you
> always, even to the end of the age."
>
> —Matthew 28:18-20

Again, as will become even more apparent as we address this further, the clear application of both passages above is that we, like the first century disciples, are responsible to *tell* the people of our generation about Jesus. WE are to be His witnesses throughout the world and to make disciples of "all nations." Of course, most of us will never have the kind of evangelistic ministry as did Billy Graham or other prominent evangelists in history. Nonetheless, every believer can and should *share* the message of Christ whenever possible with those who still need Him.

Witness in its Verb Form

The second form of this word is a verb: *i.e.*, it is something we *do*. When we witness, we are openly professing our Christian faith: by verbally sharing our firsthand account of something we personally saw, heard, or experienced, and by visibly living out its implications in our lives. So, when we: *tell* someone about our experience in this relationship or *show* them something about how this relationship leads us to act, we are then *witnessing* to what we know as a result of this relationship with Him.

Both the Acts and Matthew passages above point to the fact that a Christian witness involves both a passive (noun) and active (verb) element. In its passive (noun) sense, those who know Jesus Christ in a personal relationship are *witnesses* of what Christ is able to do to change a person's life. But in its active (verb) sense, we are called to *tell* the Good News of the gospel to others and to *show* it in how we live out our lives.

It is through our witnessing, both through *hearing* our testimony and *seeing* its message lived out in our lives, that people are able to understand and respond to God's calling in their lives.

And we can see very dramatically how this was expressed in the lives of the disciples after Jesus' ascension. In Luke's narrative found in Acts 2:14-41, the Apostle Peter preached the gospel message to the thousands gathered in Jerusalem for the feast of Pentecost. Luke reports that three thousand people came to know Christ when Peter gave this invitation:

> Repent, and each of you be baptized in the name of Jesus Christ for the forgiveness of your sins; and you will receive the gift of the Holy Spirit.
>
> —Acts 2:38

When you read that whole passage, and others in Luke's great history of the early church, *The Acts of the Apostles*, it is easy to visualize how Jesus' disciples' witnessing played out through the gripping drama of Luke's reports.

Based on these two word-form definitions of "witness," the noun form and the verb form, and the examples we see on display in the book of Acts, it becomes obvious that:

- a *person* who is a witness is actually nothing more than fulfilling the role of a messenger and

- when we witness, we are simply *telling* people what Christ has done in our lives based on our firsthand experience, and/or *showing* them how it looks lived out.

Witness: Event or Process?

The act of sharing a witness is something that most Christians recognize as an important part of their Christian faith. Even those who don't make sharing their witness a priority in their lives generally recognize that it is something they ought to do. And it is not like verbalizing our witness is something that is difficult to learn. In fact, many people over the years have developed methodologies to teach Christians how to share their faith. Most of these methods are good and effective, so all a person needs to do is pick one and learn it.

7

Witness as an Event

As we look at these various methods, we can actually see a lot of similarities between them. Virtually all of them encourage Christians to find a venue in which to share a gospel presentation, make the presentation, then go for the jugular to bring a person to a decision—all in one fell swoop.

This model has been used with great success by many dating back to biblical times. We see it with:

- Peter and the disciples before the crowd at Pentecost, (Acts 2:14-41)

- Paul with large audiences on his various missionary journeys, (Acts 17, *etc.*)

- Philip sharing one-on-one over his evangelism career, (Acts 8:4-7 and Acts 21:21-40)

We see it in in modern times, as well, with:

- vocational evangelists like Dwight Moody, Billy Graham, Luis Palau, and

- the many lay evangelists you know who share their faith with great effect, one-on-one.

When these methodologies are taught for individuals to use in one-on-one situations, it is quite common to teach students to share their faith using a *cold-call* approach. That is, an individual goes to someone's home or meets a person on the street, then engages that person in a conversation that leads to a witness opportunity. Many times, the people hearing the witness in these situations are total strangers. Other times they may be known to the witness, but there is no personal relationship that would make for a natural conversation about faith matters.

8

A cold-call approach to witnessing closely parallels the work of most salespeople in the secular world. The truth is, only a relatively small number of people truly have the personality and skills to be effective in cold-call sales. Those who are skilled in that arena tend to be quite at ease in that role, and they often make a lot of money. But most people are simply not skilled, comfortable, or effective, doing that kind of work.

This observation is not meant to denigrate street evangelism or other cold-call witnessing experiences. These kinds of opportunities do have their place. But in truth, for most Christians, that approach will likely be the exception rather than the rule. Frankly, as with salespeople, the number of believers called and spiritually gifted in the area of cold-call evangelism is also relatively small. And frankly, to force the majority of believers to use that method is to push them away from sharing their faith altogether.

To characterize this cold-call approach more fully, what we generally see is that the end of a witnessing presentation to a person also represents the end of any further opportunity to share with that person.

The reason for this is that the cold-call approach causes the witnessing experience to be seen as an event rather than a process. When seen this way, at the conclusion of the witness' gospel presentation, the listener typically either makes a decision to accept Christ or reject Him right there on the spot. Whatever that decision, there is usually no relationship foundation in place capable of taking the person further. When it is over, it is over.

Witness **Within a Relationship**

While certain situations call for an event approach, most witness opportunities, particularly in everyday life situations, should be conceived of as a process that occurs in the context of a relationship. Generally, we should think of witnessing as an expression of our life, rather than merely as an event in which to participate. Statistics show that, far and away, most people who ever come to know Christ do so by the influence of a friend or family member.

This approach is also commonly seen in the biblical text. In some cases, a person will bring a friend to someone else in order to express the gospel. In other cases, a person makes a friendship and uses that as a means for sharing the gospel. For instance:

- John 1:39-42 Andrew brought Peter to Jesus where he heard the message and decided to follow Jesus.

- Luke 16:31-33 In this instance, the jailer who was responsible for guarding Paul saw the work of God and Paul used the opportunity to share Christ. The jailer then brought in his family to hear the message and they, too, came to Christ.

- Acts 17:10-12, 16-34 In these verses, as Paul was engaging his missionary work, he was able to befriend people in Berea and in Athens who were willing to listen to his message. Over a period of time, within those sets of relationships, he was able to share the gospel of Christ, and some responded positively.

As we engage in relationships during the course of everyday life, some of the people with whom we interact are not yet Christians. In order to fulfill Christ's commission to share our faith, we must learn to cultivate those relationships. In that way, we first gain these people's trust, and then become able to share our faith with them in the normal flow of life.

It is in a trust relationship context where believers have an opportunity to engage non-believers over a period of time. This kind of situation gives a believer ample opportunity to encourage non-believers to consider a relationship with God. It also ends up being the more normal and natural way of sharing a witness under most circumstances.

To recap:

- Occasionally one's witness opportunity will be an event. Again, it is not that an event approach to sharing one's faith is bad or wrong. It is just that it is very limited.

- Generally, however, we should think of witnessing as an expression of our life, rather than merely as an event in which to participate.

As we engage in relationships through the course of everyday life, some of the people with whom we interact are not yet Christians. In order to fulfill Christ's commission to share our faith, we must learn to cultivate these relationships. In that way, we gain people's trust and are able to share our faith with them in the normal flow of life.

Dealing with Responsibility and Guilt

As we consider our witness, though, it is important to grasp the full scope of the witnessing process. If we don't see this big picture, particularly as it relates to responsibility and guilt, we could end up with some very serious personal problems.

Some people allow responsibility that doesn't belong to them to rest upon their shoulders. When a non-believer rejects Christ, it is that person's decision and responsibility, not the one who is doing the witnessing. We should never allow someone else's responsibility to weigh on us. That can only lead to driving oneself into the ground.

Neither should we feel personal guilt when someone with whom we share doesn't receive Christ. Of course, we will feel bad—but for them—not for our own actions. Every person is responsible for their own decisions, and we should never feel guilt about something that is not our responsibility.

11

The Biblical Mandate

When people hear the word evangelism, many immediately think of famous evangelists like Billy Graham who preached before large crowds, or TV preachers with worldwide audiences. Certainly, full-time evangelists (sometimes called vocational evangelists) have an important place in the evangelical community. Millions of Christians give credit to an evangelist for leading them to receive Christ.

In fact, however, this popular image of evangelists and evangelism is not fully what the New Testament writers had in mind. The English words *evangelism* (which does not appear in Scripture) and *evangelist* (which does) are derived from the Greek word *euaggelistés*, which literally means "a bearer of good news."

That word is found in three verses in the New Testament. Let's examine each one:

> So, He (Christ) gave some as … evangelists ….
> —Ephesians 4:11a

In this verse, a portion of his letter to the believers in Ephesus, Paul lists evangelists among those persons whom God had specially gifted to lead the church. He was apparently referring to evangelists as individuals who were exceptionally gifted at presenting the basic tenets of the Christian gospel to people who did not have a relationship with Christ, and equipping the believers in the church to share their own faith. Still today, certain spiritually gifted individuals preach to large audiences, and others simply share their faith one-on-one. Usually, these people have a great enthusiasm for sharing the gospel.

Nonetheless, we must be careful not to assume that *only* such specifically gifted persons can tell others the gospel message with this effect.

> But you, be sober in all things, endure hardship, do
> the work of an evangelist, fulfill your ministry.
> —2 Timothy 4:5

In this second passage, Paul is advising his protege Timothy, the pastor of the church in Ephesus. He had already given this young minister other sound advice about how to care for those he was leading in his church. Here Paul tells Timothy not only to endure the difficulties of his pastoral duties, but, along with those tasks, to "do the work of an evangelist."

Here is the third (and last) verse where *euaggelistés* is found:

> On the next day we left and came to Caesarea, and entering the house of Philip the evangelist, who was one of the seven, we stayed with him.
> —Acts 21:8

In this passage, Luke refers to Philip who was one of the seven Hellenistic Jews (*i.e.*, Greek or of Greek-heritage) selected by the Apostles to help take care of the Greek-speaking widows in the church in Jerusalem. Those widows were complaining that they were being insufficiently cared for in the church's administration of ministry compared to widows of Hebrew heritage. (Acts 6:1-5) It is noteworthy that Philip was not one of the disciples who Jesus called to follow him on His three-year ministry. He was simply an early believer in the church.

As an aside, it is also interesting to note that, like Philip, Stephen (another of those seven Hellenistic Jews) was not one of the Apostles, either. Nonetheless, he was among the most zealous *nonvocational* evangelists for the Lord in the early church. It even cost Stephen his life as the first Christian martyr. (Acts 7:54-8:1)

Shortly after Stephen was killed, many believers, including Philip, left Jerusalem. Thus Philip began his long evangelism career of several decades in Samaria. (Acts 8:4-7) Perhaps his most famous convert was the occupant of a passing chariot who was struggling with the meaning of a Scripture passage he was reading. By leading this man (a highly-placed Ethiopian government official) to Christ, he, perhaps, fostered Christianity throughout Ethiopia. (Acts 8:26-40) Luke, in the verse quoted above, remarks that later on, Philip was

13

still evangelizing in Caesarea and had earned the title: "the evangelist."

However, the implication here is that *every* believer is commissioned to share the gospel to those who don't know Christ and seek to win them to faith in Jesus.

Unfortunately, most Christians have never even once explained the gospel message to acquaintances, friends, or relatives who don't know Christ.

A Christian's Motivation To Witness

As we lamented above, most Christians, even those who have known Christ for many years, have never shared their faith with a single person in their entire life. We are not alone in our lament, by the way, as these articles attest:

- John Starke, in his Gospel Coalition article, *Why Don't I Evangelize*, (https://www.theGospelcoalition.org/article/why-dont-i-evangelize/) and

- Chuck Lawless, in his article, *Nine Reasons Christians Don't Evangelize* (https://archive.thomrainer.com/2015/11/nine-reasons-cont-evangelize/).

Why have so many never shared their faith? Consider these common reasons often expressed by believers:

- In some cases, although they might want to witness, they just don't know how to explain the gospel message to someone else.

- In other cases, those who would like to share their faith are afraid, or are too shy, to discuss something as personal as religion. They are afraid they might offend someone, become embarrassed should the person reject the message, or otherwise hurt the relationship by engaging in a potential argument (this is the same reason people often avoid discussions of politics).

- For the most part, however, followers of Christ are simply indifferent and apathetic about sharing the gospel. It is something they rarely, if ever, think about at all. They are so caught up in the day-to-day matters of life that they just do not concern themselves with it.

God's desire is to partner with believers in this process. Throughout the Bible, and through history in general, God has used human instruments to deliver His message. He has given us the privilege and responsibility to partner with Him to proclaim His Truth in each generation.

But why should Christians take on this responsibility? Let's consider some key reasons:

First, each Christian is commanded to share the gospel.

Remember what Jesus instructed the original eleven surviving disciples in the moments before His ascension? His words to them are as relevant today as they were in the first century.

> And Jesus came up and spoke to them, saying, "All authority has been given to Me in heaven and on earth. Go therefore and make disciples of all the nations, baptizing them in the name of the Father and the Son and the Holy Spirit, teaching them to observe all that I commanded you; and lo, I am with you always, even to the end of the age"
> —Matthew 28:18-20

Second, love and gratitude are powerful motivators for accomplishing a task. Because of what Christ has done in our lives, we should be powerfully motivated to express our love and gratitude to God by our obedience.

People often act to express their love and thanks to others. Wealthy professional athletes often buy homes for their parents who helped them get to where they are in life. Soldiers often willingly risk their lives because of their love for their country, some even diving onto a grenade to protect the rest of their squad. As for Christians, shouldn't love and gratitude to God be a powerful motivator to tell others about Jesus and how to receive salvation through Him?

Without reservation, the love believers have for their fellow human beings should prompt them to share their faith.

Christ died on our behalf in payment for our sins, that we could have eternal life with Him. So, we certainly should love others with the same fervor as God loves us. He told us to do it and He did it for us.

> There is no fear in love; but perfect love casts out fear because fear involves punishment, and the one who fears is not perfected in love. We love because He first loved us.
>
> —1 John 4:18-19

As followers of Jesus, we are promised a full and abundant life, both now and forever. (John 10:10b) Nonetheless, we need to understand the emptiness of peoples' lives without God. Though people who don't know Christ may appear happy, they ultimately have no goal in their lives which provides the kind of meaning and purpose that gives fulfillment for the soul. As the Apostle John wrote,

> And the testimony is this, that God has given us eternal life, and this life is in His Son. He who has the Son has the life; he who does not have the Son of God does not have the life.
>
> —1 John 5:11-12

However, the third, which is the most important and perhaps *most personally compelling,* reason Christians need to share Christ concerns the reality of eternity and the importance of choosing Him before death.

16

According to Jesus, everyone will live for eternity. (see Matthew 25:46) Their eternal destiny is the ultimate concern of God. The final judgment will determine their fate. In the book of Hebrews, we read,

> And inasmuch as it is appointed for men to die once and after this comes judgment.
> —Hebrews 9:27; see also Revelation 20:11-12

The Bible indicates that after death, there are two possible outcomes of this judgement for all persons:

➤ one, for those who have chosen to make Jesus their Savior before they die, and

➤ the other, for those who have not.

It is the finality of this choice—made consciously *before* their physical death—and the eternal consequences of that choice, that makes witnessing to non-believers so essential for the believer.

If Christians do not tell others how to receive Christ, then those who don't know Him do not have a clear understanding of the possible outcomes concerning where they will spend eternity.

The first option, above, relates to those who put their faith in Jesus Christ before they die. They will forever be in the presence of God in heaven. Jesus Himself promised that those who believe in Him will inherit eternal life. (John 3:14-16; 5:24 and 11:25-26)

And what will it be like?

The Apostle John saw a vision of the "New Jerusalem," reporting it in Revelation 21. The city will be more beautiful than we can imagine. He describes it as a bride adorned for her husband and shining like gemstones.

John also describes heaven as a wonderful garden. In Revelation 22, he states that in its midst is the Tree of Life, nourished by the River of Life.

Certainly, those who trust in Christ as Savior and Lord will enjoy eternity … with God … in heaven.

The second option, also above, relates to those who do *not* put their faith in Jesus Christ before they die. They will forever be separated from God.

Jesus described a place of eternal separation from God that we commonly call hell. For many people, even some calling themselves Bible-believing Christians, the idea of an eternal hell is difficult to accept. Nonetheless, those rejecting the gospel will be separated from God for eternity. (Matthew13:41-43; 25:41, 46)

So, what will hell be like?

From numerous Scriptures, we can discern clues as to its nature.

First, it as an experience of unending death. Physical death is a reality for everyone in this life. Nonetheless, the Bible describes a deeper spiritual death for unbelievers. In Romans 6:23, the apostle Paul states: "For the wages of sin is death." This is the "second death" referred to in Revelation 2:11 and 20:6, 14.

That death, however, does not constitute an ultimate state of either nothingness, some undefined spiritual dimension, reincarnation into a higher or lower material state, or of eternal, impersonal unconsciousness. Rather, it will be an eternal state of conscious punishment for those who have not repented from their sin and turned to Jesus during the time of their life on earth … before they die.

Second, in Matthew 25:30, Jesus also pictured hell as a place of darkness where "there will be weeping and gnashing of teeth." Matthew 22:13; 2 Peter 2:17; and Jude 13 provide even more descriptive detail.

Finally, the fate of those who die without Christ is described as a place of "unquenchable fire." This is generally the most difficult

18

depiction for many people to accept. Yet, we must look at what Jesus and Scripture say (*emphasis* added):

- Then He will also say to those on His left, "Depart from Me, accursed ones, into the *eternal fire* which has been prepared for the devil and his angels; ...."
  —Matthew 25:41

- "It is better for you to enter life with one eye, than to have two eyes and be cast into the *fiery hell*."
  —Matthew 18:9

- Jude 23 talks of showing love to "save others" by "snatching [them] from *the fire*."

- Hebrews 10:27 foreshadows "a terrifying expectation of judgment, and *the fury of a fire*."

- Revelation 21:8 reiterates the same saying, "... their part will be in *the lake that burns with fire and brimstone*, which is the second death."

To summarize the overriding points:

- ➤ Those who die in Christ will live forever in heaven with Jesus.

- ➤ Those who die without Christ will spend eternity apart from God, in a place of suffering called hell.

For these reasons, Christians must share Jesus with those who don't know Him. Because God loves them, we, His people, want *all* people to know the joy of eternal life, and not the tragedy of eternity without God.

So, we see that upon hearing the gospel, non-believers will know that they have a choice when faced with the eternal question and can make some level of informed choice ... right up until the moment they die.

Now then, from whom will they hear this Good News?

Who Are The Ones Involved In A Witness?

As we consider our witness, it is important to know who all of the players are and where they fit in the process. There is more than one player in the game. In fact, there are three, and each has their own role to play. Each one can only do his or her own part, and no one can do that of the others.

God's Part of the Process

Human beings are completely incapable of affecting one part of the witnessing process. We are not in a position to change another person's relationship with God. When a person invites Christ into his or her life, God performs a miracle that actually creates within that individual something that did not exist before. Only God can do that part and He does it based on a decision He made regarding His purpose for humankind.

When God created human beings, He performed a profound miracle by giving them not just life, but a unique kind of life ... "in His own image." Such life did not exist before He specifically breathed it into the physical bodies He created for it. God's creative activity regarding this matter is front and center in the first two chapters of Genesis:

> God created man in His own image, in the image of God He created him; male and female He created them.
> —Genesis 1:27

> Then the Lord God formed man of dust from the ground and breathed into his nostrils the breath of life; and man became a living being.
> —Genesis 2:7

This miracle of human life is marvelous enough in and of itself, but because of the Fall, the body that every human ends up in is a corrupted vessel. The human spirit (human nature) that is the essence of our personhood is permeated with sin—which inclines us to do acts in life that cause separation between ourselves and God.

> For all have sinned and fall short of the glory of God.
> —Romans 3:23

This is the reason we need the gospel message in the first place. God wants to fix the brokenness. But the fix cannot be made in the broken human nature we now possess. It requires a completely new nature.

So, when a person recognizes his or her separation from God, repents from sin, and asks forgiveness, God performs a second miracle. At that point, He creates a new nature in us—something that did not exist before—and literally makes us a new creature.

> Therefore, if anyone is in Christ, he is a new creature; the old things passed away; behold, new things have come.
> —2 Corinthians 5:17

Because of this new nature, we receive a new element in our lives that is not corrupted by sin. This provides a holy place within us where God can actually dwell. With that, He attaches Himself to our lives in a way that was not previously possible.

> Or do you not know that your body is a temple of the Holy Spirit who is in you, whom you have from God,
> —1 Corinthians 6:19a

In the process, He literally adopts us into His family. Before He created this new nature in us, we were only a creation of God. When we entered the personal relationship with Him by repentance and received His forgiveness, we became an actual child in His family.

> For you have not received a spirit of slavery leading to fear again, but you have received a spirit of adoption as sons by which we cry out, "*Abba*! Father!"
> —Romans 8:15

21

A Believer's Part in the Process

The actual change that takes place in a person's life at salvation can only be accomplished by God. But for some reason, He has chosen to use human beings as instruments in the process.

While believers are not the ones who *create* this change, we do have a significant role to play in God's plan. We are messengers who God has designated to deliver knowledge of His offer of salvation. While we don't know of any particular reason *why* God allows us to partner with Him this way, we do know that using believers as messengers is a part of His plan to reach the entirety of living humanity with the message, and to spread His glory throughout His creation more fully.

Christian witness is the primary means by which God confronts people. Of course, He is not limited to just one way of operating in people's lives. If human witnesses are not faithful in sharing the message, or if there are no Christians within physical proximity, God is not without options for confronting people with His presence. He is certainly able to challenge people *via* their consciences, by orchestrating circumstances, by His revelation through nature, or by means we cannot even begin to imagine. In fact, many people, even in extremely remote places where no Christians or churches are anywhere present, can, nonetheless, receive the clear gospel message. They can hear it on radio, see it on television, read it in books and tracts, or see it presented online in Christian websites they 'happen' to find. God is even able to reveal Himself, if it suits His purpose, through dreams or visions where another witness is not available.

That being said, God's primary tool is the witness of believers. He has commissioned Christians to take the message of the cross and proclaim it to a world separated from Him by their sin. His plan is to use believers to engage other people in a way that creates free and open relationships that allow for a witness.

The essence of God's purpose for His entire creation is centered around relationship. He created humankind for the purpose of

22

having a new class of beings capable of relating to Him personally and reflecting His glory. In creating this new being, He put in us the very personhood characteristics of Himself. An essential element of that is the ability to be self-aware and thus, have conscious, interactive relationships. This element makes it possible for human beings to be able to relate to God personally, and to other people this way, as well. This capability is the platform for our witness.

Of course, we must begin by doing our due diligence. That means we must gain an understanding of the worldview beliefs a non-believer may hold. Then we can learn how to share the gospel message effectively by creating a bridge across the gulf that separates us from people who hold different worldviews. We can't get away from that necessity. But the platform for our sharing is in the relationships we make. As we develop relationships with non-believers, we put ourselves in the best position to share the gospel message in a way easily understood and accepted by those who need to know Christ.

Earlier we noted that it is the responsibility of every believer to share the gospel with those who don't know Christ, and we offered some Bible verses that point to the importance of making that effort. We don't, though, want to take that necessity for granted, or just use proof texts to make this point. There are some bedrock biblical principles that give us a deeper understanding as to why this is so. Let's take a moment to look at some of them.

A Kingdom of Priests

In the Old Testament, God established a system of worship for the Israelites that was designed to help them understand who He was, the nature of sin, and the concept of salvation. The system He established also involved priests who would serve as go-betweens between the people and God.

The coming of Christ, with His death and resurrection, however, brought forth a change. God's intention from the very moment He created Adam and Eve was for humanity to live in a personal relationship with Him.

23

The death and resurrection of Christ provided the means for breaking the bond of sin that has enslaved mankind since the Fall. This opportunity to engage that relationship is available for all who willingly receive God's forgiveness by inviting Christ into their lives.

Then, after Christ returned to heaven, He sent the Holy Spirit to indwell the lives of those who take that step. No longer is a priest needed to intercede between God and man, as God Himself, in the form of the Holy Spirit, enters the very life of every individual believer.

The significance of this truth is seen in Matthew 27:51 at the moment of Jesus' death when the curtain in the temple was split in two. It dramatically symbolized that there was no longer a barrier between God and man, and that priests were no longer needed to mediate between God and man. (see also Mark 15:38; Luke 23:45)

We see a further reference to this when the apostle Peter spoke of the state of believers regarding their personal relationship with God.

> But you are A CHOSEN RACE, A royal PRIESTHOOD, A
> HOLY NATION, A PEOPLE FOR *God's* OWN POSSESSION,
> so that you may proclaim the excellencies of Him
> who has called you out of darkness into His
> marvelous light; ....
> —1 Peter 2:9

The important thing to note here is that there is not a special class of leader that has responsibility for accomplishing the work of God out in the world, while the rest of the believers simply allow those "called ones" to do the work of ministry. All believers are equal in their standing before God, and all are called to do the work of God out in the world. The New Testament knows nothing of varying levels of believers.

The Role of Church Leaders

If there are no priests to stand between God and man, then what does that say concerning the nature of religious leaders? Certainly, there are still leaders in the church, and these leaders are ordained by God to serve the church. In fact, we see where God has specifically called certain people to serve in leadership roles in the church.

However, it is important to recognize that these leaders are not priests, and do not hold authority over the other believers in a hierarchical way, mediate between man and God, nor do they supplant any believer from Christian ministry. All believers are called into Christian ministry. The difference is in the role individuals play as they live life in the world, not in the calling itself.

Perhaps one of the clearest Bible passages that deals with the role of church leaders is found in Paul's letter to the Ephesians. There we read:

> And He gave some as apostles, and some as prophets, and some as evangelists, and some as pastors and teachers, for the equipping of the saints for the work of service, to the building up of the body of Christ; until we all attain to the unity of the faith, and of the knowledge of the Son of God, to a mature man, to the measure of the stature which belongs to the fullness of Christ.
> —Ephesians 4:11-13

In verse 11, the apostle Paul mentions that God has given specially-called leaders to the church. Then in verse 12, he explains their primary job: ... to equip *the people* to do "the work of service"—not to do all the work themselves .... There is no hierarchy in the New Testament church when it comes to living out the Christian faith. All believers are priests, and all believers are tasked with performing the work of Christ (Christian ministry) out in the world.

The Place of Spiritual Gifts in the Church

Another important matter that fits into this discussion has to do with spiritual gifts. As a part of His personal interaction with individual believers, the Holy Spirit equips people for service by empowering them with spiritual gifts.

In Romans 12:3-8 and 1 Corinthians 12:1-27, the apostle uses the metaphor of a body to describe the church. Specifically, he says that there is one body with many parts, with Christ as the head (the One giving direction to the whole). The image is that each individual Christian serves as a body part to make the whole function properly. Thus, each person's role is different but special ... and necessary.

The spiritual gifts, however, don't correspond to only one specific kind of task. Rather, the gifts empower individuals to help them be effective as they serve God in the world, whatever their specific work might be.

As God's greatest purpose is to bring people into relationship with Himself, the use of spiritual gifts also facilitates this process. The Bible does not specify how particular gifts are to be used, only that they allow certain individuals to meet the needs of the church more powerfully as it fulfills God's purpose in the world.

The Recipient's Part of the Process

God has His part to play in the witnessing process and salvation cannot occur unless He creates a new nature within an individual. Believers also have their part to play as messengers who convey the message to those who do not yet know Christ. But there is a third party who must also participate. That third party is the person who is still separated from God.

When God created humankind, He created us in His image. That means we have the same personhood characteristics as God Himself. This is not to be mistaken for a belief that we are, ourselves, also gods. We are not! We do, though, have the essential personhood characteristics that God has. One of the key elements of God's personhood, and thus our own, is the ability to make free-will decisions.

When it comes to the subject of personal relationships, it is absolutely essential to understand this trait. For a relationship to be an objective reality—one that actually corresponds to the way reality exists—it must be entered into freely. A forced relationship is no relationship at all.

Because God is sovereign and all powerful, it would certainly have been possible for Him to make humankind as a creature with no choice. He could have forced Himself on us by making us love Him. If He had, though, we would not be persons, we would be some sort of robot. One can certainly enjoy operating a robot, but it is impossible to have a personal relationship with one.

Beyond that, if God had made humankind with no free-will, He could have enjoyed a certain kind of companionship with us—much like a person can enjoy companionship with a pet dog or cat. But something is missing in that kind of interaction. A pet cannot self-consciously love back. It can show affection but cannot express self-conscious love.

God created humankind with the ability to actually love Him by means of a personal, free-will decision—in the same way that He shows love to us. And it is only when that kind of love is expressed as a two-way relationship, that the purpose of God's creation of humankind is able to be fulfilled.

And this brings us back to the very purpose of the creation itself. God created the natural universe to provide a place for human persons to exist whom He could love and who could freely love Him back. This new creation was also a means by which the glory of God could be extended into an entirely new arena.

In all of this, there is one more thing that must be confronted. If humankind truly does have a free will, then it is also possible for an individual to make a decision *not* to enter into a relationship with God.

At this point, we come back to the topic of the recipient's responsibility. God has opened the door for a relationship, but *the person* must individually walk through it. The responsibility for this decision rests squarely on the shoulders of that person. When an individual makes a decision to enter into a relationship with God, He then performs the miracle of creating a new nature within and adopts that individual into His family. If the individual does not make that positive choice, it is their own decision. Either way, it carries significant, eternal consequences.

How These Players Fit Together

So, we have the three components of God's plan for the salvation of humankind. There is God's part, the believer's part, and the non-believer's part. We looked at the three parts individually. Now let's see how they all fit together.

Everything begins with God's purpose. The very existence of humankind had its origin in the mind of God. He didn't just randomly start creating things to see where it might lead. He started with a purpose.

The purpose in God's mind was to create a kind of being with whom He could have an intimate personal relationship. But in order for these beings to exist, there had to be a place for them to live.

The Bible does not share why God created humankind to exist in the kind of physical body that we have. But in His own purposes, He decided that the makeup of this creature would be physical. Consequently, a physical environment was also required.

So, God created a physical universe that is finely tuned with the capacity to support life. He then created the earth as the specific place in the physical universe where a mortal creature could exist. Following that, He created human beings who were capable of a relationship with Himself.

At first, there were no problems. The entire material order was created without sin, and God enjoyed an unhindered relationship with Adam and Eve on earth.

But one day, they were tempted by Satan to sin, and they fell for the ruse. At that point, sin entered the created order in a way that permeated the entire creation. The nature of humankind was also breached, and humanity became unworthy to stand in the presence of God. The relationship was broken.

But God was determined not to be defeated by Satan and instituted a process that would lead to the redemption of His created order. For the redemption to take place, the penalty for sin had to be paid—and the penalty was death.

The death penalty should be paid justly by those who commit the sin. And indeed, God's plan specifically follows that principle. But He also provided a means whereby the penalty could be paid by someone else. That person, however, had to be someone who was not tainted by sin. Since no mortal human could qualify, God took it upon Himself. He took the form of a human being, the man Jesus Christ, and lived a sinless life on earth in order to qualify as the sacrifice for sin. He then paid the penalty for sin by His death on the cross. The resurrection of Christ from the dead was the confirmation that the power of God was supreme over sin and death.

While the death and resurrection of Christ is sufficient to accomplish the salvation of all human beings, God does not impose it on anyone. He offers it freely, but each individual must personally decide to receive it. At this point, we come face to face with the responsibility of the recipient. Every person who decides to ask God for forgiveness, and who gives his or her life to Him, is given the new nature and adopted into God's family.

But He did not leave it there. In order to spread the word about His offer of salvation, God commissioned believers to partner with Him to tell the story. As members of God's family, we are given the privilege of working together with Him to accomplish the purpose of bringing humankind into relationship with Himself. With this, all three parts of the puzzle come together to fulfill God's plan.

CHAPTER 2
Why a Knowledge of Worldview is Important for Witness

Robert Bolt's award-winning play and movie, *A Man for All Seasons*, tells the story of Sir Thomas More who, from 1478 to 1535, was the Chancellor of England. More, however, was charged with treason because he would not sign a document validating King Henry VIII's divorce and remarriage. He refused to sign because he saw it as a violation of his Roman Catholic conscience.

In his script of More's trial, Bolt uses a clever rhetorical illustration of how people's assumptions can be wrong. More asks the court to consider whether the earth is flat or round, a question still being debated in the sixteenth century. Assuming, he argued, that the earth is indeed flat, does it become round just because the King says it is round, and everyone believes it? Or, if it is indeed round but the King and everyone says it is flat, will that make it flat?

Virtually no one today would argue the "flat earth—round earth" issue, but the principle remains. Many people today still make assumptions about the truth or falsity of various ideas they hold without ever even examining them—simply because it is what they have been told or taught and have never had their beliefs challenged. These never-examined assumptions are the very essence of the nature of worldview beliefs.

What Is Worldview?

As we begin to explore the entanglement of witness and worldview, it would be prudent to take a moment to explain what we mean by the term worldview. We need to do this because we must know what we are dealing with before we can ever expect to grasp the implications of worldview in the witnessing process.

It is vital to recognize that until a few generations ago, this kind of knowledge was not an essential consideration in the witnessing process for most Americans. Since the vast majority of people in America operated from the same worldview foundation, a worldview bridge did not need to be built to communicate the gospel in a way that would make it understandable to the hearer. It was possible to go directly to a presentation of the gospel message itself.

That simply is *not* the case anymore. In modern society, in order to share the Good News effectively and in an understandable way, we need to also be able to deal with people's worldview foundation.

Everyone in the world—without exception—has a set of beliefs that form the foundation of everything they think and do. While most Christians probably assume that their foundational set of beliefs consists of their Christian faith, this is not actually the case. In dealing with worldview beliefs, we are engaging a set of beliefs so basic that even the Christian faith does not make sense without them.

A Worldview is a Set of Assumptions

Thus, it is fair to say that most people cannot articulate their worldview beliefs even if directly asked to do so. Nonetheless, they hold these worldview beliefs anyway. Everyone lives by a set of assumptions they hold about the nature of reality. And it is an understanding of that concept that points us to our definition of worldview:

> *A worldview is the set of assumptions*
> *people hold about the nature of reality.*

32

Or put another way, everyone has a set of beliefs about how reality is structured, and everyone lives as if those beliefs are true—whether they are true or not, and whether the individual is consciously aware of them or not.

At first glance, this definition may seem a bit philosophical, even esoteric. And perhaps, in some ways, it is. But the implications of the truth in this definition are actually quite clear and practical. In fact, nothing is more practical in a person's life than coming to an understanding of their worldview beliefs.

A Worldview is Exclusive

As we deal with this issue, we quickly bump up against a difficult problem. There are several worldview possibilities, and every one of them contradicts every other one at some essential point. That being the case, all of them cannot be true. In fact, it is only possible for one worldview, among all possibilities, to be true.

There is only one way that reality is actually structured, and the beliefs that match up with that way are the only ones that correspond to that structure.

> "It is what it is.
> And it can only be
> described truthfully
> … as what it is."

So, what are the implications of this fact?

This means that the beliefs most people in the world hold at a worldview level are *not* true. There is no single worldview position to which a majority of the world's populations, people groups, or nations presently adhere. What we end up with, then, is a situation in which the majority of people in the world live life *as if* reality is structured in the way they believe, even though it is not.

This is important because their worldview affects how they interact with every part of life (*e.g.,* possessions, relationships, personal attitudes, government, morality … really *every* part of life). Beyond that, it affects how they interact with the supernatural world (*i.e.,* what they believe about God, heaven, hell, *etc.*) … or even whether or not they believe a supernatural component of reality even exists. In fact, there are even some people who believe that the natural component itself is illusory.

Looking at it this way, we can appreciate how our worldview beliefs affect our own life, and why it is important in our witness to understand where non-believers' ideas originate. In some ways this may seem strange, because the way everyone evaluates the structure of reality seems so obvious to them … no matter what worldview they hold!

But remember, worldview beliefs are assumptions. In fact, the structure of reality itself is not something that can be fully analyzed in a laboratory. While we can do scientific experiments on some things that relate to the operation of the natural universe, no person can go into a lab and perform experiments to prove scientifically that what they believe at a worldview level is true. We can experience parts of life in the physical world by empirical means, but other parts have to be discerned by faith, such as:

- Is there a God, or not?

- Is there a spiritual realm, or not?

- Does sin exist, or not?

A Deeper Look at the Definition of Worldview

While the topic of worldview may seem a bit daunting at first glance, it is not nearly as difficult as it might appear. Let's take a moment to break down the definition and focus on certain key words in order to grasp their significance.

What is an *Assumption*?

The first concept we need to look at in the definition of worldview is the word *assumption*.

A worldview is a set of *assumptions* about the nature of reality—and an *assumption* is nothing more than a belief that seems so obvious to a person that it is unimaginable that other people could see things differently. For instance,

- for a Christian, it is hard to imagine that some people don't believe that God exists (even when they say they don't), but

- for a Naturalist, it is hard to fathom that Christians actually believe in the "superstition" that God does exist.

Based on their worldview foundation, people hold beliefs that, to them, seem so obvious that they never even consider the possibility that they might not be true.

What is *Nature of Reality*?

The second concept we need to understand in the definition is the phrase: *Nature of Reality*.

When we think of how all of existence is structured, we delve into the realm of the "nature of reality." The entirety of reality is structured in some actual way and is not structured in any other way.

"It is what it is. ..."

For example, either there is a supernatural world or there is not. God either exists or He does not. It is certainly possible to imagine some non-actual ways in which reality might be structured. In fact, fantasy and science fiction writers do it all the time. But no matter how creatively it might be described, it does not change the way things *actually* are. This actual structure of the way things exist is what we call reality.

35

"... And it can only be
described truthfully
... as what it is."

We can also refer to it as Truth (with a capital T). Truth, in its most fundamental form, relates to the set of beliefs that line up with how reality is actually structured.

The Full Scope of *Worldview*

Now that we have looked at the pieces, let's put it all together and see if we can grasp the full scope of the definition:

Worldview is a faith position (a set of *assumptions*) that is the organizing principle for an individual's understanding of how reality is structured and how it operates (the *nature of reality*). It is how individuals distinguish (in all things) between:

- what they consider to be real and

- what they consider to be fantasy.

The possibility that the set of worldview beliefs which someone holds may or may not correspond to the way reality is *actually* structured is quite beside the point. The fact is, human beings are fully capable of living their lives, from birth to death, based on an understanding of reality that is not true. In fact, billions of people all over the world do just that.

And since we cannot physically sense (*i.e.,* see, feel, hear, taste, and/or smell) or measure (*i.e., quantify* what we see, feel, hear, taste, and/or smell) the structure of reality itself, we are left to gather various other kinds of evidence to support our position. However, we have no choice but to select a position and to live by it (though most people don't actually select theirs, they just grow up in it).

36

Why An Understanding Of Worldview Is Important For Witness

This brings us to the question: Why do we need to grapple with worldview concepts as we address the topic of our witness?

First of all, as Christians, we believe that there is a real, personal God who created and sustains the material world, and who has revealed Himself in the Bible. A lot of circumstantial and forensic evidence supports our claim, but we can bring no empirical *proof* to the table to scientifically demonstrate our belief to be true.

Of course, everyone else in the world is in the same boat. Some believe there is no God, or there are many gods, or the cosmos consists of an impersonal, immaterial life force, or in a god that is different from the one revealed in the Bible. These are some of the faith positions that are widely held by people throughout the world.

Furthermore, as Christians, we believe that what is revealed in the Bible represents actual reality. Anyone who believes something different lives by a set of faith assumptions and holds a worldview that comes from a different source.

But to shoulder our evangelism responsibilities in a way that allows us to witness across the chasms that exist between our worldview and each of the others, we need to know:

- *why* our worldview's faith position is the truth and others are not, and

- *how* to share our faith with people who hold other worldview assumptions.

We can only do this if we grasp the full implications of the concept of worldview.

Let's consider a couple of analogies to help us understand the nature of worldview beliefs.

A Worldview is a Belief Foundation

In our first analogy, we will compare a person's worldview to the foundation of a building. Before the superstructure of a building is ever put up, its supporting foundation has to be laid. There are two critical parts of this foundation:

- The first is its *shape*. When a foundation is laid, it defines the possible outer limits of the building. One can make the building smaller than the foundation but cannot build outside of it.

- The second is its *strength*. The superstructure can be made lighter than what the foundation can support, but not heavier.

So, when using this analogy to describe a worldview system, we can see how the comparison works.

- First, worldview beliefs define the *shape* of the belief system. Beliefs that exist outside of its boundaries belong to some other system, *not* to the one defined by this worldview's specific belief system structure.

- Second, worldview beliefs define the *strength* of the belief system. The worldview beliefs must be strong enough to support the beliefs that are claimed by the system. There cannot be internal contradictions, historical untruths, or logical weaknesses. If it is incoherent at any of these points, the belief system cannot stand, because it does not describe actual human experience.

A Worldview is a Belief Lens

In our second analogy, we will compare worldview beliefs to eyeglasses.

As an example, living life based upon a non-true worldview is much like looking through a pair of glasses with red lenses. A red lens alters what we see through the glasses. It does this by distorting what we see in a way that does not represent the full spectrum of visible colors that actually exist in the world.

Imagine, however, that you have only looked through red lenses all of your life. In that situation, everything would look 'normal' to you because that perspective would be all you had ever known.

If, at some point, you exchanged your red lenses with clear, uncolored ones, at first it would not look normal—even though you would be seeing the *full* color spectrum that actually exists. It is only when you come to the realization that the uncolored lenses allow you to see actual reality, that you are able to fully appreciate what you are seeing. Until then, you would simply live life *as if* the red-tinted glasses accurately portrayed reality and continue to believe that the clear ones skew it.

So, to apply this concept to beliefs about the structure of reality, we could say that a person's worldview is a set of faith lenses. People look through their worldview beliefs to understand what is real and what is fantasy.

If their worldview beliefs do not represent actual reality, they won't even know it, and will live their lives *as if* their beliefs are true— even though they are not. Holding untrue beliefs will certainly skew many things for people as they live in the real world, but they will simply not be aware of the inconsistent consequences of their false beliefs. It is possible for people to live their entire lives looking through a false set of beliefs and nonetheless believe their faith is the Truth. But that doesn't alter the fact that it is not.

Where A Worldview Comes From

If a worldview is a set of assumptions, these assumptions must come from somewhere. So just how do people come to a place in life where they personally affirm a particular set of beliefs?

39

From Circumstances

Initially, a person's worldview beliefs emerge from the environment in which they were raised. As children are growing up, they don't have either the perspective or the skills to analyze the things they are learning. They simply live in a household and accept, at face value, the things they learn from people they trust. A person's first beliefs are merely accepted based on the direct and indirect influences of the significant people in, and the experiences of, their lives.

In fact, as a child, individuals do not even realize that there are other perspectives than those with which they grew up. And for many, this perception carries on throughout their entire lifetimes. Even though there are multiple worldview possibilities, unless a person is somehow brought to a conscious awareness of other beliefs, or they make a deliberate effort to discover them, all they will ever know are those they were exposed to when they were young.

From Confrontation

It is not unusual, though, for individuals to be confronted, at some point in life, with a different set of worldview beliefs. Since these different beliefs literally contradict their own beliefs at the most fundamental level, for some people, this can create a belief crisis. It is sort of like when an older child realizes there is no Santa Claus.

This brings us to a second possible source for worldview beliefs—a collision of worldviews. Sometimes when a person confronts a new worldview, it creates an internal conflict that causes him or her to deeply question previous beliefs.

If this crisis is compelling enough, it is quite possible that the individual would even change over to a different set of beliefs. Typically, when this happens, it results in a very dramatic and emotional experience. This often is the case when a person converts from some other belief to faith in Christ. It is also what happens when a person converts from Christianity to some other belief.

From Choice

There is a third way that a person can come to own a worldview belief system—by choice. Upon discovering the fact that different worldviews exist, it is possible for individuals to study the different worldview possibilities, then choose the one that seems to correspond most closely to the way they perceive reality. This is one of the main reasons we should make the effort to understand the concept of worldview. This not only helps us better understand our own faith, but also the default beliefs of those with whom we wish to share our Christian witness. The point is, if we are going to ask people to switch worldviews, we need to know what we are asking them to do.

It might be noted that this third way tends to be the least used because most people never become consciously aware of their own worldview system, let alone worldview systems other than their own. If one is not aware of the various possibilities, and doesn't develop the ability to compare the options, they are not even aware that a choice is possible.

What Makes Witnessing So Difficult?

Having alluded to the difficulty of changing from one set of worldview beliefs to another, let's look a bit more deeply at why changing them is so difficult. This will not only help us be more compassionate toward the people to whom we wish to witness, but more patient with them as they consider the message, as well.

We need to recognize that both the decision to change and its implementation are a combined mental, physical, emotional, and spiritual experience. When a person makes a change, all four of these factors need to be addressed. This is actually true for any serious change we try to make in our lives, not just those related to our religious beliefs.

The Mental Dimension of Change

To begin, we must recognize the mental dimension of change. Every change is based on a new understanding of something. Without this new understanding, a person can't even know what they ought to change, much less how to implement it.

In our witness, we need to make sure that the person we are witnessing to fully understands what we are asking them to change. Depending on the individual's starting point, this could be a very easy or a very difficult matter. If the person grew up in a Christian environment, or even in some other kind of theistic belief system, the Christian faith may not be so difficult to grasp. If they grew up in some other worldview environment, however, the Christian message may seem very strange indeed—and it may take them some time to even understand the message we are presenting. Remember, we are asking them to change their view about what is real and what is fantasy—a belief that they have held so deeply, that it was held and acted upon unconsciously.

The Physical Dimension of Change

Second, change has a physical component. As humans, we are essentially spiritual beings, but we are housed in a physical body. Our bodies are subject to physical laws—some of which are operative within our bodies themselves. When we make a change, there are new neural patterns in our brains that must be formed, and sometimes a life change requires new physical habits that even affect our muscular and other bodily systems. Anyone who has ever tried to start a new exercise routine knows how difficult this physical change can be. If someone wants to receive Christ, we may have to be patient with them as they struggle to create new habits in their lives. Many times, the new habits of a Christian life may conflict with the habits of their old life.

The Emotional Dimension of Change

Change also has an emotional component. Human beings become emotionally attached to the status quo. Some of the emotional elements also have physiological (as with drug addiction), or social elements (as with peer pressure or family patterns), as well. Change may require giving up something to which the person may have an emotional attachment. Christ calls believers to holiness. But people who have been enjoying an unholy life may find themselves having difficulty abandoning certain activities, or certain interactions with particular non-believer friends or relatives. We must be ready to help people work through this emotional stress.

The Spiritual Dimension of Change

Change also has a spiritual dimension. When it comes to making changes in order to follow Christ, you can be sure that Satan is doing all he can to attack the person spiritually to keep that change from happening. When we share a witness, we must be prepared to help the person face a spiritual attack like they have never experienced before.

Worldview Change is a Struggle

A person's worldview is a powerful set of beliefs. It is the foundation of their very identity. When we tamper with people's worldview, we knock the legs out from under their very understanding of reality. This is quite profound and can be tremendously unsettling. When we ask people to give up their foundation and accept a new one in Christ, we are asking them to change the entirety of their life's orientation. Virtually no one makes that kind of change without significant inner wrestling. If we want to be effective witnesses, we need to know what other people believe and how to craft the message of Christ in a way that makes sense to them.

Simply put, every part of the change process is a struggle. So, when we ask a person to receive Christ, we are asking them to make a massive change—in their thinking and their lifestyle. In fact, we are asking them to actually change their very persona, their very identity ... both private and public. People don't give up the old, familiar ways very easily. Thus, as a witness, we need to be prepared to be patient and helpful to those who are considering that decision.

The Importance Of Worldview In Witness

The reason we Christians share a witness is because God has commissioned us to do it—nothing more and nothing less. As we developed above, we are admonished in the Great Commission:

> And Jesus came up and spoke to them, saying, "All authority has been given to Me in heaven and on earth. Go therefore and make disciples of all the nations, baptizing them in the name of the Father and the Son and the Holy Spirit, teaching them to observe all that I commanded you; and lo, I am with you always, even to the end of the age."
> —Matthew 28:18-20

When God gave us this commission, He did it for a reason. He did it because it lines up with His purpose for creating humanity. He created us for relationship with Himself, and as a means of spreading His glory throughout the entirety of His creation.

But in the current state of existence, humanity is separated from Him due to the fact that we have a fallen nature because of sin. However, in His great desire to bring all of humanity back into relationship with Himself, God has called on Christians to partner with Him to show non-believers *how* they can be reconciled to Him. This calling to share our faith is what witnessing is all about. Of course, as we engage this process, there will be obstacles.

One difficulty many Christians have is a fear of sharing the gospel message with people unfamiliar to them. Fear is most often due to a lack of knowledge. Typically, we don't fear sharing things about which we are confident. So, by effectively equipping ourselves regarding the elements of witness, we eliminate both the fear *and* the lack of knowledge.

Another reason some Christians struggle is because they have made certain personal lifestyle choices that cause them to feel inadequate or hypocritical.

But none of these obstacles are valid excuses for putting aside God's stated will for our lives. Rather, we must strive to overcome whatever difficulties we face in order to be faithful to God's calling on our lives. As with any issue, being obedient to God's calling is simply a matter of making a decision to put aside sin and to live in fellowship with Him.

So, yes, we need to witness. But why does using worldview concepts in the process matter?

Reasons for Using a Worldview Paradigm

There are actually several reasons why using a worldview approach to sharing our faith is good. Let's take a moment and look at some of them.

Reason #1. It Helps Us Understand Faith

One of the most important points to understand about the topic of worldview is that *every* worldview is built on a faith foundation. This can be a critical matter when it comes to the opportunity for witness.

---

faith (*noun*)
1. complete trust or confidence in someone or something.
2. strong belief in God or in the doctrines of a religion, based on spiritual apprehension rather than proof.
  —Oxford Languages

Now **faith is** the assurance of things hoped for, the conviction of things not seen. —Hebrews 11:1

Some worldview belief systems acknowledge this faith foundation up front. In fact, this is actually one of the central elements in our own Christian faith. Christians acknowledge that individuals must receive Christ by faith. This does not, of course, mean there is no evidence for our belief. In fact, substantial evidence supports the Christian faith. It is just that there is no scientific proof that can be brought forth to satisfy a totally empirical inquiry.

Honestly though, most non-Christians don't ever consider the faith aspect of their beliefs. In fact, most never even think about that at all. For the great majority of people, if their belief seems reasonable to them on a surface level, they simply accept it without even considering where it came from. At this point, though, it is good to go back and consider our definition of a worldview. We noted that a worldview is a set of assumptions—it is a faith position. Still, most people never even consider the possibility of challenging the assumptions they follow. They simply believe them, and that is good enough.

Some people, though, honestly believe that their worldview dogma is solidly based on an empirical foundation. This is particularly true for those who adhere to a naturalistic worldview. After all, for them, the natural universe is all that exists. They assume that everything, without exception, can be analyzed and explained through experiment and observation—if only the technology is available and given enough time. Nonetheless, there are no empirical answers to the questions that define a person's worldview beliefs—regardless of their foundation. Naturalism is as solidly a faith-based point of view as any other worldview system.

With this principle in mind, one of the first things we need to do as we enter a witness opportunity is to establish that a person's worldview rests on a faith foundation, and to identify that foundation. Only by doing that are we in a position to accurately address the validity of their faith. The purpose for doing this is not to be vindictive. It is certainly possible to win the battle and lose the war. That is the last thing we would ever want to do. Our purpose is to introduce them to Christ. But we must establish the faith nature of their worldview's conceptual language before we can speak to the validity of their beliefs.

Another thing that is important to keep in mind is that most people who are anti-Christian are very practiced at throwing in our face what they consider to be inconsistencies within our faith. Sometimes, people attack us by questioning the validity of our faith using various arguments. When they do this, it is important to get on an equal footing with them. By understanding the faith foundation of other worldview positions, we are able to bring questions into the minds of these unbelievers about the validity of *their* faith. This, then, begins to pry an opening for slipping in our message to them.

Reason #2. It Helps Us *See* the Objective Truth of the Gospel

The fact that a biblical worldview is based on a faith foundation does not alter the fact that it represents actual (or objective) reality. Just because our belief system is not based purely on empirical data does not mean it is false.

The truth of the matter is, some worldview position *does* represent the way reality is actually structured, and whatever way that turns out to be, it is a faith position. It cannot be otherwise since no worldview can be verified using purely empirical means. That leaves us with the task of trying to discover what belief system does represent objective Truth using logic and human experience along with the empirical evidence. As we carefully examine the Christian faith, the evidence strongly demonstrates that it truly is the objective truth about how reality exists.

Reason #3. It Gives Us *Confidence* in the Truth of the Gospel

At this point, we come to one of the most important aspects of how worldview beliefs fit into the witnessing process. In a word, knowing that our belief is the truth about reality gives us confidence to share our faith with others.

If we, indeed, are willing to affirm that our faith is the truth, why, then, are such a large percentage of Christians not willing to share their faith?

There are two critical reasons:

1. Most Christians do not have a working knowledge of the gospel message itself. If one doesn't know the content of the message, how is it possible to share it? Simply put, it can't be done. Teaching Christians the essential elements of the gospel message along with the worldview paradigm gives believers the knowledge they need to tell the message with confidence.

2. Another reason Christians tend to be unwilling to share their faith is that they are not completely sure that they can answer the objections of people who might oppose them. This problem is also easily overcome. When we know that what we are sharing is the objective truth about reality, and *why* it is the truth, we no longer fear arguments people might throw our way. Using a worldview paradigm in our witness training gives us this knowledge, as well.

No one wants to be in a vulnerable position when it comes to faith matters, and certainly not when it comes to expressing them to others. If we don't know the content of the message or we don't understand why our faith is the truth and others are not, it is only natural that we would avoid discussing the topic. But if we take our study of worldview beliefs seriously, we will have all of the knowledge necessary to stand up to any attack and prevail in any situation.

This kind of confidence is especially important in a couple of settings:

- Perhaps the most difficult witnessing situation is when we engage people who are hostile to our faith. Not only do they come at us with an unwillingness to listen and a bad attitude, but they also tend to be the ones who hit us with the questions

48

most difficult to answer. But when we truly understand worldview beliefs, we are not only able to deflect their attacks, we can even go on the offensive.

- Our need for confidence is not limited to those who are hostile, however. We need it even when we engage those who are quite interested in our message. Many of the honest questions people might ask can cause us great insecurity if we are not able to answer them. Often people are truly searching for the answers about the problem of evil, the question of suffering, the seeming injustice in the world, and so on. Understanding worldview concepts gives us a means for dealing with these questions, as well.

Once we have true confidence in our faith, there is no situation that will make us uncomfortable. At that point, we are capable of sharing a witness, come what may.

Reason #4. It Provides an Understanding of the Beliefs of Others

We have dealt extensively with the importance of understanding the worldview paradigm. It helps us see, concretely, the contrast between the truth and all of the false belief systems we encounter. We need this understanding for our own confidence, but it also gives us a powerful tool for explaining that truth to others. If we can show people *why* their worldview beliefs are not true (*i.e.*, they do not adequately or accurately explain actual reality), they are more likely to respond positively to our gospel presentation. This does not necessarily mean they will accept the Lord, but it may create an opening through which His Spirit can move.

The reason worldview understanding is so important for witnessing is because to be effective in sharing our faith, we must present the gospel in a way that makes sense to the one hearing our presentation.

For example, suppose you want to share a witness with someone who claims to be Wiccan. We know that this is a form of Animism, and that Animists do not recognize the Bible's concept of God as a supernatural, individual person. Animism is the belief that there are many gods or spirits that are manifested in nature. They believe that the material world and spirit world interact with each other in a symbiotic relationship, and by using the proper incantations, offering sacrifices, and performing rituals, humans can manipulate the power of these gods or spirits to their benefit.

If you begin sharing your faith with Wiccans as if they already understood God to be the person revealed in the Bible, they likely will not understand what you are talking about. They understand supernatural beings to be an entirely different kind of being from the God who is revealed in the Bible.

If you want your presentation to make sense to them, you must start at a different place. You must first explain who the God of the Bible is and what He is like. And you must do this until they finally understand what you mean. This very well may mean making direct comparisons between the God of the Bible and their deities. Even if they never come to the place of accepting Christ, you must still bring them to an understanding of the biblical God for it to even be possible. So, you have to begin by distinguishing the God of the Bible from the gods and spirits that they follow.

What is true for Animism, when it comes to clarifying the biblical understanding of God, is also true in some specific way for every other worldview and its associated belief systems. The people you want to hear and understand your message will come to you with a set of religious beliefs already in place. You must discern what *their* starting place is and tailor your explanation to it.

The Christian plan of salvation assumes a certain knowledge of God. This knowledge is part of the core worldview beliefs of a Christian. If the person with whom you are sharing does not have that foundational knowledge about the God of the Bible, they will not understand your presentation.

Every worldview has its own conceptual understanding of the ultimate a person can achieve in this life. Each assumes a different starting point and a different outcome for their belief system's "salvation." We need to know each person's starting point, and why their concepts are wrong. Then, as we share a witness to someone who holds a different worldview, we must convey a certain amount of knowledge about *why* their view does not line up with reality. From that point, we can lay a foundation about the Christian understanding of salvation and present the gospel message so it will be believable and meaningful to them.

Reason #5. It Provides an Understanding of the Weaknesses of Other Faiths

Every person we ever engage in witness comes to us with a worldview position already in place. If that position is based on a Christian worldview, our task is greatly simplified. Since that person already substantially agrees with us, we don't have to convince him or her of the truth of the Christian faith. In that case, all we need to do is simply present the gospel message and offer the opportunity to respond to it.

But as we have noted, more and more, the people we engage come to us from entirely different worldview backgrounds. When that is the case, a completely different dynamic is at play. Not only do we have to share our own message, but we also have to overcome the message they already hold.

Many of the people with whom we come into contact these days will either dismiss our witness as fantasy, or actually attack our Christian faith and argue that Christian beliefs are not true or reliable. While every one of their objections can be overcome, staying on the defensive can create a dynamic that never allows us to actually share our faith. No matter how good an answer you give, people can always come up with more questions.

When people deal with you in this mode, they are simply not ready or willing to listen. They are merely looking to throw you another curveball, so they won't have to deal with your message … or their need for it.

The way to overcome that problem is to approach it from a different perspective. Rather than constantly trying to defend your position, or outwait their never-ending list of disingenuous questions, you can subtly turn the tables and make them explain what *they* believe. When you shift the discussion that way, all of a sudden, the burden is on the other person to defend their position. When you know the weaknesses of other people's belief systems, you position yourself to break down the false beliefs that their worldview is founded upon.

Once again, this does not necessarily mean that they will accept your faith. But until their foundation is knocked out from under them, they will not even be willing to look in another place for a new one. When we understand worldview concepts, we can quickly detect the weaknesses of the opposing positions that others hold.

Back To The Purpose

At this point we need to reiterate a very important principle. The purpose of worldview knowledge is not to destroy other people. It is easy enough to win an argument. But if we do it with a wrong attitude, the person we are sharing with will simply not listen to us.

Our purpose in having worldview knowledge is to be able to share the gospel message effectively … to the point that others can understand and accept it. For this to happen, we must have a right attitude and a loving spirit toward all those we engage.

Chapter 3
Preparing for Witness

"**G**ood morning," said Tom, approaching a young student who was sitting on the steps eating his lunch. This was his chance to witness to a new student on campus.

"My name's Tom. What's yours?" They shook hands.

"Raj," the man replied smiling. "I'm a new student from India."

"That's great. May I ask you a few questions?" Tom asked.

"Uh, okay. What about?"

Tom went straight to the point, "Do you believe in God?"

"Which god?" Raj asked in return.

"You know, God … **God**," Tom said.

"I believe in all the gods."

Tom looked at Raj with a puzzled glare. "Well, how many gods are there?"

"I don't know. Millions, I guess."

"Millions?" Tom tried another approach, "Well, do you believe in Jesus?"

"Who's he?"

Tom was stunned. Was Raj serious? Did he not know who Jesus was? "Don't you read the Bible?"

"Is that the university newspaper?"

"It's the book of God's Word!"

"Which god?"

"Look, Raj, don't you want to be saved?" Tom pleaded.

"From what? I'm fine. I'm just eating lunch." Raj was now getting a bit annoyed.

"Sin!" Tom spelled it out, "You know, S-I-N."

"S-I-N? Has something to do with trigonometry, right?"

Tom tried again, "Don't you want to go to the New Heaven?"

Raj looked puzzled, "That's in Connecticut, right? Why would I want to go there?"

Tom finally gave up exasperated. "Thanks for talking to me."

"You're welcome," replied Raj, relieved to see Tom leaving at last.

Tom thought to himself, "That guy sure has strange ideas."

Raj thought to himself, "That guy sure asks strange questions."

Tom's motives were certainly right in wanting to share Christ with Raj. But he failed to realize that his method was ineffective for the situation. Raj, a Hindu from India, with no prior exposure to Christianity, had no idea about what Tom was saying.

Tom's questions were all perfectly logical in terms of Tom's worldview, and Raj's questions were all perfectly logical in terms of Raj's worldview! Thus, we can see why BOTH Raj and Tom thought the other was talking fantasy! Their communication was on totally different wavelengths.

In this chapter we examine how to engage anyone, no matter what they believe, in order to introduce them to Christ in ways that will make sense, whatever their situation.

Before getting specifically into the "how-to" of sharing a witness, however, it is probably a good idea to get a big picture of what is involved. A basic checklist of the necessary elements involved in sharing a witness (the topic of the next chapter) will assure the pieces are in place for an effective witness, no matter the circumstances.

Our purpose here is to list all the pieces to the puzzle. While there is generally a certain order to these pieces, this is not simply a step-by-step process. The truth is, different situations call for different approaches, and sometimes even different skills. Witnessing to one person may require a different knowledge base and a different way of interacting than with another person. If you have a big picture understanding of the elements involved in the process and prepare for them in advance, you will be ready—no matter what the situation.

Due Diligence

If you buy a house, one of the first steps you take is to do your "due diligence." Doing your due diligence means to thoroughly investigate what the potential deal entails *before* signing a contract. Likewise, doing your due diligence is the initial preparation stage for witnessing. At this point, you must prepare in advance to take advantage of opportunities to share your faith when those opportunities open up.

Doing your due diligence falls into two categories:

- The first involves developing the necessary and sufficient knowledge base. You need to know certain things in order to share an effective witness.

- The second is more personal. You must develop a desire to witness in ways that are attractive and understandable to the person to whom the witness will be given.

Master the Knowledge Base

The knowledge base for effective witness is composed of four basic elements. Two of these equip you to gauge where the other person is in his or her current understanding. With that, it becomes possible to deliver the gospel message in a way that makes sense to the listener. The other two elements are necessary because they contain the content of the gospel message itself.

1. A Basic Understanding of Worldview

A person's worldview is the bedrock foundation for everything else they believe. In fact, every religion, cult, and philosophy emerges from one of the four worldview categories we will discuss in the next chapter. Some Christians may immediately object and proclaim that their Christian faith is their most basic set of beliefs. But that is not accurate. In fact, one's Christian faith doesn't even make sense without a particular set of worldview beliefs to support it. For instance, if a person's worldview assumes that God doesn't exist, then belief in the God of the Bible is impossible.

Understanding worldview concepts is the key to dealing with the belief environment that exists in today's world. It is now necessary to break through barriers that, in the past, were not problems, then build a worldview bridge in addition to a gospel bridge in order to get our message across.

We address the major worldview categories (Naturalism, Animism, Far Eastern Thought, Non-Christian Theism, and even Hybrid

56

systems) in Chapter 4, reserving our discussion of Christian Theism for Chapters 6 and 7.

2. The Specific Belief Background of the Person with Whom You Want to Witness

Although a worldview is a broadly-based set of beliefs, numerous specific belief *systems* (typically identified as religions, cults, or philosophies) rest upon the foundation of each worldview. While all of the belief systems within a particular worldview category have the same basic understanding of God, man, and salvation (as these conceptualizations are used in our analysis), they each express those concepts in different ways. We detail the major worldview categories in Chapter 4 (Naturalism, Animism, Far Eastern thought, Non-Christian Theism, and even Hybrid systems), and in Chapters 6, and 7 (Christian Theism).

While understanding an individual's worldview foundation is an essential starting point for witness, it does not provide all of the specific details needed to proceed effectively. For that, one needs more knowledge about the individual's particular belief system. For instance, members of both The Church of Jesus Christ of Latter-day Saints (traditionally known as the LDS, or the Mormon Church, and its members as Mormons) and the Jehovah's Witnesses base their beliefs on a theistic worldview. That being said, their stated doctrines of God, man, and salvation, are quite different from each other, and are radically different from historic Christianity. So in order to witness effectively to one of those folks, even though we share the same basic worldview, it becomes necessary to also have some knowledge of their beliefs on these three critical theological topics. This allows us to distinguish between their and our essential doctrines.

This same principle holds for all of the other worldview categories, as well. For instance, Hinduism and Buddhism both fit within the Far Eastern Thought worldview category. However, even though they are based upon the same essential worldview beliefs, there are significant differences in their specific beliefs about the existence of gods and the meaning of life. Likewise, Voodoo and Wicca are both animistic beliefs, and Secular Humanism and Postmodernism are examples of naturalistic beliefs where these same kinds of distinctions can be made.

We describe these issues in Part II, Chapters 4 and 5.

3. The Scope of the Christian Worldview

The scope of the Christian worldview involves sharing the big picture story of the Christian faith. It starts with an explanation of the God of the Bible and His purpose for the creation of man and the universe. It then moves on to explain mankind's fall, life after the Fall, redemption, and eternity. This is a narrative account of the Christian worldview. Sharing this big picture helps people see the differences between the Christian understanding of reality and their own.

4. The Essentials of the Christian Faith

The essentials of any belief system define the boundaries beyond which one's beliefs cannot cross and still remain within that system. In the Christian faith, the essential beliefs comprise the actual gospel message. They draw a clear line around true biblical faith, and they express the essential core doctrines one must believe in order to be an authentic follower of Christ.

As we have seen, the essentials of every belief system answer the three essential worldview questions:

1. Who is God?

2. What is a human being?

3. And what is salvation (*i.e.*: the ultimate one can achieve in this life) and how does one achieve it?

We expand both the scope and the essentials of the Christian worldview and faith in Part III, Chapters 6 and 7. While we apply these questions to the major worldview categories in Chapter 4, we also want to encourage you to recognize a fuller application, which is discussed later in Chapter 7.

The biblical answers to these questions comprise the message one gives when sharing Christ by means of The Four Spiritual Laws, The Romans Road, or any other Christian witnessing method. This is the gospel message we must share in order to bring a person to the point of deciding whether or not to accept Christ into their own lives.

> See Appendix 1, *Breakdown of Popular Witnessing Methods,* for a comparison of how several popular Christian witnessing methods address these questions.

This fourth step is the beginning *and the end* of a witness opportunity in most traditional witnessing methods. That is not necessarily a bad thing, so long as the person hearing the witness already believes in the God of the Bible. A person with that belief already possesses a Christian worldview foundation, affirms that the Christian faith is true, and believes what the Bible teaches about God, His purpose, and the need to accept Christ. This person may have been raised in a home or church where he or she was exposed to the Bible and rudimentary Christian concepts. The only thing left, in that case, is for the individual to actually make the decision to receive Christ.

However, for those who don't start with those essential beliefs and assumptions, we may have to give further explanations. *Before* sharing the gospel message, it will be critical to shatter their belief mirage by:

- identifying their worldview,

- determining their specific belief system, and

- building a worldview bridge that explains to them the scope of the Christian worldview …

Master Yourself

The other element of due diligence is for you, as an individual Christian, to prepare your own life for faithful witness. Without this preparation, people will see you as (and you will see yourself to be) insincere and hypocritical.

1. Acquire the Necessary Perspective

Our natural tendency is to look at life from our own personal perspective. This has particular implications as it relates to witnessing. For instance, when things are going well with our faith, we tend to be willing to share it with other people. But, when things are not going well with our faith, whether because of wrong decisions we have made or even simple fatigue, we simply don't "feel" like doing it. And for most people, when they don't "feel" like it, they simply won't do it.

But God did not make life to revolve around us. He made it to revolve around Himself. If we really want fulfillment in life, we have to start where God starts. This means having a perspective that is not focused on ourself. Rather, we must first evaluate how our perspective affects the work of God's kingdom, then take appropriate action.

As it relates to humanity, the starting place is God's love. He loves everyone and wants a relationship with each individual human being.

The right perspective means not basing our actions simply on how we feel, but on what God wants to accomplish through us in any particular situation.

2. Intentionality

A second issue related to self-mastery regards the way we approach our witness to other individuals. We need to be intentional. That is, we must define our witnessing approach in our own minds. To do that, we need to develop an appropriate strategy, methodology, and tactical plan for reaching each person with whom we wish to share.

The fact is, most people in the world don't know God's love. If those individuals don't turn to Christ, they are headed to an eternity separated from Him. As a part of His plan to remedy this problem, God has commissioned believers as His instruments to share the message of salvation. Since we have personally experienced His work in our lives, we are witnesses of the fact that He is able to change a person's life. It is up to us, then, to share that good news with those who do not know Him.

As we think about our part in the work of God, we must recognize that simple intellectual assent to our responsibility is not generally enough to generate action. Many Christians acknowledge that they *ought* to share Christ with others, but just never do it. We must come to a place where we actually exert some energy if we want something to be accomplished. In the case of our witness, we have to take the initiative to interact with other people.

There are those, of course, who are naturally outgoing and make friends easily. But being an extrovert is not a requirement for making friends. Even the most introverted people have some friends. Truthfully, most people actually tend more toward isolation. In modern American society, with the development of social media, this trend is becoming even stronger. As Christians, we have to buck the trend of focusing inwardly.

The easiest way to do that is to open ourselves up and let people know us. It is not necessary to be an extrovert; we only have to be transparent. When people recognize that we are open to them, most will naturally open up to us.

Once we have personally made the determination to open ourselves to others, we must then identify specific people with whom we need to share a witness. We have to make an intentional effort to become friends with those God places in our path. We can't simply always just be in waiting mode. Some people will not move toward us until we move toward them. This doesn't mean we should attack people

61

with the gospel, but we should be willing to go out of our way to be a friend. Once we do that, the witnessing opportunity will emerge in His due time.

There are two additional points that need to be made.

1. Not everyone you encounter is going to be attracted to you. ... and ...

2. It is impossible for any single individual to verbally witness to everyone.

That is why God has placed Christians in so many different places. Everyone has their own circle of influence. If we are open to relationships, some people will be attracted to us, and appropriate opportunities will come.

3. Spiritual Preparation

Spiritual preparation relates to how we put ourselves into a position to be a worthy witness. It is a fact that in this life we will never reach sinless perfection. We can, though, grow in our relationship with God and continually move closer to the goal. In order to do this, we must keep our personal relationship with God up to date. We need to spend personal time with Him and conform our lifestyle to His ways. This discipline will address the problem of our feelings of moral inadequacy.

It is important to get this personal internal element right or we will feel uncomfortable sharing our faith. The way we engage our personal relationship with God is the key to this internal preparation.

Of course, the work of salvation is, ultimately, not a work that we do. God is the only one who can change a person's life. But if we are going to carry the message of God to the world effectively, we must also carry the character of God. Message and character cannot be separated. Two things will happen if we do not live our lives based on God's character:

- First, the person with whom we are trying to share will not take us seriously. We will be seen as hypocritical if we share a message that calls a person to holiness yet are not living it out in our own lives.

- Second, we will personally feel inadequate to share the message. Not only will the other person identify us as a hypocrite, we will feel that way about ourselves. It is very difficult to share the gospel personally with someone when we feel unworthy of it.

We must remember that witnessing is all about God and His purposes, not about us. The point is not for us to set records regarding how many people we can bring to Christ. The purpose is for individuals to come into a personal relationship with God through Jesus Christ.

Develop A Relationship

The second key component of effective witnessing is well-expressed by the word *relationship*. When it comes to such a deep and sensitive topic as one's faith, most people are not going to take a random conversation seriously with someone they don't fully trust. We need to develop relationships based on mutual trust and respect. At that point, it becomes possible to talk about anything, even religious matters, without offense.

As we discussed in Chapter 1, there are times when some kind of event approach to witnessing is appropriate. There certainly are circumstances when a brief opportunity opens up for it. However, if our entire approach is to operate from an event perspective, all we have are incidents that occur from time to time which we seek to complete and be done. There is a better way.

So how can we approach our witnessing to keep it from becoming a series of random events?

Witness in The Context of An Ongoing Relationship

Instead of thinking of our witness in terms of an event, we should consider it in the context of an ongoing relationship. This way, the discussion is not simply about "getting the person saved" (justification), but also about the continuation of the salvation process (sanctification).

When we think of our witness in terms of our relationship with a person, sometimes we will talk about God, but other times we might chat about food, sports, the kids, or whatever. When the talk about these things ends, we will still have plenty of opportunities to come back later and talk about faith matters again. The relationship and the conversations continue. Then, if at some point the individual does invite Christ into their life, we are able to continue to walk with them in a spiritual growth process that is actually a part of the relationship.

God has in mind individuals to whom He specifically wants us to witness—individually—and they are not just randomly selected. We need to recognize this fact and insert intentionality into our part of the process, too.

1. Witness Intentionally

Statistics show that the huge majority of people who come to know the Lord are influenced by someone they know well—like a close friend or relative. That being the case, it only makes sense to develop our primary witnessing strategy based on a relationship paradigm.

In order to have opportunities to share our faith most productively on a continuous basis, we need to consider with whom we want to share our faith—in advance. Having that in mind will insert us into the lives of those people and establish relationships that can lead to witnessing opportunities. This does not mean we will necessarily become best friends with every person with whom we interact. But without some kind of relationship, other people will generally not open up to us on the topic of their faith.

2. Prepare for Building a Relationship

So, our own readying for witness includes not only our preparation to deliver the message, but also for personal interaction. Developing a relationship involves knowing a person on a personal level. We have to make an actual effort to get into their life … and open ourselves to them, as well. There are several things that this involves, and to become proficient we can take a page out of the missionary's playbook to understand the process. After all, God has called us to be His missionaries out in society.

Learn Their Language

One element of relationship-building involves learning the other person's language. If you were going to another country to do missionary work, you very well may have to learn an entirely new language, along with its rules about the structure and sequence of speech sounds, vocabulary, grammar, intonation, and the various rules for appropriate communication.

But language involves more than just these formal language elements. Even people who speak the same native language come from backgrounds that have different frames of reference. Interacting with someone from another country is very different from dealing with people from your own. For example, Americans and Australians both speak English, but they have many different colloquialisms that can make communication confusing. Beyond that, interacting with someone in a rural community is very different from dealing with people from an inner city. Interacting with someone from a different generation is very different from dealing with people of your own generation. Interacting with someone of a different ethnicity is very different from dealing with people of your own—even if you are speaking the same verbal language. There may be different nuances, or even entirely different meanings, to certain words or expressions. People feel more comfortable when they are operating in their own dialect, so sometimes we need to learn the nuances of the vernacular of the person with whom we are interacting—even if we are interacting with them in a common language.

65

Learn Their Culture

Another element concerns the other person's culture. You may have the same 'big picture' culture as other people you know, nonetheless, many come from various subcultures. While subculture differences may not be massive, they can be just different enough to make people uncomfortable around you. They may also hold concepts or ideals that ascribe different meanings to the words you might use.

One of the important things all missionaries do is to notice cultural differences and adapt to them for the purpose of making the other person feel comfortable. This doesn't mean you have to become a part of that other culture or subculture. However, you may need to adapt your verbal and non-verbal communications and to modify your expressive actions and activities in ways that help people know that you accept and care about them.

Learn Their Religion

A third element you need to consider has to do with their religious faith. Even people who claim to be Christians have different ways they conceive of and express their faith. We still must keep in mind that even people who self-identify as Christians do not necessarily possess, or even know about, a personal relationship with Jesus Christ. There are a lot of "Cultural Christians" who self-identify as "Christians" simply because they live in a "Christian country," were baptized when they were children, or grew up in a "Christian home."

It is important to know people's faith background in order to understand whether or not they are *really* Christians—and, if not, what you will need to explain to them in order to lead them to Christ.

Learn Their Lifestyle

Another important element to bear in mind is a person's personal lifestyle. People generally feel comfortable around others who are like them, and uncomfortable around those who are not. This is particularly true when it comes to lifestyle issues. If they drink beer and you don't (or *vice versa*), you are going to need to figure out how to act so they will feel comfortable around you when you don't share their values and personal practices. If they engage in certain activities you believe are immoral, you will have to find ways to love and interact with them without compromising your own standards—much like Jesus did when he interacted with people who were considered sinners by the polite society within the region where He ministered.

Developing intentional relationships for the purpose of getting into a person's life so you can share a witness with them can be challenging and hard work. You won't be able to do this with everyone, but you can do it with those to whom God leads you.

3. Gather the Person's Worldview Information

As we have already noted, a person's worldview relates to their most deeply held beliefs. These beliefs are so ingrained that they form the foundation of a person's very identity. They define what a person recognizes as real and what is fantasy. In fact, worldview beliefs are so deeply rooted that most people are not even aware they exist. After all, if something is indisputably assumed to be real, why would it even be questioned? And if something is considered to be a fantasy, why entertain it at all? The end result is that because we don't (or so rarely) deal with them, most people are not conversant regarding their—or anyone else's—worldview beliefs. They will know, to some extent, *what* they believe, but they may have no idea *why* what they believe represents, or does not represent, reality.

Since worldview beliefs operate at such a deeply personal level, most people are not open to discussing them seriously unless they feel comfortable with the person with whom they are talking. Thus, before broaching this topic, it is necessary to have developed a trust relationship. That is why it is so essential to make the development of relationships a priority.

As we indicated earlier, human beings have a tendency to live around and interact with people who share their same basic background. People are drawn to those who are like themselves and repelled by those who are different. This is particularly true as regards worldview beliefs. Generally, people interact on an ongoing basis with others who hold the same worldview beliefs as themselves.

In spite of that, especially in our modern, increasingly pluralistic society, most people still have some in their relationship circle who do not share their worldview background. More than ever, people from different cultures, religions, and philosophical backgrounds make up modern society ... even your own neighborhood!

So in order to share an effective witness, we not only need to know the specific beliefs of those who share our own worldview, but the beliefs of those who hold other worldviews, as well. Even if we know how to give an effective gospel presentation, our message may be ineffective if we don't know where another person is coming from at a worldview level. In that situation, our listeners may not fully understand what we are talking about.

So, when we engage people who hold other worldview beliefs, we must figure out the right starting point for witness. This means learning their worldview beliefs. Thus, when we identify a person with whom we wish to share a witness, we must ask the kinds of questions that will elicit the information we need to understand their worldview background.

4. Map and Analyze the Person's Worldview Beliefs

Once we find out a person's worldview foundation, it becomes possible to analyze and understand it, thus giving us a path to interact intelligently with that individual. It is pointless to begin sharing the gospel message with someone if they do not know who Christ is, or do not believe He was God in the flesh. For someone like that, we will need a different starting point.

The reason for analyzing a person's worldview is that it gives us that right starting place for our witness. This starting point is critical, as we can't assume our friend already understands who God is and what He is like.

For instance, if we start talking about the God of the Bible to a Buddhist, that person is not going to fully comprehend that we are talking about a being who is personal and loving. Buddhists don't believe in a personal, loving God, and an explanation that wrongly assumes that they do, or even that they understand such a concept, will not make any sense to them. It is necessary to go back a step and give the person an explanation of the nature and character of God based on biblical teachings before we can effectively share how they can come to know Him.

Remember, everyone who comes to us already has some belief about how reality is structured. We must have some connecting point if we want our witness to make sense to them. With that in hand, we become able to make explanations that they can understand.

Mapping a Person's Worldview and Belief System

In order to map a person's worldview and belief system, we need to find out what they believe about three things at these levels. These three markers give us the information necessary to shatter their belief mirage and bridge the gaps between our beliefs and theirs.

> See Appendix 2, *Creating a Witnessing Map*, for a resource for capturing your learning into a handy map aid.

1. **Who is God?** As we have already seen, every belief system has some understanding about God—He doesn't exist, there are many gods/spirits, there is an impersonal life force, some non-Christian God, *etc*. Mapping a person's understanding of the concept of God simply means finding out specifically what their concept is.

2. **What is a Human Being?** Mapping this second question simply means to discover what the person believes about the nature of humanity. Are humans purely animal creatures with a highly evolved brain? Are human beings spirit creatures in

material bodies that symbiotically interact with the many gods/spirits that exist in the spirit world? Are we merely illusory expressions of an impersonal life force? Are human beings created by God for some purpose? If so, which god and for what purpose? ... It is essential to grasp this knowledge because a person's concept of the nature of humanity determines what he or she believes is necessary for salvation.

3. **What Is Salvation and How Does One Achieve It?** It is important to keep in mind that the concept of salvation, in worldview terms, relates to the ultimate a person can achieve in this life—and every belief system has its own idea as to what constitutes that ultimate goal (which may or may not have consequences beyond this life). We map this by finding out from the individual what this concept is to them. We cannot assume that they understand salvation the same way as do Christians.

As Christian witnesses, our purpose is to help nonbelievers understand Christian salvation, then build a bridge from our Christian beliefs to their beliefs. We, thus, need to know what they believe at the deepest level, their worldview, so we can bridge the gap.

Analyze Worldview Weaknesses

The fact that a person's worldview defines what they understand to be real and, thus, what is fantasy, gives us another important piece of knowledge about how to interact with those who are not Christians.

As we have noted,

> **Reality exists in some objectively real way, and any belief that does not match up with that reality is not true.**

Thus, *only* the belief system that matches up at every point with the way we actually experience life can be true. Every other belief

70

system has elements that do not reflect the way human beings actually experience life.

Knowing this gives us another way to interact with other people's worldview beliefs. If their beliefs do not reflect reality, and we know at what points inconsistencies exist, it is then possible to point out reasons for them to explore another alternative.

Worldview Bridge Points

We must also understand, though, that simply grasping the concepts of our beliefs and those of non-Christians *intellectually* is not enough. In our discussions with them, we must also bridge the gap that separates these most-basic beliefs. Remember, we are not just dealing with differing beliefs, we are dealing with entirely different understandings about what is real and what is fantasy. As we begin to share a witness, we must tap into the way the other person understands reality before our message will even begin to make sense to them. Then, once we have a point of common understanding, we can show them *why* their worldview beliefs are wrong and point them to a new understanding. These inconsistencies shatter their truth mirage, allowing us to bridge the gap from their worldview to reality.

5. Understand the Person's Commitment Level

The level of commitment a person has to their faith is another very important factor to consider as we look at sharing our faith with someone. Their commitment level makes them either more willing or less willing to listen to what we have to say.

Many people with whom we interact do not have a high level of personal commitment to their faith. For them, their religious belief is more a matter of ethnic heritage or cultural identity. While those are important, people who are not highly committed to their faith will generally be more willing to listen to what we have to say. Their religious faith is not the primary driving force of their lives. This does not mean, however, that they would necessarily be ready to immediately change their religion. Even if their faith is only at the

71

level of ethnic heritage or cultural identity, it is still a strong influence in their life. Changing will still mean they must reorient their lives—which, quite possibly, will affect many of their family and other close relationships. That being said, less-committed people generally are more open to listen to our ideas, provided they are presented in a winsome way.

Others, though, are very much involved in and committed to their faith. These are people who recognize their faith to be the place where they draw personal spiritual strength. They have probably engaged in a deeper level of training and involvement in their faith. As such, it is necessary to make a heavier investment in a relationship with this kind of person in order to even get a hearing. The higher the commitment level, the stronger the relationship base we will have to establish, and the stronger the case we will have to make.

It is important to recognize the relationship necessity up front, and that it will generally not be a quick and easy matter. It will almost always involve a long-term strategy and require a deeper commitment to the relationship. Beyond that, our commitment to the relationship itself cannot be dependent on the outcome of our witness. The connection has to be with the person at a deep level no matter what kind of decision they make in the short term.

Prep For Witness—Conclusion

The steps above do not necessarily represent a particular sequence in the witnessing process. Generally speaking, a certain order is represented, but every person we encounter is at a different place in his or her understanding of, and receptivity to, a witness. We have to discern from our interaction with the individual what relationship elements need to be developed in order to share an effective witness.

That being said, these are the elements we need to master in order to be a competent and effective witness. If we master these elements and make sharing a witness a priority in life, God will use us in powerful ways to bring people into relationship with Himself.

Part II

The Due Diligence of Christian Witness

As we consider our entry into the task of sharing our faith across worldview barriers, we must recognize that there are particular concepts, pieces of knowledge, and skills that we need to learn. It is important to know what these are, and to make a personal commitment to the task in order to become proficient in sharing our faith across worldview barriers.

The first thing we must determine is the starting point for witness. When dealing with cross-worldview witness, there is no such thing as a generic starting point. Every worldview begins with its own set of assumptions, and we must know how to tap into those assumptions if we wish to make sense to people who hold them.

It is also important to have knowledge of how to craft the wording of one's witness effectively as we present the gospel message. When we master these things, we will find ourselves in a position to be truly effective in getting the gospel message across to those who don't know Christ.

Chapter 4

Building Bridges for Witness

"Sir," asked Wendy, approaching the man at the lunch counter. "Are you familiar with the Romans Road?"

"Romans Road? No, I've never even been to Italy," a bit taken aback by her forwardness, "why do you ask?"

"Well, it's the way to get saved from your sins and go to heaven."

He winced. "Oh, well I'm not Catholic and don't know much about that church. In fact, I'm Jewish, but I don't attend synagogue very often."

"I don't mean *that* Roman road, I'm not Catholic either. I'm talking about what it says in the book of Romans in the Bible."

"Which Bible? Yours or mine?"

"There's a difference?"

"Yes, we Jews don't accept what you call the 'New Testament' as Scripture. Only the books of what you call the 'Old Testament' … or, as we call it: 'The *Tanakh.*'"

Wendy did not know what else to say. She looked at the man, thanked him, and walked away.

Most Christians who actively share their faith use some kind of method for sharing Christ. Some of the more prominent training programs that have been developed over the years include The Romans Road, The Four Spiritual Laws, FAITH, Steps to Peace with God, Evangelism Explosion, and many others.

Nothing is wrong with any method as long as it contains the essential biblical points that show a person how to receive Christ and does not add to or subtract from them. But there are often problems with smoothly leading into or transitioning to a gospel presentation at the beginning of, or during, a conversation, that make sharing the message more difficult. To deal with those issues, most methodologies start with a leading question designed to help move the conversation into the presentation. Some of the questions used by various systems include:

- Have you ever heard of the Four Spiritual Laws?

- If you were to get to the gates of heaven and God were to ask why he should let you in, what would you say?

- If you were to die today, do you think you would go to heaven?

- Have you ever come to a point in your life where you trusted Jesus Christ as your personal Savior and Lord?

- How do you think someone becomes a Christian?

- In your personal opinion, what do you understand it takes for a person to go to heaven?

- Do you know for sure that you are going to be in heaven with God when you die?

If you look carefully at these questions, you will notice this common denominator among them: they all assume that the person being addressed has a theistic worldview—that is, that they believe in a transcendent, supernatural God. And many specifically assume the

76

person holds a *Christian* theistic worldview—that is, they believe in the God of the Bible.

These questions also presuppose that a spiritual world exists that can be known, and which people can enter at physical death.

If the person hearing the gospel message already holds a theistic worldview, then these questions will probably be at least understandable.

But:

- What if the person doesn't believe that a supernatural reality even exists?

- What if this person believes in many gods or spirits who express themselves in nature?

- What if he or she believes that ultimate reality is an impersonal life force?

- What if the individual believes in a god, but not the one described in the Bible?

- What if that person contends it doesn't really matter what anyone believes?

In any of these cases, the kinds of questions posed above will not be good places to start sharing the gospel message ... and today, an ever-increasing majority of people in America fit into one or another of these categories.

Bridge Building from One Worldview to Another

Different worldviews are so fundamentally dissimilar that it is difficult for people from one worldview to understand or communicate effectively with those from another on topics related to faith. That is because those who hold different worldviews have

77

entirely different conceptions of the very structure of reality. This problem is demonstrated outwardly in life as people try to communicate with one another regarding matters of faith.

Typically, people are not even aware of the depth of the divide between themselves and those who believe other worldviews. That is because we all use pretty much the same vocabulary, and because we so rarely discuss worldviews at all. However, when we do discuss worldviews (even without acknowledging that we are doing so), the meaning and nuances of the words people use will be very different from one worldview to another.

For example, both Theists and Naturalists use the same word, morality, but the practical implications of that word are entirely different based on the presuppositions of the two worldviews.

- For Theists, morality represents an objectively real revelation from God as to what is right and what is wrong, or what is good and what is bad.

- Naturalists, on the other hand, see morality as a relativistic concept—that is, they consider it to correspond to how they personally view a given situation, and not based on any absolute (objective) foundation.

So, what we end up with is a common verbal vocabulary, with different worldviews assigning different meanings to the words. In one sense, it is like speaking entirely different languages. And what is true for the word 'morality,' also applies to other important words such as God, man, salvation, and even the word 'meaning' itself.

Building a bridge across worldview barriers is an educational process. Even if people with different worldview beliefs don't agree with each other, at the very least they need to understand one another for valid communication to even take place—let alone for a profitable discussion to occur.

As Christians, we want to be able to share the gospel clearly (again, accurately, effectively, and efficiently) with those who are not believers. But the gospel message assumes not only a theistic worldview foundation, more specifically, it also assumes that Christian theistic beliefs are objectively true. If we are trying to witness to a non-believer, knowing that they do not understand our Christian foundation means we must build a conceptual bridge. That is, we must find common meanings for the words we both use and for the concepts and assumptions we each hold. Only then can we present the gospel's good news to them in a way they will be able to understand.

In actual fact, it will be necessary to build two bridges.

- The first bridge is a worldview bridge. This bridge is necessary when sharing Christ with anyone who holds non-theistic worldview beliefs. Building a worldview bridge involves discovering what specific worldview one is engaging, then creating a common understanding of faith vocabulary, belief concepts, and assumptions about truth.

- The second bridge is a gospel bridge. This is the process of clearly explaining the gospel message itself to enable people to understand its content. It involves discovering what specific belief system one is engaging, then creating a common understanding of belief system vocabulary, belief concepts, and assumptions about truth. This is necessary so your gospel message will convey the Bible's truth, and its words will not be misunderstood to mean whatever *their* faith system assigns to them.

Worldview Bridge

For those who hold non-theistic worldview beliefs, the first bridge that must be built is a worldview bridge. We must somehow help them understand that an actual transcendent God exists who is the Creator and Sustainer of the material universe. The default belief of people who hold non-theistic worldview beliefs will be something other than that.

79

To make this explanation to non-theists, we may even have to first explain to them what their own worldview foundation looks like. They have likely never consciously thought about it before. Remember, a worldview is a set of assumptions—mostly unconscious beliefs. See the left side of the map in Appendix 2, *Witnessing Resource 2. Creating a Witnessing Map.*

The fact is, every witnessing situation is unique. Everyone to whom we witness already has a worldview foundation that defines the boundaries of their beliefs. In order to figure out how to make this bridge, we need to create a belief map. A belief map is nothing more than the results of the analysis of the essential beliefs of the person to whom we wish to witness. (Again, see Appendix 2.)

As earlier noted, every worldview system has certain basic doctrines that absolutely cannot be violated—doctrines so basic that changing even one of them actually moves a person into a different worldview. Thus, adherents of any given system can and will disagree about non-essential beliefs. But they absolutely cannot disagree on the essential ones.

We can get to their essential *worldview* beliefs by asking the following three simple questions:

- What is the nature of ultimate reality? (In conversation, the most revealing form of this question is, What do you believe *about* God? **Note:** Do not ask, "Do you believe in God?" Their "Yes" or "No" response does not tell us anything about *which* God they believe in, or what he, she, or it is like.)

- What is the nature of a human being? (The most revealing conversational form of this question is, What is a human being?)

- What is salvation and how is it achieved? (The most revealing form of this question is, What is the ultimate you can achieve in this life … and how do you achieve it? Remember, *salvation*, in worldview jargon, simply relates to the greatest fulfillment that the system has to offer.)

Every person within any given worldview system will answer these three questions the same way.

Following an explanation of their worldview foundation, we must explain what *our* biblical foundation looks like. When that is done, it is then possible to compare, contrast, and assess the two. This step establishes a basis for analyzing your listener's worldview and communicating the Christian worldview message in terms that make sense to them.

Gospel Bridge

Once the worldview gap is crossed, it becomes necessary to build another bridge—a gospel bridge. This one specifically leads a person to understand the Christian faith. It might be noted, if the person already holds a non-Christian theistic belief (Mormon, Jehovah's Witness, Jew, Muslim, *etc.*), building a worldview bridge will probably not be necessary. Therefore, you can begin immediately with the belief system portion. (See the right side of the map in Appendix 2, *Witnessing Resource 2. Creating a Witnessing Map.*)

Even here, though, depending on their knowledge of their own faith and of the Christian faith, it may be necessary to make some comparisons between their beliefs about God, man, and salvation, and those taught in the Bible. This will require that you know enough about their beliefs to make the comparison. It may also require that you know enough about Christian apologetics to adequately answer legitimate questions about the validity of the Christian faith.

Once you are at a place, however, where you can actually explain the gospel message, you will need to begin with a systematic overview of the Christian faith. (We will look at this more deeply in Chapter 6.) Essentially, this involves telling the Christian story. It begins with an explanation of God's purpose in creation, then moves on to an explanation of the Fall, the results of the Fall, redemption, and eternity. Once people grasp this big picture narrative, they are in a position to understand the gospel message, itself. (We will deal with this topic in chapter 7.)

It is very important to be sensitive to what your hearers are understanding and what they are not. Essentially, an explanation of the gospel involves sharing what the Bible says about God, man, and salvation. Before being in a position to make a decision, an individual must understand the entirety of the gospel message. However, depending on the background of the person to whom you are talking, some elements of it may require more explanation than others. Some parts may be easier or harder for them to comprehend, and you will need to be sensitive to make sure they grasp it all. For instance, if the person believes we are not *born in sin*, then understanding what is meant by the phrase, *we are sinners*, will be more difficult for them to grasp and will need to be emphasized.

Starting Point for the Basic Worldviews

When we wish to share a witness with someone who is not a Christian, we must begin by understanding this person's worldview foundation. It is a fact that every non-biblical worldview belief uniquely conflicts with the Bible. In order to explain this concept more fully, we will now take a look at the major worldview categories and examine the big picture issues critical to our understanding.

> See Appendix 3, *Overview of Various Belief Systems*, for details related to the major belief systems in each worldview category.

Naturalism

1) Basic Assumption

The most basic assumption of Naturalism is that there is no supernatural existence. For Naturalists, the only thing that exists is the natural universe of time, space, matter, and energy, which is evolving. Naturalists believe this but are unable to explain where it all came from. They also believe that the universe will ultimately end with its eternal death … along with everyone and everything in it.

2) Major Belief Systems Based on a Naturalistic Worldview

Atheism	Agnosticism	Skepticism
Marxism	Modernism	Postmodernism

Secular Humanism

3) Naturalism's Answers to the Essential Questions

- **What is the nature of ultimate reality?** There is no supernatural existence. All of reality exists within the bounds of the natural universe of time, space, matter, and energy.

- **What is the nature of a human being?** Human beings are purely animal creatures that have a highly evolved brain.

- **What is salvation and how is it achieved?** The ultimate that life has to offer is survival and personal fulfillment. A person achieves this by whatever means necessary based on personal goals and life dreams.

4) Weakness of Naturalism

All Naturalistic belief systems look primarily to human reason, based on observations of the natural universe, as their authority source. It is assumed that unaided human reason is able to lead to a definitive understanding of objective reality. The problem that emerges from this assumption, though, is that Naturalism is, itself, a faith position lacking objective support. It is impossible to prove the foundational assumptions of Naturalism using its own requirement that everything be explainable using an empirical

83

methodology. Specifically, it is impossible to empirically demonstrate:

- that and/or how the universe began out of nothing,

- that the material that makes up the natural universe has a natural source,

- that life can emerge out of non-life,

- that less complex life forms can evolve into more complex forms, and

- that consciousness can emerge out of non-consciousness.

All of these beliefs are foundational for Naturalism, and all of them are faith assumptions. This fact presents a huge problem for adherents of this worldview position because all of its foundational beliefs depend on faith assumptions, while asserting that all of reality can ultimately be understood based on empiricism.

5) Starting Point for Witness to Naturalists

Naturalists believe the natural universe is all that exists. They are convinced that they can arrive at Truth and can come to a definitive understanding of objective reality using unaided human reason. That being the case, the starting point for witness must be somehow related to what goes on in the natural universe—that is, issues related to everyday life (*e.g.*, evolution, abortion, societal organization, the nature of freedom, or virtually any other topic).

One can bring up an issue and begin discussing the possible different perspectives for evaluating that matter. This allows the discussion to move outside of Naturalism as alternative beliefs are proposed. The discussion can also involve conversations about "what must be true" for the various points of view to hold up. This allows for the weaknesses of Naturalism (see above) to be discussed. With that, it is possible to point out why naturalistic beliefs are internally inconsistent.

From that starting point, we must build a bridge to belief in the God of the Bible. We can do that by helping people understand the following two worldview and three belief system bridge elements:

a. Worldview Bridge Element #1: Naturalism itself is a faith position that completely lacks objective support.

The bridge that must be created between Naturalism and Theism is the bridge leading from a belief in no God (no supernatural component to reality) to one that asserts the existence of God (reality is composed of both natural and supernatural components). Building that bridge begins with helping these individuals understand that their own assertion that God does not exist is, itself, a faith point of view. Most Naturalists are unable to see this inconsistency until it is pointed out to them.

It can then be demonstrated that it is impossible to prove empirically the foundational assumptions of Naturalism. No one is able, by empirical means (*i.e.*, observation and experiment), to explain:

- how the universe began,

- that the material that makes up the natural universe has a natural source,

- how life can emerge out of non-life,

- how less complex life forms can naturally evolve into more complex forms, or

- how consciousness can emerge out of non-consciousness.

All of these are foundational presuppositions for Naturalism, and all of them are faith assumptions.

b. Worldview Bridge Element #2: God is an objective person.

The second part of the bridge for helping a person make the conceptual leap from Naturalism to Theism involves an explanation of the God of the Christian worldview. Since Naturalists don't believe in God (or any form of supernatural existence), they will not want to acknowledge even the possibility that God could exist. However, after recognizing that their own position is based on faith assumptions, they must at least acknowledge the possibility of a supernatural source for the existence of matter, life, complex creatures, and consciousness—even if begrudgingly.

Of course, this does not mean they will immediately believe that the existence of God is true. But they must at least acknowledge that without evidence to the contrary, one faith position is as valid as any other. So, even if they don't believe your explanation about God, they ought to at least be willing to listen to you. Here, you are basically providing an alternative explanation for the source of their faith assumptions about the nature of reality.

c. Belief System Bridge Element #1: The truth about God can only be known from the Bible.

The validity of the authority source of the Christian faith is the first belief system issue to address when specifically trying to bring a Naturalist to Christ. Some people may be willing to simply accept the assertion that the Bible is true. Others, however, will insist that you demonstrate to them *why* they should believe the Bible is true. At this point, you will need to be conversant with evidence for the validity of the Bible. Numerous lines of evidence support the validity of the Christian authority source. As you share your witness, you may have to go into the reasons why the Bible is the truth. If so, go down that road and present some of the very profound evidence for the reliability of the Scriptures. (See Chapter 5, subtitle **Evidence for the Validity of the Bible.**)

Again, leading a Naturalist to understand the concepts of Christianity does not mean he or she is going to agree it is true. It is, though, a necessary step in the process.

d. Belief System Bridge Element #2: Explain the Christian Worldview.

When individuals come to the place where they are able to grasp the principle that the Bible is the authority source for the Christian belief system, it is then necessary to give an overview of the Christian faith. This begins with an explanation of God's purpose in creation, then moves on to deal with the Fall, the results of the Fall, redemption, and eternity (See chapter 6).

e. Belief System Bridge Element #3: Explain the Gospel Message.

Once the person understands the big picture of the Christian faith, it is then possible to share the gospel message.

Animism

1) Basic Assumption

According to Animism, the universe contains both material and immaterial parts. Spirits exist in a separate place from physical beings, but they interact with each other in a symbiotic relationship. Humans on earth offer sacrifices and perform rituals that benefit the spirits, and they, in turn, take care of the needs of humans on earth.

2) Major Belief Systems That Are Based on an Animistic Worldview:

Japanese Shinto   Voodoo/Santeria   Wicca

    Neo-Paganism   Native American Religions

        Non-American Tribal Religions

3) Animism's Answers to the Essential Questions:

- **What is the nature of ultimate reality?** There are many gods and/or spirits that exist in the spirit world who interact symbiotically with human beings in the physical world.

- **What is the nature of a human being?** Human beings are spirit beings housed in physical bodies. The humans' spirits enter the spirit world at physical death.

- **What is salvation and how is it achieved?** The ultimate aim of Animism is to live physical life without oppression. This is accomplished by living in harmony with the gods/spirits. Every individual enters the spirit world upon physical death.

4) Weakness of Animism.

Animists look primarily to ancestral history and community tradition as the authority source for their worldview assumptions. They believe the teachings about the nature of reality that have been passed down from their ancestors is enough evidence to prove their worldview. Because of their presuppositions, they see the outworking of the actions of the gods and spirits in nature, and they don't recognize a need to look to revelation or science. However, their position has nothing to support it.

The fact is, there are many animistic traditions in the world. Any particular animistic belief system is only one among many. With no single authority source, many of these different belief systems literally contradict one another on essential points. That being the case, they cannot all be true.

This leads to two questions: How is it possible to arbitrate between the different beliefs? ... and how can one group know that its beliefs are true, and others are false? The truth is, there is no way to do either of these things. All that can be mustered is anecdotal evidence that itself—depends on faith presuppositions. But, of course, something is not true simply because someone believes it.

5) Starting Point for Witness to Animists

Animists look primarily to their heritage/traditions to support their worldview assumptions. They believe teachings about the nature of reality as passed down through the generations are enough of an authority. That being the case, a witness to Animists must begin in a place that touches on their traditions.

The apostle Paul did this when he was in Athens, as recorded by Luke in Acts 17. While not everyone in Athens followed an animistic religion, particularly those he was preaching to in the marketplace and at the Areopagus (KJV: Mars Hill), they did live in an animistic environment, and everyone understood it. So as he began his sermon about God, Paul started with a concept they understood—he spoke of the many gods who were worshiped in the city. He then noted their acknowledgment of an "unknown god." Using this "unknown god" as a starting point, he proceeded to introduce and share details about the God of the Bible, Jesus Christ, and His resurrection from the dead.

As we interact with Animists, as with any non-Christian, it is necessary to acknowledge their understanding of reality, recognize some point of contact with their understanding, then use it as a starting point to explain the God of the Bible. Possible touch points might include such things as God's creation of nature, how God interacts with nature, the fact that God answers prayers, and the like. Any specific touch point should relate specifically to the belief system one is addressing. As such, it is important to do your due diligence *before* engaging in your witness with this person.

Animists see the work of the gods/spirits in the very structure of nature itself. They don't acknowledge any need for direct revelation from these gods/spirits through any other authority source—for example, a sacred book or affirmation from empirical science. Therefore, in order to effectively witness to an Animist, one must lead them to understand the following two worldview and the three belief system bridge elements:

a. Worldview Bridge Element #1: The Animistic position has nothing to support it.

As was mentioned above, many different animistic traditions exist in the world. Any particular system is only one among many. This presents a serious problem because the various animistic belief systems often contradict one another on key points. Therefore, they cannot all be true. At the very least, some of them must be untrue.

That point understood, there must be some way of arbitrating between the different ones. But there is no way to make this determination. Animism, in every iteration, is a faith point of view with nothing more than anecdotal evidence to back it up. It has no empirical evidence, or even any assertions of revelation, that can be evaluated. And even what does exist depends on the faith assumptions of the worldview itself. There is simply no way for any animistic group to demonstrate that its beliefs are true, let alone that the others are false.

The specific points a Christian must make to deal with this issue are educational in nature. At some stage, it will be necessary to teach the Animist another way to understand reality. When that is accomplished, it becomes possible to compare and contrast the two worldview systems side-by-side.

b. Worldview Bridge Element #2: There is only one God.

Typically, animistic belief systems hold that there are many gods and/or spirits. After getting a person to acknowledge the possibility that his or her belief could perhaps be wrong, it is then possible to present an alternative. Since Christianity believes in only one God, it is necessary, at this point, to introduce the notion of monotheism.

Essentially, one who would share a witness with an Animist must explain the nature of the Christian God. It must include a description of what God is like and how it is possible that one God can account for all that exists. This explanation does not, of course, guarantee that the person will believe and accept the Christian faith. But unless and until an individual understands its content and acknowledges it as a possibility, it is impossible to lead a person to any kind of decision.

c. Belief System Bridge Element #1: The truth about God can only be known from the Bible.

Once an Animist understands that their belief system has no reasonable foundation, and grasps the concept of a theistic worldview, it is then possible to share the source of the Christian faith. At this point, one must explain how the Bible is the authority source of the Christian faith and provide evidence to back it up.

To do this, it is necessary to be conversant with the many lines of evidence that undergird the Christian authority source. In sharing a witness, it may be necessary to go into the reasons why the Bible is true. (See Chapter 5, subtitle **Evidence for the Validity of the Bible**).

Again, coming to an understanding of the Christian belief system does not guarantee that an Animist is going to accept the biblical viewpoint about the nature of God. It is, though, a necessary step in the process.

d. Belief System Bridge Element #2: Explain the Christian Worldview

Once an individual recognizes the Bible as the authority source for biblical Christianity, it is then necessary to give an overview of the Christian faith. This begins with an explanation of God's purpose in creation, then moves on to deal with the Fall, the results of the Fall, redemption, and eternity. This helps the individual understand the full context of the beliefs that make up the Christian faith. (See chapter 6)

e. Belief System Bridge Element #3: Explain the Gospel Message

Once the person understands the big picture context of the Christian faith, it is then possible to share the gospel message in a way that brings him or her to a decision point.

Far Eastern Thought

1) Basic Assumption

According to the beliefs of Far Eastern Thought, the essence of all existence is the impersonal life force. The big picture concept is that pieces of that life force have spun off from the central core and have gotten far enough away from it that they have taken on a different character. While Far Eastern Thought worldview beliefs assert that ultimate reality is immaterial and impersonal, it *appears* to human beings to be both material and personal. The natural universe expresses its *material* manifestation, while the human ability to engage personal relationships expresses its *personal* element. However, in Far Eastern Thought, these material and personal expressions are understood to be illusions, as ultimate reality is actually considered to be immaterial and impersonal.

These separated elements of the life force are constantly attempting to work their way back to rejoin the main body, with the ultimate goal to re-merge with it. As such, all of life in the physical universe consists of nothing more than pieces of the impersonal life force that are mechanically working their way back to reunification with the main body.

This is accomplished through the process of reincarnation. As the pieces of the life force progress through successive material incarnations, they are attempting to move from lower life forms to higher ones. But to progress forward in this process, the life form, at whatever stage in the reincarnation process, must live its life in such a way as to accumulate "good *karma*."

If it does well, it will move up to a higher form in its next incarnation. Generally, if not, it stays at the same level or moves down. When it makes it to the highest level and does well, the material reincarnations cease, and the life force merges with the impersonal main body. The essence of this worldview is pantheistic and monistic. Pantheism is the idea that everything is god. Monism says that everything is one.

2) Major Belief Systems That Are Based on a Far Eastern Thought Worldview:

Hinduism   Buddhism   Hare Krishna

Sikhism

3) Far Eastern Thought Answers to the Essential Questions:

- **What is the nature of ultimate reality?** Ultimate reality is a life force (life energy) that is both immaterial and impersonal. Everything, in all of existence, is made up of some expression of this life force.

- **What is the nature of a human being?** Human beings are one expression of the impersonal life force that has spun away from its main body. Humans are at some particular stage in the cycles of reincarnation and appear to be material and personal. This, however, is an illusion since the life force itself is immaterial and impersonal.

- **What is salvation and how is it achieved?** Salvation, in Far Eastern Thought, occurs when the pieces of the life force that have been spun off from the main body, are able to reunite with it. This is accomplished as the life force reincarnates over many lifetimes to higher and higher levels, until finally being absorbed back into the main body. For human beings, the ultimate goal is to live their current life in such a way as to accumulate good karma. This allows their life force to advance to a higher level in its next life.

4) Weakness of Far Eastern Thought

Adherents of Far Eastern Thought look primarily to human experience to validate their worldview assumptions. They take the beliefs that have been passed down through the ages and filter them through personal experience.

Once again, we have a situation where nothing objective supports the belief system. In fact, Far Eastern Thought has the same essential problem as does Animism. In this case, however, the problem area is human experience rather than tradition. People from many different belief systems experience reality in contradictory ways. Unfortunately, there exists no authority able to arbitrate between the contradictory experiences of the different systems. Something is not true simply because someone has a certain kind of experience.

5) Starting Point for Witness to Far Eastern Thought Believers

Adherents of Far Eastern Thought look primarily to human experience to validate their worldview assumptions. Therefore, in order to effectively witness to an adherent of Far Eastern Thought, one must understand their foundational assumptions and begin the witness there.

More specifically, the essence of their human experience is material and personal. In order to believe that ultimate reality is immaterial and impersonal, it is necessary for them to ignore their daily human experience and to explain reality with a set of beliefs that contradict that experience.

The fact is, it *is* possible for people to put themselves into an emotional, psychological, and physiological state that allows them to imagine that their being is somehow transcending the material universe. This is based, however, on Far Eastern Thought philosophical beliefs, not on actual human experience. Those who do this, then, choose to believe their philosophical belief—the product of an altered state of consciousness—over the way they normally experience life in their material existence. These altered states are attained through various methods including meditation,

94

repeating a mantra, drugs, asceticism, sexual rites, or other esoteric processes. These techniques can elicit quite profound spiritual and psychological experiences that the practitioners believe confirm their beliefs.

To counter this self-evident and subjective experiential base, it is necessary to somehow break through this false reality. One part of this is to intellectually challenge their point of view. It does not match up in any way with how human beings actually experience reality.

Remember, however, people who hold these worldview beliefs actually believe they reflect reality. Therefore, challenging them is quite a difficult process and requires a great deal of patience. Also, their mystical experiences may blind their minds to any rational arguments. Unlike Naturalists, they are not particularly concerned with the rational coherence of their beliefs.

a. Worldview Bridge Element #1: The Far Eastern Thought position has nothing to support it.

The Far Eastern Thought point of view uses human experience as its ultimate authority source. Then, using various techniques, they put themselves in an altered state of consciousness and come to imagine that the altered state represents actual reality.

Not surprisingly, even people from different Far Eastern Thought belief systems experience reality in contradictory ways. So, the question that must ultimately be answered is: Who is able to arbitrate between the contradictory experiences of the different belief systems within this worldview category? Something is not true simply because someone has a certain kind of experience. Truth is an objective reality that may be confirmed in some ways using human experience … but cannot be proven by it.

The specific matters one must deal with here are educational. At some point, it will be necessary to teach the Far Eastern Thought believer another way to understand reality, and that his altered-state experiences are inadequate bases for discovering real truth.

95

b. Worldview Bridge Element #2: God is a personal and objective person.

Once a person is brought to the place where he or she is able to acknowledge that some other belief may be the truth, it is then necessary to introduce the Christian faith to them. Far Eastern Thought understands the power behind the universe to be an impersonal life force and not a personal, objective God. Christians, therefore, must share their theistic understanding of reality. This explanation must be pursued until the individual is able to comprehend the possibility of a personal creator God. To do this, one must explain who God is and what He is like—based on biblical teachings. This doesn't mean, of course, that the person will immediately accept it, but it is not possible to move to the next step until there is an understanding of this point. With that, it becomes possible to put the two worldview systems side-by-side and make the comparison.

c. Belief System Bridge Element #1: The truth about God can only be known from the Bible.

In order to validate Christian beliefs, it is necessary to explain the authority source of the Christian faith. If an individual has already been led to an understanding of the God of the Christian faith, an explanation of the validity of the Bible is a critical next step. At that point, the person must understand our authority source in order to have confidence that the Christian faith represents actual reality.

To do this, one needs to be conversant with the evidence for the validity of the Bible. Numerous lines of evidence support the truth of the Christian authority source. As we share our witness, it may be necessary to go into the reasons why the Bible is the truth. (See Chapter 5, subtitle **Evidence for the Validity of the Bible.**)

Again, coming to an understanding of the Christian belief system does not guarantee that a Far Eastern Thought believer is going to agree about the nature of God. It is, though, a necessary step in the process.

d. Belief System Bridge Element #2: Explain the Christian Worldview

When an individual grasps the concept that the Bible is the authority source for the Christian belief system, the next step is to give an overview of the Christian faith. This begins with an explanation of God's purpose in creation, then moves on to deal with the Fall, the results of the Fall, redemption, and eternity. (See Chapter 6)

e. Belief System Bridge Element #3: Explain the Gospel Message

Once the person understands the big picture of the Christian faith, it then becomes possible to share the gospel message itself. In that process, it is important to ultimately bring the person to a decision point where they actually have the opportunity to invite Christ into their life.

Non-Christian Theism

All Theists, regardless of the particular beliefs they hold about God, look to some form of revelation to validate their beliefs. They believe that a transcendent God has revealed Himself to humanity. And based on that assumption, they assert either the validity of some holy writing or the words of a prophet as the means by which the revelation has been passed down to mankind.

The problem that exists when trying to analyze theistic belief systems is that every individual system has its own unique authority source—and each one contradicts all others. So once again we run into the problem of how to arbitrate between the various ones.

We do have a different dynamic, though, in Theism. When it comes to the worldview system itself, this is the one that corresponds to the way human beings actually experience reality, and even our own Christian faith is based on Theism. Thus, when doing an analysis of theistic belief systems, our engagement with people who follow other theistic beliefs must be done at the individual *belief system*

97

level—rather than at the worldview level—as we share a common worldview platform with them.

As Christians, we believe the truth about God can only be known from the Bible. While ultimately this is a faith assertion, it is not purely blind faith. It is faith that is based on various kinds of evidence—empirical, logical, and experiential. Non-Christian theistic belief systems advocate an entirely different God who has different characteristics, and they are based on entirely different authority sources.

As we delve into the various theistic belief systems, it is possible to use objective evidence to discover the strengths of the Christian faith and the shortcomings of other beliefs. Sources others use to understand God which lie outside of the Bible are not reliable, and the evidence will bear this out.

1) Basic Assumption

All theistic belief systems, even non-Christian faiths, believe in an infinite and transcendent (supernatural) God who is the Creator and Sustainer of the material universe.

2) Major Belief Systems That Are Based on a Non-Christian Theistic Worldview:

Baha'i   Cultural Christianity   Islam

Judaism   Jehovah's Witnesses

The Church of Jesus Christ of Latter-day Saints (Mormons)

3) Non-Christian Theism's Answers to the Essential Questions:

- **What is the nature of ultimate reality?** There is a transcendent God who created and sustains the material universe for His own purposes.

98

- **What is the nature of a human being?** Human beings are creatures that have been intentionally created by God for His own purpose.

- **What is salvation and how is it achieved?** There is neither a unified definition among theistic belief systems as to what specifically comprises salvation, nor a common belief about how to achieve it. Each one has its own definition as to the ultimate purpose of God, and man's part in that plan. To determine salvation for non-Christian Theists, it is necessary to study each system individually.

4) Weakness in Non-Christian Theism:

As noted, there is no generic way to expose the weaknesses of non-Christian theistic belief systems. Each one has its own authority source(s), history, and logical structure. We can be sure, though, that there are historical and logical problems with each one. To get at the evidence for any given system, it is necessary to deal with each one specifically.

5) Starting Point for Witness to Non-Christian Theists:

Theists look to some form of revelation to validate their beliefs. Every theistic belief system asserts the existence of a transcendent God who has revealed Himself and His ways to humanity. From that starting point, each will latch onto some form of scripture, or the teachings of some prophet, as the means by which that authoritative revelation is passed on to mankind.

Nonetheless, keep in mind a couple of important principles:

First, we know that reality exists in some objectively real form and does not exist in any other form. As such, it is only possible for one theistic belief system to be true. As an example: every theistic belief system proposes its own unique God with its own unique understanding of how to achieve salvation. As each belief system contradicts every other one on these issues, it is only possible, for one of them to represent reality. Every other one is a false religion.

A second important fact to remember is that there is evidence (or at least perceived evidence) to support or negate every belief system in existence. Not all of the evidence is based on empiricism, but the evidence does exist. Every belief system that does not represent reality contains historical, empirical, logical, or experiential flaws that are evident when seriously analyzed.

Note: Since both Christian and non-Christian Theists share the same worldview system, worldview bridge elements do not need to be addressed here. So, we are able to immediately address belief system elements. Nonetheless, in order to effectively witness to a Theist who is not a Christian, it is necessary to lead him or her to understand the following belief system elements:

a. Belief System Bridge Element #1: The truth about God can only be known from the Bible and it is a reliable authority source.

Theists who are not Christians each have their own belief system's source of revelation to which they point as the truth. For example, Muslims rely on the *Qur'an*. The Church of Jesus Christ of Latter-day Saints (more familiarly called Mormons) has three extra-biblical texts that supersede the Bible in authority. Jehovah's Witnesses use only their own biased Bible, the *New World Translation of the Holy Scriptures*, published by their organization, The Watchtower Bible and Tract Society—which must be studied based on the official interpretations found only in their literature.

So, it may be necessary to research a belief system's authority source(s) to discover its shortcomings. Sources for understanding God outside of the Bible are simply not reliable, and evidence shows that. Non-Christian Theists already believe in a transcendent God, so our task is not so much to get people to believe God exists, but to demonstrate that any deity other than the one revealed in the Bible is not the true God. (See Chapter 5, subtitle **Evidence for the Validity of the Bible**).

Along with discovering the weaknesses of other belief systems, it is also important to be proficient in sharing why the Bible is true. We need to explain the authority source of the Christian faith and be prepared to give evidence why it is true. There is powerful evidence that the Bible, and what it says about Jesus Christ, is the truth.

In order to make our case, we need to be conversant with the numerous lines of evidence that support the validity of the Christian authority source. Once again, as we share our witness, we may have to go into the reasons why the Bible, *exclusively*, is true. There are many resources one can tap into for the purpose of gaining this knowledge. (See Chapter 5, subtitle **Evidence for the Validity of the Bible.**)

For non-Christian Theists who claim to follow the Bible, it is additionally necessary to dissect their particular doctrines. When dealing with people who hold non-biblical views, know for sure that they will use Scripture passages out of context, rely on flawed or distorted translations, and/or present blatant misinterpretations to try and justify their doctrines. As such, our biblical interpretation skills must be sharp.

Again, bringing a person to an understanding of the Christian belief system does not guarantee that our friend is going to agree with us about the nature of God. That said, it is necessary for the individual to at least understand our position.

b. Belief System Bridge Element #2: Explain the Christian Worldview

When the non-believer grasps the concept that the Bible is the authority source for the Christian belief system, we can then give an overview of the Christian faith. You can be sure that the story of their faith system will be quite different from the biblical view, and it is important to make sure that *they* understand the differences. This begins with an explanation of God's purpose in creation, then moves on to deal with the Fall, the results of the Fall, redemption, and eternity. (See Chapter 6)

c. Belief System Bridge Element #3: Explain the Gospel Message

Once the person understands the big picture of the Christian faith, it is then possible to share the gospel message in a way that brings him or her to a decision point.

Hybrid Belief Systems

Some belief systems cannot be identified as being within any single worldview category. Hybrid belief systems take elements from two or more worldview categories and attempt to combine them. The big problem with such attempts is that they pit essential beliefs against one another in a way that does not logically hold together. Since every worldview literally contradicts every other worldview, every hybrid belief system contains irreconcilable internal contradictions. Typically, believers in hybrid systems simply ignore the contradictions. As such, the necessary first step in sharing the gospel with someone who believes in a hybrid system is to make them aware of the inherent contradictions within their beliefs.

1) Basic Assumption:

Every hybrid belief system is unique to the degree that there is no single assumption, or set of assumptions, one can generalize to for the purpose of understanding it. Each one has its own unique combination of beliefs that have been cherry-picked from two or more worldview systems. Thus, in order to talk about faith matters with people who hold a hybrid belief, it is necessary to study and analyze the particular system they individually hold.

2) Major Hybrid Belief Systems:

Christian Science   New Age

Scientology   The Unification Church

Unitarian Universalism

102

3) Hybrid Answers to the Essential Questions:

It is possible to address the three essential worldview questions for hybrid belief systems. That said, there is no single way that all hybrid systems will answer these questions. Each system will answer them based on its own particular belief set. As the three questions are answered, however, those answers are necessarily derived from two or more worldview systems. As such, each one has internal contradictions that become evident as one identifies how the hybrid system answers the questions.

4) Weakness of Hybrids

Since every worldview literally contradicts every other worldview, and hybrids, by definition, take elements from more than one worldview foundation, every hybrid belief system has built-in contradictory beliefs. As such, no hybrid belief system can hold together logically. By analyzing the various hybrid belief systems, we can discover from which worldviews they draw, and identify the contradictions that inevitably emerge. The specific contradictions relate to the particular combination represented in an individual system.

5) Starting Point for Witness to Hybrid Believers

Hybrid belief systems attempt to combine elements from more than one worldview system into a single belief system. As such, every hybrid belief system has built-in contradictory beliefs. In order to effectively witness to a person holding a hybrid belief system, we must lead them to understand the following:

a. Worldview Bridge Element #1: Hybrid belief systems have serious problems with their authority source(s).

In order to point out the contradictions within a particular hybrid belief system, we must study and understand the specific beliefs within that system. There are many hybrids, and the specific contradiction(s) in each one is/are unique to itself/themselves and

103

relate to the particular combination of worldview beliefs represented.

Of first importance is to expose the weaknesses of their authority source(s). As one digs into a hybrid belief system's authority source(s), contradictions will be found, as well as other problems that expose the fallacies of the belief. For instance, Christian Science founder, Mary Baker Eddy, tried to marry Far Eastern Thought presuppositions to biblical terminology, grossly distorting the clear meanings of scriptural words. Likewise, L. Ron Hubbard, founder of Scientology, attempted to meld Far Eastern Thought with Naturalism to create a pseudo-scientific mental health system.

b. Worldview Bridge Element #2: There exists an objective, personal God who can be known.

Once it can be demonstrated that a particular hybrid belief system is not valid because of its internal contradictions, it will then be necessary to explain the Christian point of view. This involves explaining the fact that God exists, along with who He is and the truth that there is only one true God.

The specifics of this explanation cannot be known without uncovering the beliefs of the particular hybrid system you are dealing with. There will be differences between the hybrid's beliefs about God, and those of the Christian faith. Once those differences are known, it is possible to make explanations and comparisons.

c. Belief System Bridge Element #1: The truth about God can only be known from the Bible.

Once it is demonstrated to the other person that his or her authority source is not valid, the opportunity presents itself to explain the Christian faith. At this point, it is important to present the Bible as the true revelation from God and to share why it is *exclusively* the truth. Sharing this evidence is crucial because this person must come to a place where they acknowledge the truth of our authority source in order to have confidence that we are leading them in the right direction.

To do this, as with other worldview belief systems, Christians need to be conversant with the evidence for the validity of the Bible. As we have indicated, numerous lines of evidence support the validity of the Christian authority source, and this evidence can be shared to show the reasons why the Bible is true. (See Chapter 5, subtitle **Evidence for the Validity of the Bible.**)

d. Belief System Bridge Element #2: Explain the Christian Worldview

When an individual grasps the concept that the Bible is the authority source for the Christian belief system, we must then make sure they understand the big picture message of the Bible. This kind of overview can help them understand the context of the Christian message. This explanation begins by recounting God's purpose in creation, then moves on to deal with the Fall, the results of the Fall, redemption, and eternity. (See Chapter 6)

e. Belief System Bridge Element #3: Explain the Gospel Message

Once the person understands the big picture of the Christian faith, it then becomes possible to share the gospel message itself in a way that brings him or her to a decision point.

The Importance of the Starting Point in Witness

In the introduction to this chapter, Wendy was doing her best to share her faith with the man at the lunch counter. However, her starting point was simply inadequate for helping a secular Jew grasp the concepts of the Christian faith.

While in some ways it may seem counterintuitive, the starting point for witness is not the gospel message itself. Before the message can be shared in an understandable way, it is necessary to know the worldview language of the person you are witnessing to. Just as we can't have a conversation with a person in English who doesn't speak the language, we can't share the gospel message with those who don't understand the conceptual language of Christian Theism—they simply will not understand what we mean.

In our modern pluralistic society, more and more people simply don't understand the Christian worldview because they have been brought up in an environment based on a non-Christian worldview. To share the gospel with these people, we must bridge the gap between their beliefs and ours. When this is effectively done, it is then possible to share the gospel message in a way that makes sense to the hearer.

Chapter 5
The Art of Argument

"You must be crazy not to believe in God!"

"You're crazy for believing it!"

The two men sat across from one another in the office break room. Jack was trying to witness to Ron, one of his co-workers. Ron had stated strongly that he did not believe in God and did not see how anyone could. After a few minutes of bantering, the discussion devolved into an argument.

"Well, let me tell you why I think you're dumb for not believing in God," retorted Jack. He then laid out several points he had read about how Atheists are ignorant of the truth and evil.

Ron just looked at him and shook his head not really knowing what else to say.

"I guess I showed you," said Jack as he headed out the door.

Rarely is anyone ever convinced to become a Christian simply by argument, especially like the one above (a dictionary's classic "first definition" sense of this noun) in which two or more people's strong disagreement leads to an emotional confrontation. A better kind of argument is when people representing different viewpoints present rational and coherent reasons for their positions (a dictionary's classic "second-definition" sense of this noun). It is similar to two lawyers calmly and meticulously making their case before a judge based on the law and legal precedents.

---

ar·gu·ment /ˈärgyəmənt/ noun

1. an exchange of diverging or opposite views, typically a heated or angry one.
"I've had an argument with my father."

2. a reason or set of reasons given with the aim of persuading others that an action or idea is right or wrong.
"There is a strong argument for submitting a formal appeal."

—Oxford Languages

Christians certainly do have a compelling point of view that can be argued on a purely intellectual level. Coming to know Christ, however, is not merely a matter of the intellectual acceptance of a set of ideas. That being said, we do not concede that scholarly arguments for the gospel are irrelevant. No one can legitimately accept beliefs they do not understand.

But when it actually comes to the point of making a decision to follow Christ, people don't do it by accepting an *argument*! They must accept the *person* of Jesus Christ. This distinction between the *impersonal* and the *personal* is ultimately the crucial point when it comes to sharing a witness. If we miss this, we may be a good debater, but we will never be a good witness. Our purpose is not to win arguments, it is to be faithful witnesses of Jesus Christ and to see other people willingly invite Christ into their lives. Ultimately, a relationship with God is personal—between an individual and God—not merely intellectual assent to a description of Him. In fact, when a person decides to follow Christ, even before we ever engaged them in an argument, God was already calling them to Himself.

Nonetheless, to see this ultimate purpose come to fruition, we must be able to make compelling arguments for its veracity. The apostle Peter made this point clear in his first letter:

> But in your hearts revere Christ as Lord. Always be
> prepared to give an answer to everyone who asks you
> to give the reason for the hope that you have. But do
> this with gentleness and respect.
>
> —1 Peter 3:15

Given these facts, there are two strategic approaches we can use.

The first approach, **Arguing on the Offensive**, takes an offensive
(but non-antagonistic) tack. This is, perhaps, the least understood
and least used method, but probably the most important when
sharing with non-believers—particularly those who may be
antagonistic. Arguing on the offense is designed to examine the non-
believer's non-Christian belief system and demonstrate its
weaknesses.

The second approach is **Arguing Defensively.** This approach is the
more traditional use of apologetics to 'defend the faith' by giving
positive evidence for why we believe what we believe, and to
counter anti-Christian intellectual challenges. This method is more
useful when we wish to give evidence to those who are truly seekers,
and confidence to those who are already believers. Nonetheless, we
do not want to passively allow critics to make their case without
challenging their arguments. We should have valid reasonable
responses to skeptics' negative assertions.

Keep in mind, that whichever approach happens to be best for a
particular situation, it is in the context of the relationship with the
person with whom you are sharing. Remember, Jesus advised His
disciples to be "wise as serpents and harmless as doves." (Matthew
10:16b KJV)

Arguing on the Offensive

When talking about arguing on the offensive, we are not advocating
that a person be offensive (*i.e.*, obnoxiously combative) in their
argumentation. Rather, we are speaking of not allowing ourselves to

be caught or forced into a defensive posture and losing the ability to direct the course of the conversation.

We certainly need to be able to defend our faith, and we should prepare ourselves in that arena. But we should never argue the gospel while under attack—without at least putting ourselves on equal footing with our opponent.

---

offensive of·fen·sive

adjective
The definition of offensive is something likely to invoke feelings of hurt, anger, disgust, disapproval, or revulsion, or is something associated with an aggressive attack.

noun
Offensive is an organized campaign or plan of action, normally created … to achieve some specific … aim or goal.

—YourDictionary.com

As to this 'leveling the playing field' to create a receptive conversational environment, remember that every belief system in existence is built on a faith foundation. That is why it is called a *belief* system. Other faiths are just as vulnerable to allegations regarding a lack of empirical proof as they say we are with our Christian faith. The time for a defense of your faith comes when you have the opportunity to share positive evidence for the Christian faith. But even this must not be done from a defensive posture. Never allow people to question the validity of your faith until they have first justified the validity of their own.

Both choosing the time in our relationship to begin witnessing to our non-believing friend and managing the conversational environment are crucial to the process. Sometimes we can choose the time when the environment is receptive, sometimes our friend, or others, will choose the time, but the tone of the conversational environment is vital.

Dealing with Relationships

Whenever you engage another person in argument, one of the key principles to remember is that he or she is a real person. The context of the conversation is a one-on-one relationship.

As a Christian, the most important thing to keep in mind is that whatever you do in life is done for a purpose—God's purpose. God has made it clear that His ultimate aim is to bring people into relationship with Himself. If we are in tune with Him, then that will be our objective, too. So, our witness needs to be fully aligned with God's purpose.

This does not mean our interactions are always congenial. Sometimes people need to be put in their place—not just for their own sake, but also for the sake of others who they might intimidate or influence. Sometimes it is necessary to shock people into realizing their point of view is invalid. We have to assess each encounter to determine the appropriate approach.

In any case, keep in mind that the element of relationship is always in play. You are not trying to win arguments; you are trying to win people. Any argument not taking this fact into account is not of God. For that reason, it is essential to continuously nurture your relationships to the highest degree possible. This is true no matter how an opponent responds in a given conversation or setting.

How People Try to Put Christians on the Defensive

In order to take the offensive in arguing, do not take on a bad attitude or become overly aggressive. But you do need to put yourself in a good position to argue.

When non-believers challenge Christians for their beliefs, they commonly do several things. Virtually every attack begins with the assumption that something is wrong with the Christian faith in contrast to what *they* believe to be "true." These snipers assume a morally or intellectually superior position and, based on that assumption, they go on the attack.

Unfortunately, most Christians simply allow these assaults to happen. But the truth is, there is no reason to allow it. You can preemptively "level the playing field," or even put the other person on the defensive—if you clearly understand their beliefs.

One common way non-Christians attempt to put Christians on the defensive is to call us hypocrites. How many times have you heard someone say they would never go to church because it is full of hypocrites? Well, that may be true. But a couple of other things are true, as well.

First, the presence of hypocrites does not determine the truth or falsity of the Christian faith. Our faith can be true even if everyone in a particular church is a hypocrite.

But also, hypocrites are everywhere—including the circles where the accuser roams:

- Would they never see a doctor again because some doctors are hypocrites? How silly.

- Would they never again go fishing, hunting, or walking; or never again watch sports, or go to work because some of those who do are hypocrites? How crazy.

- And would they allow the bad actions or attitudes of others to determine their own faith? How ridiculous.

Frankly, people who use such attacks are simply making excuses.

A second common means some non-believers (Naturalists, primarily) use to put Christians on the defensive is to say that science proves the Bible is not true. Usually, this kind of attack focuses on the Darwinian Theory of Evolution and comes from those who believe it, though not exclusively.

To be blunt, this assertion is a fallacy. Science *cannot* prove the Bible is not true anymore than it can prove the Bible is true. And while science can validate or invalidate certain specific facts a

112

particular belief system may claim, it is incapable of proving that any given set of beliefs is true or false. Specifically, as regards The Theory of Evolution, science does not give positive proof for that particular faith position either. In fact, a growing number of even secular scientists, citing an increasing mass of scientific data, are actually challenging the validity of Darwin's theory.

A third technique some non-believers use to put Christians on the defensive is to assert that the Bible is not reliable—that it contains a lot of errors or is historically inaccurate. This is another red herring. Numerous passages in the Bible certainly are difficult to interpret, but people who denigrate the Bible this way are actually showing their own ignorance regarding the principles of biblical interpretation, or their laziness by not doing the work of an honest interpreter or historian.

A fourth way non-believers try to get the upper hand is to strongly assert their own beliefs. Usually this is done without anything to actually back it up. They just smoothly and hyper-confidently talk *as if* what they are saying is true. They often get away with it because they are more fully versed in their beliefs than Christians are in theirs. Their confidence factor alone tends to silence the Christian who doesn't know how, know enough, or have the confidence in their position to answer back.

All four of these attack modes can be dealt with in short order—if you do your due diligence. A little study to get up to speed on the topics mentioned will equip you to stop this kind of put-down. The big problem is not that these issues can't be addressed, but that most Christians simply don't put forth enough effort to understand, confront, and face them down.

Problems in Non-Christian Belief Systems

The fact is, every non-Christian belief system has severe credibility problems. As we identify those problems and point them out when others try to put us on the defensive, we will quickly stop their attacks. Using this approach does not prove our position over that of others. What it does, though, is to put us on an equal footing with

113

them. At that point, we can deal with the evidence related to the veracity of the belief rather than just being intimidated by the put-downs.

So, let's look briefly at the major philosophical problems related to the various non-Christian worldviews.

1. Naturalism

Remember, there are many naturalistic belief systems. Some have their own unique weaknesses that can be exposed with a little specific study added to what is mentioned here. That said, every one of them has the same underlying worldview foundation, and the weaknesses of that foundation are inherent in all of them.

All naturalistic belief systems look to human reason as their primary authority source. Since they acknowledge no transcendent reality, they are forced to assert that unaided human reason can lead to a definitive understanding of objective reality. The only problem is that unaided human reason cannot prove any belief system. The foundation of any faith system rests entirely on how it answers the three essential worldview questions. As it turns out, the answer to every worldview question is based on faith. There is no empirical proof for any one of them. Since Naturalists assert that ultimately everything can be explained empirically, they immediately face a logical dilemma.

At its most basic level, Naturalism asserts:

- time, space, matter, and energy have a natural source,

- life can emerge out of non-life,

- less developed life forms can evolve into more complex forms, and

- consciousness can emerge out of nonconsciousness.

The dilemma is that no science supports any of these assertions. All of them are faith assumptions. It simply cannot be demonstrated that the supernatural does not exist, or that natural processes alone can account for what does exist. So Naturalism maintains it is possible, given enough time, to completely understand all of reality and how it works using empirical methodology. Nonetheless, its actual understanding of the nature of reality is based on faith.

2. Animism

As with Naturalism, there are many animistic belief systems. And as with Naturalism, Animism's individual belief systems each have their own unique weaknesses. But the same principle applies here as before—all of these individual belief systems have the same underlying worldview foundation, so the weaknesses found in the worldview are inherent in each and every one of them, as well.

Animism's authority foundation is built completely on ancestral history and tradition. Collectively, Animists believe that the nature of reality is expressed in the beliefs passed down from generation to generation. There is no other basis, and this foundation is not questioned in any respect. Based on their underlying worldview beliefs, Animists perceive what they consider to be the outworking of the gods and spirits in nature, and don't perceive a need to look to any other source—such as revelation or science.

As such, the animistic position has nothing to support it. The various animistic traditions around the world have different historical situations. Any particular animistic belief system is only one among many which literally contradict one another on various key points. This leads to the obvious conclusion that they cannot all be true.

That being the case, there must be some way of arbitrating between the different systems. The problem is, though, there is no way to make this determination. All any system has is anecdotal evidence to back it up—and the interpretation of the evidence depends completely on its presuppositions.

So, the question must be raised: How can any group know their belief structure is true and opposing beliefs are false? Something is not necessarily true simply because someone believes it. History and tradition are not sufficient to prove the truth of a belief system.

3. Far Eastern Thought

The same issues seen in both Naturalism and Animism also hold true with the numerous Far Eastern Thought belief systems. Every one of them has its own unique weaknesses. And still true here is the fact that the weaknesses found in the underlying worldview foundation apply to them all.

Far Eastern Thought belief systems rely primarily on human experience as their authority source to validate their worldview assumptions. They take beliefs passed down through the ages and filter them through personal experience.

Far Eastern Thought has the same foundational issues that exist for Animism, only with a different authority source. In Animism, the problem is contradictory historical traditions with no way to arbitrate between them. This same problem exists with human experience. People from various Far Eastern Thought belief systems experience reality in contradictory ways. So, who arbitrates between the contradictory experiences of the different belief systems? Once again, something is not necessarily true simply because someone has a certain kind of experience. Truth is an objective reality that can be *affirmed* in some ways by experience, but not *proven* by it. Human experience, though, is not sufficient to absolutely establish the truth of a belief system.

4. Non-Christian Theism

As with all of the worldview platforms cited before, there are many non-Christian theistic belief systems. And, as before, each one has its own problematic issues—but, in this case, with a slight difference. Theism is the worldview foundation most closely aligned with the way human beings actually experience reality. It acknowledges both physical and spiritual dimensions of reality and reconciles the two.

The problem, though, is that every theistic belief system claims that *its own God* is the true one. But as each system's God differs, one-to-another, all of them can't be right. In fact, only one can possibly be right. Any belief asserting something different from what is true is necessarily wrong.

The authority source for every theistic belief system is some form of revelation. A transcendent God is acknowledged to exist and is believed to have revealed Himself to mankind—generally by some scripture or prophet.

So, to find the truth, it is necessary to analyze each individual belief system's authority source based on the logic of its own authority foundation. In doing this, the belief system's problems will become evident based on inaccuracies in the historical record, inconsistent logic, contradictions within the authority source, and the like. Christians contend that these problems are evident in *every* non-Christian theistic belief system.

5. Hybrid Belief Systems

A hybrid belief system is any belief that tries to combine elements from two or more worldviews into a single system. The irresolvable problem, as we have repeatedly shown, is that every worldview literally contradicts every other worldview. As such, all hybrid belief systems automatically are logically incoherent and have irreconcilable internal contradictions. For instance, it is not possible for God to exist and simultaneously not exist. There can only be many gods or just one God, but not both. God cannot be both personal and impersonal. Every hybrid system has some kind of internal contradiction of this magnitude.

All that is necessary in dealing with people who hold hybrid belief systems is to figure out where their contradictions lie. Once that is done, the belief system is effectively eliminated as a legitimate way of understanding the truth about the structure of reality.

Problems Matching Human Experiences with Worldview Doctrines

Besides the weaknesses we have looked at above, there is another way to attack the weaknesses of non-biblical worldview beliefs—analyzing how they match up with human experiences. As we analyze the various elements in our search for the truth about reality, one of the most important elements of our search relates to how our human experiences match up with the tenets of a given worldview system. All human beings live life in particular ways. Ideally, the way they live matches up with how reality is actually structured. If that is the case, their beliefs and experiences will align in ways that create harmony in their lives. If these things do not line up, they will experience serious *dis*-harmony in their lives.

Human beings, though, have an interesting characteristic: they have the unique ability to disregard reality and live their lives based on beliefs that do not match up with how people actually experience life. In fact, there are millions, perhaps even billions, of people in every generation who adhere to each of the worldviews. Since every worldview literally contradicts every other worldview, it is impossible for all of them to be true (that is, to correspond with actual reality). They could all be wrong, but it is only possible for one belief system to be right. That fact is a powerful confirmation of the human ability to ignore reality and live with inconsistent and contradictory beliefs. It also leads to the conclusion that the majority of people on the planet, at any given time, live life *as if* what they believe about reality is true, when, in fact, it is not.

The way human experiences match up with the beliefs of a worldview system is a critical element in getting at the truth or falsity of any particular worldview system. If there isn't a match, it means either that the system is wrong, or that their human experiences are wrong. If their human experiences are wrong, people can't reliably make judgments about anything. Since humans experience what they experience—if it is wrong they wouldn't even know it. As people live life, they have no choice but to accept that human experiences reflect reality. If, on the other hand, one's belief

118

system is wrong, the only way to correct the problem is to discover the truth and change beliefs.

So, what if a person's human experiences do match up with the doctrines of a particular worldview system? In that case, it is quite strong evidence that an individual is moving in the right direction. Again, we are not talking exclusively about empirical proof, because getting at the truth or falsity of a worldview using only empirical methods is impossible. Rather, we are dealing with specific types of evidence that can be applied to our search.

In examining the four worldview systems, the only one that completely corresponds with human experiences is Theism. As such, we have powerful positive evidence that the ultimate truth about the nature of reality lies within that system. That being said, there are numerous, and contradictory, belief systems even within Theism. In the end, it becomes necessary to delve beyond the worldview level to discover ultimate truth. Still, finding the worldview platform that corresponds to the way reality is actually structured is a necessary starting point. (Note: Ultimately, only one belief system—which is associated with one particular worldview— can represent actual reality. The Christian faith *is* that one belief system).

One of the strongest lines of evidence regarding the truth or falsity of a worldview system is to analyze how it does or does not match up with the way human beings experience life. Below, we have identified nine areas that virtually everyone acknowledges to be a part of human existence. By comparing these with the presuppositions of each worldview, we can see how they match up.

Here are the nine human experiences that everyone encounters, and that we can compare to the beliefs of the various worldviews.

1. We experience life as personal, self-aware beings.

As humans, we possess the characteristics of personhood and are aware of our own existence.

119

2. We have a sense of transcendence.

Most human beings acknowledge a sense that something exists beyond the material universe. (This does not mean that everyone acknowledges an actual transcendent existence, only that there is a sense of it.) This has been true across cultures and time in every part of the world.

3. We experience life in relationships.

Humans have a need for relationship that goes beyond mere biological necessity. This need is seen in the desire we have for non-sexual interactions, as well as in selfless acts toward others.

4. We experience life based in spiritual qualities.

There are unique human qualities that go beyond mechanistic biological function. These include such characteristics as creativity, self-consciousness, self-determination, and the like.

5. We experience life based on natural laws.

It is apparent that the operation of the material universe is based on natural laws. It is possible for human beings to work with natural laws to create benefit for themselves. On the other hand, it is impossible for humans to manipulate the material universe in ways that run counter to these laws.

6. We are capable of knowledge.

Human beings have a unique ability to hold and self-consciously use knowledge.

7. We have a sense of morality.

All humans live life based on some system of morality. Various people may define this differently or disregard what they believe to be right. Nevertheless, the moral sense is operative regardless.

8. We experience time as linear.

Human beings experience time as a non-repetitive sequence of events that moves from past to present to future.

9. We experience the world as objective.

Every human being lives life as if the world exists as an objective reality. Despite any philosophical attempt to define it in another way, all must live *as if* it is true.

The worldview categories described here match the way we actually experience reality and are summarized in **Table 1. Evaluating the Truth of Worldview Categories**. For a deeper treatment of this topic see the discussion in *The Truth Mirage*.

Table 1. Evaluating the Truth of Worldview Categories

Human Experiences	Naturalism Match	Animism Match	Far Eastern Thought Match	Theism Match
Personal, Self-aware Beings	No	Yes	No	Yes
Sense of Transcendence	No	Yes	No	Yes
Life in Relationships	No	Yes	No	Yes
Spiritual Qualities	No	Partially	No	Yes
Life Based on Natural Laws	Yes	Partially	No	Yes
Capable of Knowledge	No	Partially	No	Yes
Sense of Morality	No	Yes	No	Yes
Experience Time as Linear	Yes	Yes	No	Yes
Experience the World as Objective	Yes	Partially	No	Yes

Do Your Due Diligence

The ability to operate "on the offensive" rather than "from a defensive posture" requires doing your due diligence. You must become knowledgeable enough to counter the attacks of whoever comes up against you. So, just what is this body of knowledge? It contains four important matters.

First, master the concept and the categories of worldview. Every person with whom you ever want to share the gospel already has some worldview belief. It may be relatively close to the truth, or it may be way off base. Wherever it is, it will affect the way you share the gospel message. Without an understanding of worldview, it is difficult to know the correct starting point for witness.

Second, know and be able to communicate the content of the gospel message itself. This includes four essential facts that you must be able to explain:

- who the God of the Bible is,

- the nature of humanity as separated from God because of sin,

- how God has provided a fix for the sin problem, and

- what a person can do to make that fix a personal reality for their own life.

The message is not difficult or complicated, but you must take the time and effort to learn the material. You will find it very hard to bring anyone to a knowledge of faith in Christ without this knowledge.

Third, master relationships. Certainly, some people are naturally better at forming new relationships than others. But that is not the point. Unless you live as a hermit, you definitely have relationships, or potential relationships, among people with whom you interact every day. If you wish to share your faith with someone, you must develop your relationship with them to allow for comfortable discussion of your and their religious faiths. Even someone not very good at forming relationships can learn the skills necessary to do this.

Finally, grasp the techniques that allow you to operate on the offensive. These techniques should include the following, as appropriate:

1. Be able to deconstruct opposing belief systems.

Deconstructing your opponent's beliefs must be done before constructing your own for them. If they don't see a problem with their own beliefs, they will have no reason to listen to an explanation of another one. Every non-Christian belief system represents a faith position that *does not* reflect the truth about the nature of reality. And every one of them can be deconstructed to show why. When opponents make incorrect statements, point them out and reply with a correct one.

2. Never allow people to evaluate the Christian faith based on assumptions from other worldviews.

A person who evaluates Christianity based on naturalistic assumptions, for example, will dismiss out of hand every miracle mentioned in the Bible. This would include certain core beliefs such as the virgin birth and the resurrection of Christ, or even that a supernatural God exists. A person cannot become a Christian without believing in the faith's core tenets. If someone insists on making attacks of this nature, it will probably be necessary to deconstruct their worldview platform before you can even have a respectful dialogue.

3. Learn how to hold people accountable for their attacks on your faith.

When someone challenges the truth of Christianity, make them back up their attack. The attacks can come from numerous directions, but, regardless of any particular point they make, make them explain *why* it is valid. Some of the points they try to make might include

124

denigrating the validity of the Bible, putting down Christians as hypocrites or ignoramuses, accusing Christianity of being anti-science, and the like. Remember though, every challenge can be intelligently answered. Make your opponent defend the validity of their assaults before dignifying them with an answer.

4. Always argue to the end, to the greatest degree possible.

Sometimes a discussion can become tedious or uncomfortable—for any of a number of reasons. If that happens, do not fall prey to the temptation to simply cut out of the discussion. If you do, it is quite possible your opponent(s) will think they have won. Stick with them until they finally give up their attacks. This attitude of sticking it out to the end is not for the purpose of simply winning an argument. Rather:

- On a tactical level, it is to make sure that your adversary recognizes that he or she cannot avoid the ultimate truth. If you have done your due diligence, you cannot be outmaneuvered—because the Christian faith really does represent the truth about the nature of reality. The truth always rises to the top when given the opportunity. If issues come up that you personally don't know how to deal with, seek out the answers.

- And on a strategic level, remember your ultimate goal—be sure to complete your witness because of the eternal consequences they face in their unbelief if they do not choose Jesus.

Don't give up!

5. Never make personal attacks on your opponent(s).

Do not miss opportunities to point out the flaws and inconsistencies of attacks against your argument, even strongly if necessary. But it must never become personal—that is, do not call your opponent ugly names or impugn their character. Even if they begin throwing insults, never respond in kind. Simply point out that their personal insults do not contribute to making their point.

Don't forget, your ultimate goal is not to beat people down, but to share a witness of Jesus Christ. How the witness is received is ultimately up to the person with whom you are interacting, not with you. But if offense to your argument *is* taken, it should not be because you made a personal attack. It may be that your argument has pinned them into a corner, and they are mad that they can't answer back. Even though they may accuse you of a personal attack or lash out in a personal assault on you, it is okay. Gently point out that you did not personally attack them, and that they should not personally attack you, either.

It is difficult to keep from being forced into a defensive posture if you have not made an effort to become skilled in arguing on the offense. But, with a mastery of arguing on the offense, the skills of dealing with hostile people will prove out, and such a confrontational situation can become a productive opportunity to build the kingdom of God.

Arguing Defensively

Being "on the defensive" is never a good idea. But there are those times when we must step up and defend the tenets of the Christian faith. In fact, an entire Christian theological field of study, called apologetics (which we have mentioned before), is dedicated to doing just that. This kind of *defense of the faith* is a very important skill for Christians. But, as vital as it is, when it comes to the witnessing process, its value only comes into play once we have established that our faith is worthy of defense by demonstrating the faith nature of our opponent's position.

> Defensive /dəˈfensɪv/ /dəˈfɛnsɪv/
>
> *adjective*
> > 1 Used or intended to defend or protect.
> >   1.1 attributive … relating to or intended as defense.
> >
> > 2 Very anxious to challenge or avoid criticism.
> > —Lexico Dictionary

In other words, there is a huge distinction between arguing from a negative defensive posture and positively defending our faith. We should always be ready to rationally explain it, but we should never allow ourselves to be put on the defensive.

It is always good to keep in mind that even this is a part of the witnessing process. Defending the faith is not simply a matter of sharing intellectual material. Remember, its purpose is always to lead people to Jesus Christ. This is most valuable when sharing with people who are open to the evidence for the Christian faith.

So, once we establish that our faith is worthy of defense, how should we go about doing it? Essentially, it is a matter of presenting the evidence for the validity of our faith. We should become familiar with all of the basic lines of evidence. None is, by itself, proof that our faith is the truth about the nature of reality. After all, we are working with worldview *beliefs*. But piled layer upon layer, these lines of evidence can be quite compelling.

We will take a moment here to look over the various categories of evidence. Keep in mind that this is only a brief summary. Entire books could be, and have been, written about each of these. But we at least need to know the categories.

Evidence for the Validity of the Bible

Many people attack the Christian faith by attacking the Bible. These attacks fall into several categories.

127

1. Preservation and Transmission of the Text

Some critics say the Bible is an ancient book and was not accurately preserved and/or transmitted over the centuries. But the fact is, the Bible *has been* accurately preserved and transmitted to us throughout the ages. An entire discipline of study is dedicated to tracking the Bible's transmission, and the evidence for its accuracy is overwhelming. Anyone making the argument that the Bible has not been transmitted accurately to our time simply does not know what they are talking about.

For further study on how the Bible was written and preserved see:

- Craig Blomberg: *The Historical Reliability of the New Testament: The Challenge to Evangelical Christian Beliefs.* Nashville, TN: B&H Academic, 2016 Nashville, TN: 2016.

- F.F. Bruce: *The New Testament Documents: Are They Reliable?* Grand Rapids, MI: Wm. B. Eerdmans Pub. Co., 2003.

- Norman Geisler, William Nix: *From God to Us: How We Got Our Bible.* Chicago, IL: Moody Press, 2012.

2. Contradictions

Another disparagement people make is that the Bible is full of contradictions. Skeptics who make this attack are again in error. In order to make this claim, they generally attempt to filter the Bible's teachings through their own worldview beliefs. This is not an acceptable methodology. The consistency of the Bible is based on its own teachings and its own worldview foundation. Even though it was written by approximately 40 authors; over about a 1500 year period; in different languages, places, and cultures; the Bible is entirely and amazingly consistent with itself.

For further study on answering Bible difficulties see:

- Norman Geisler, Thomas Howe. *When Critics Ask: A Handbook on Christian Evidences* [revised and updated]. Grand Rapids, MI: Baker Books, 1992.

- Norman Geisler, Thomas Howe. *The Big Book of Bible Difficulties: Clear and Concise Answers from Genesis to Revelation.* Grand Rapids, MI: Baker Books, 2018.

3. Unfulfilled Prophecy

A third challenge is the claim that prophesies contained in the Bible have not been fulfilled. This argument takes a number of different forms, so it is necessary to be knowledgeable in this area to make an adequate defense. Also note that various groups of Christians make differing claims about prophecy based on diverse approaches to the study of theology and eschatology (the scriptural study of last things). It is critical to sort these things out before engaging in argument in this arena. That being said, the Bible contains literally scores of prophecies that have been fulfilled in minute detail. Some of them were made hundreds of years before the fulfillment.

4. Science Disproves the Bible

Finally, some people claim that science disproves the Bible. In actual fact, science supports the Bible in virtually every way.

One area of science that gives positive evidence for the validity of the Bible is archaeology. Over the years, it has provided increasing evidence that the places and people mentioned in the Bible actually existed, and the facts about them recorded in the Bible are historically accurate. Other areas where science upholds the Bible relate to the creation of the universe from nothing, the growing evidence of an intelligent designer, and the origin of life.

129

For further study on science and the Bible see:

- Stephen C. Meyer. *Return of the God Hypothesis: Three Scientific Discoveries That Reveal the Mind Behind the Universe.* New York, NY: HarperCollins Publishers, 2021.

- Hugh Ross: *The Creator and the Cosmos: How the Latest Discoveries Reveal God* [4th edition]. Oak Park, CA: RTB Press, 2018.

- Lee Strobel. *The Case for a Creator: A Journalist Investigates Scientific Evidence That Points Toward God.* Grand Rapids, MI. Zondervan Publications, 2004.

Identity Evidence

The Christian faith stands or falls on the truth that Christ was who He said He was—the Messiah of God—God in the flesh. If He was who He claimed to be, the truth of the Christian faith is assured. In fact, Jesus completely conforms to the identity of Messiah from prophecy. Beyond that, His life stands the test. He actually lived up to what He taught.

In dealing with this issue, it is important to note that Jesus Christ believed that He, Himself, was God. He was either crazy, lying, or truthful. The evidence is compelling that He was telling the truth. (Matthew 20:25-28, Mark 2:6-12, Luke 22:67-71, John 4:25-26, Revelation 1:17-18, and many more.)

Beyond that, eyewitnesses who lived and worked with Jesus also believed He was God. They believed this not merely on the basis of Jesus telling it to them, but on the basis of His whole body of work in their presence—both His teachings and miracles. (Matthew 28:9, John 1:1, Acts 7:55-60, Romans 10:13-14, 1 Corinthians 1:1-2, Philippians 2:5-11, Colossians 2:9, Hebrews 1:6, and many more.)

Eyewitness Evidence

One of the strongest lines of evidence for the validity of the Christian faith is eyewitness accounts. Many of the people who knew Jesus and were present as He taught and performed miracles were the same ones who wrote the Gospels and other New Testament writings, or who gave first-person evidence to these authors. Even the Apostle Paul, who was originally an enemy of the church, personally saw the risen Christ and interacted extensively with those who knew Jesus before His death and resurrection. Not only do we have these eyewitness testimonies, we also have reliable, written accounts of His life, ministry, and teachings. And, as we stated before, these writings were accurately preserved and transmitted over the course of the centuries.

Corroborating Evidence

While corroborating evidence is not hugely extensive, references to Jesus are found in various historical writings outside of the biblical text. While these references are not reliable in the sense of giving testimony of Jesus' messiahship, they are significant in that historically, Jesus made a big enough impact on the world of His day to warrant being included in those histories. He was an actual person in history who caused enough of a stir to be mentioned in official records and respected histories.

Rebuttal Evidence

Over the years, some of the greatest non-believing minds have tried many approaches to discredit the Christian faith. Some have tried to deny Jesus' historical existence, negate His resurrection, discredit His teachings, repudiate His miracles, prove God does not exist, or have used other means. But the fact is, not a single approach used to discount the evidence for the truth of the gospel can stand up to scrutiny.

Medical Evidence

As it turns out, Luke, the writer of one of the biographies of Jesus, was a doctor. Granted, we don't have a description of Jesus' death based on modern medicine (since modern medical technology did not exist in those days). Nonetheless, the descriptions of the death

131

and resurrection of Jesus are consistent with what would be expected based on the medical knowledge of that day.

Evidence of the Missing Body

Many naysayers have formulated all kinds of theories to explain what happened to the body of Jesus after His resurrection. Virtually every attempt to discredit Jesus' resurrection from the dead begins with the naturalistic assumption that, since the supernatural does not exist, His body could not have been resurrected. Their reasoning is that since a resurrection was impossible there had to be another explanation for the empty tomb. But these skeptics (whose numbers in the academic community have shrunk dramatically in recent decades) cannot provide any definitive proof to back up their argument. The fact is, after the resurrection of Christ, the body really was gone out of the grave—even with the extensive precautions taken by the Jewish and Roman authorities. (Matthew 27:62-66, 28:11-15)

The Evidence of Jesus' Post-resurrection Appearances

If the missing body were the only issue, detractors could claim that followers of Jesus simply hid the body well enough that others never found it. However, there is more. After His resurrection, Jesus appeared to His followers live and in person over a period of forty days. Again, it was the people who actually witnessed these appearances who were the authors of most of the New Testament writings. During that time, Jesus was seen by the apostles, close associates, and others—including over 500 people who testified to the Apostle Paul. (1 Cor. 15:1-8)

Circumstantial Evidence

Several lines of evidence fall into the category of being circumstantial. Each taken by itself may not amount to much, but together they are another powerful indicator of the validity of the Christian faith.

First, we have the fact that after the ascension, the disciples were willing to die for their beliefs. Who would put their life on the line for what they know to be a lie? Had the whole thing about Jesus been a lie, when it came down to either living or dying because of the beliefs, most people would have either recanted or simply faded into the background. However, tradition has it that all of the original twelve, except John (who died in exile on Patmos) and Judas (who hanged himself after betraying Jesus), died very public martyr's deaths.

A second line of evidence relates to the conversion of skeptics. In particular, two very high-profile skeptics not only became believers after meeting Jesus following His resurrection, but also became significant leaders in the new movement.

One was James, the brother of Jesus. We can only imagine how difficult it must have been to finally come to the conclusion that your own brother could be the Messiah of God who had been prophesied in Scripture.

The second, a skeptic-to-the-extreme who turned believer, was Saul of Tarsus. Originally, his religious background and training made him violently opposed to the faith—even to the point of being a leading persecutor of Christians. However, after a personal encounter with the risen Christ, Saul (aka Paul) believed and became a follower. Later, over the three-plus decade course of his remaining life, he wrote a large portion of what is now the New Testament ... and he, too, died a martyr's death.

Another line of circumstantial evidence focuses on the changes that occurred in key social structures, and the introduction of a completely new theology among former Jews. The kinds of things converting Jewish believers gave up were so central to their identity as Jews that it is inconceivable that they would do it without some kind of radical evidence. And literally thousands experienced the evidence.

A fourth line of circumstantial evidence concerns the ordinances of The Lord's Supper and Baptism. We would not expect that the

133

celebration of an execution and a curse (the crucifixion of Christ) would become the focal point of a belief system. Yet this is precisely what happened.

A final line of evidence, the emergence of the church from a small band of Christ-followers to a worldwide movement, is nothing less than astounding. It is virtually unheard of for a belief system to emerge and grow as this one did in its early stages without any kind of violent coercion.

Experiential Evidence

This last line of evidence is very personal. That being said, it is ultimately the one that must be accepted above all others. No kind of empirical proof is capable of changing a person's life. Those kinds of proofs may cause a person to think about other possibilities, but conversion to the Christian faith is a personal event that has to be experienced on a personal level. God is a person, and becoming a Christian requires that an individual enter into a personal relationship with Him through faith. No amount of intellectual knowledge, or any other impersonal means, will get that job done.

In addressing this level of evidence, the first thing we (the authors and producers of this book) point to is the fact that our own lives have been changed by knowing Jesus Christ in a personal relationship. We have met Him and interact with Him personally on a continual basis.

Also, we can point to the untold millions of others in history whose lives have been changed because of their personal relationship with God through Jesus Christ. Again, this line of evidence does not stand on its own, but, added to all of the other evidence, it is a very powerful piece of the puzzle.

For in-depth study on the historical evidence for Christianity and the resurrection of Christ, see:

- William Lane Craig: *Did Jesus Rise from the Dead?* Pine Mountain, GA: Impact 360 Institute, 2019.

- Gary R. Habermas, Michael R. Licona. *The Case for the Resurrection of Jesus:* Grand Rapids, MI: Kregel Publications, 2004.

- C. S. Lewis. *Mere Christianity* (revised and enlarged edition). San Francisco, CA: HarperOne, 2015.

- Josh McDowell, Sean McDowell: *Evidence That Demands a Verdict: Life-Changing Truth for a Skeptical World.* Nashville, TN: Thomas Nelson Publishers, 2017).

- Lee Strobel. *The Case for Christ: A Journalist's Personal Investigation of the Evidence for Jesus.* Updated, expanded edition. Grand Rapids, MI: Zondervan Publishing, 2016.

The Value of Argument

As we have emphasized in this chapter, when we use the word 'argument' in the current context, we are not talking about being contentious. Rather, we are speaking of sharing a witness aimed at a specific goal. The arguments we make are designed to shake people out of their rebellion against God, shatter their worldview and belief system mirages, and to show them why only Christ is the door to knowing Him. If you keep this purpose in mind and approach this mandate with the right attitude, God will use you to lead others into a saving relationship with Himself.

PART III

The Practice of Christian Witness

The gospel message must be effectively communicated if it is to have any significance at all. Effective communication means it is presented in a way that makes sense to the one who is receiving it. Therefore, when it comes to sharing a witness for Christ, we must always take both context and content into consideration.

Part of the communication must address any worldview differences that may exist, as these create difficult barriers to understanding. Since a worldview is a way of understanding reality, we must help those who don't understand the biblical worldview to at least understand its logic—even if they don't accept it.

But the worldview context is not enough. Once they understand that, we must also explain the gospel message itself, and offer them the opportunity to actually receive Christ into their lives.

There is one more important principle to keep in mind.

For us Christians, sharing our faith is not merely a recommended activity—it is an intrinsic expression of our changed lives in Christ, and obedience to the last commandment from Jesus … our "Great Commission." (Matthew 28:18-20) Having had our lives transformed by Him, we should feel an inner compulsion to share that same life-changing truth of Jesus with others.

Here, in Part III, we will cover how to do this—effectively.

CHAPTER 6
Sharing an Effective Witness:
The Context of the Gospel Message

John, a Christian, has eaten lunch with his friend Albert each week for several months. They were introduced at a business conference and discovered a common interest in motorcycles. In the course of their conversations and riding trips, John learned that Albert had been raised Jewish but was not observant. From their interaction, he concluded that Albert was, in fact, a Naturalist who didn't really believe in anything supernatural.

They talked at length about the difference between a naturalistic worldview and a theistic one, and John felt he was making progress in exposing Albert to the logical flaws in his thinking. Albert even acknowledged that maybe a God existed after all, but he didn't see how it was relevant to his life.

Eventually, John felt he was at a point where he could share the gospel of Christ with Albert. So, he gently led their discussions to the issue of who Jesus was and why it mattered now ... and for his eternal destiny. Albert listened to what his friend said and weighed his words carefully.

Like John, perhaps you are now at the place where you can actually share the gospel message. We are assuming, here, that you have established the necessary relationship with a person who is ready to hear you explain the message of how to enter into a personal relationship with Christ.

At this point, it is important to recognize that the amount of information you share, and the way you present it, may vary according to whom you are witnessing. Those who already essentially understand the message will not need nearly as much explanation as those who are further away from understanding it, in order to bring them to the point of decision. But by knowing the full scope of possibilities, it is possible to share an effective witness no matter what the situation.

The Gospel Presentation Process

Let's take a moment to look at the activities in the process for sharing a gospel presentation.

Activity 1. Get People into the Presentation

Every person, to whom we ever witness, has a belief system already in place. When we share a witness, the first order of business is to establish a relationship with the person that can provide a means for bridging the gap from what he or she believes, to the truth of the gospel message. This was the entire point of Chapter 4 as we dealt with the starting point of witness.

Some of those with whom we interact will already be close to understanding the gospel message. They may have grown up in church, or at least had a family who claimed to be Christian—and probably actually hold a theistic worldview. At the other end of the spectrum are those who know little or nothing about Jesus and grew up immersed in a different worldview environment. And, of course, they could hold any of the shades of belief in between. The first step in witness is to get into a position to engage the other person long enough to share an effective gospel presentation.

In some cases, we can do this in a one-shot deal, where we use a 'cold-call' methodology, then share the gospel, and get out. Even with a cold-call witness, though, the person has to be engaged and agree to listen to the presentation. Although this kind of relationship is shallow and temporary, it must still be established.

More often than not, though, it is far better to invest the effort and the time to cultivate a longer-term relationship with that person. We need to at least get to the point where they trust us enough to open up about faith issues.

So, regardless of the situation, the first step is to establish a relationship that leads to an opening to share the gospel. This may happen quickly or may take years. It may be done based on sales skills that have been acquired by training and experience, or in the natural flow of living life and making friends. But until this relationship is established, it is impossible to move on to the next step.

Activity 2. Distinguish Non-Christian Belief from Christian Belief

The key to bridging the gap between the beliefs of the one to whom we wish to witness, and the Christian faith, is to compare and contrast the two. In that analysis, we can determine how each one lines up with empirical knowledge, logic, and human experience.

To do this, all that is necessary is to:

- answer the three essential worldview questions (Who is God? What is a human being? What comprises salvation?) for both of the belief systems,

- lay their answers side by side with ours, and then,

- compare and contrast them.

The most dramatic differences, obviously, will be between belief systems that come from different worldviews. But even when there is a common theistic worldview, a perceptible difference exists between the Christian faith and *any* non-Christian belief system.

The reason for this is that the Christian faith is the objective truth about reality, and every other belief system strays from that objective truth.

- Some beliefs stray *far* away, and the difference is easily seen. For instance, much of the Baha'i Faith is based upon a theistic worldview. However, its beliefs about the nature of God, salvation, and life after death are radically different from Christianity.

- Others may be close, but still be over the line and outside the bounds of true, biblical Christianity. For example, Jehovah's Witnesses use common Christian and biblical terms, but they deny the most fundamental doctrine of historic Christianity: the full deity of Jesus Christ.

Regardless of the distance between our Christian faith and that of the person to whom we wish to witness, clearly marking the distinction between the belief systems on this basis is absolutely critical. It is this difference that determines:

- who needs to hear the gospel as a matter of their salvation,

- what they need in order to get them ready to hear it, and

- the starting point for sharing it with them.

Making these distinctions involves several steps:

Step 1. Elicit the other person's beliefs.

It is impossible to make a comparison between our Christian faith and another faith if there is nothing to compare. As such, the conversation must bring the other person's beliefs into full view. Sometimes the other person will be very conversant with their own beliefs, in which case you can let that person make their own explanation. Interestingly, many people who self-identify with a particular belief system are not conversant with their own beliefs at all. In that case, it is very helpful to already have some knowledge of the belief system the other person holds.

Step 2. Share the problems inherent in the other person's belief system.

The purpose for delving into the problems with the other person's belief system is to give them a reason to listen to an alternative. If they are totally convinced that their beliefs are right, they have no reason to consider changing to any another until their confidence is shown to be misplaced.

When a person's belief system is based on a non-theistic worldview, the differences with Christian beliefs will become most evident when contrasting their answers to the essential worldview questions with how the Bible answers them. In that situation, it is easy enough to ask the worldview questions, get the person to answer the questions based on their belief system, then begin a discussion as to why their beliefs don't match up with reality.

For those who hold to a non-Christian theistic belief system, it is generally necessary to draw the distinctions in a different place—as they hold a worldview common with Christianity. This is why having some knowledge about the other person's specific belief system is important. In that case, there will be problems, but they relate to such things as authority source and history, rather than worldview. Being able to point out those problems is useful.

Step 3. Contrast the Christian faith with their belief system.

The Christian faith actually does represent the truth about reality, as is evident when clearly contrasted with a false belief system. The way to do that is to ask, once again, the three essential worldview questions, and to answer them based on both the Christian faith and the other belief system. Those answers can then be easily compared.

It is not enough, though, to simply answer the questions. It is also important to explain *why* the biblical answer is true and the other belief system's is not. Answers to the "Why?" questions give even more reasons for a person to consider receiving Christ.

Activity 3. Explain the Scope of the Christian Worldview

It is possible to accept Christ without understanding everything about the Christian worldview. But it is nearly *im*possible to maintain total confidence in the faith without a mature comprehension. The Christian faith exists as a complete narrative, and without knowing the entire story, some things about it don't make much sense. The danger these days is that many opponents of Christianity are aggressively antagonistic toward biblical faith. Without understanding the whole story, it is very difficult for the immature believer to answer an antagonist's taunts in an intelligent way. On the other hand, if they know the whole story, they are in a position to answer any attack these opponents may throw at them.

An explanation of the biblical worldview can be broken down into five parts: Creation, the Fall, Life After the Fall, Redemption, and Eternity. If we share this story as a part of the witnessing process, our witness becomes understandable, even to people with worldview beliefs far from our own.

> See Appendix 4, *Verses Supporting the Biblical Worldview*, for specific Bible references that support the content of the following subtitled paragraphs.

Let's look briefly at an explanation of the biblical worldview.

Creation

In order to truly grasp the significance of the Christian faith, it is necessary to begin before the creation of the material universe and delve into the very mind of God. Ultimately, nothing else about the Christian faith makes sense without understanding God's purpose for His creation.

We are able to comprehend God's purpose because He has revealed it in Scripture—particularly in the first two chapters of the Book of

Genesis. It is impossible to know anything about God without His having revealed it. In particular, God's revelation in Scripture is essential to define His purpose for creating mankind in the first place.

The beginning of the Christian story has its roots in the creation of mankind. Before God created man *in His own image*, no material creatures He had made fit into this category.

In order to grasp the significance of man's creation, though, we must first understand something about God Himself. God is the only infinite and eternal being (existing beyond time and space). As such, He is a real person with a real purpose in His own heart and mind. He is a unique person who contains within Himself elements of both unity and diversity. This kind of *beingness* does not exist outside of the infinite and eternal person of God. He is a unity in that He is the one and only God. At the same time, He exists in diversity in that He is a Trinity of three separate Persons able to have an actual, viable relationship within His tri-personhood.

At some point, though, God, according to His eternal purpose, created another class of beings—with the personhood characteristics of God Himself—*i.e.*, "in His image." The idea of being created in the image of God simply means that man would have the personhood attributes of God. These include such things as the ability to be self-aware, creative, capable of knowledge, having a free will, and the like. This does not mean that He set out to create another god. Rather, He created a creature with personhood characteristics which provided the possibility of a personal (or person-to-person) relationship with Him. God did not reveal why He did so. Perhaps He simply wanted another way to express His love— which is an essential part of His being. Not that this was necessary for Him, though. As a Trinitarian being, everything He needed, including the need for relationship, is contained within Himself. All we know is that He created this new creature capable of sharing a personal relationship with Him.

So, at this point, we can see God's purpose for the creation of mankind in the first two chapters of Genesis. However, for that purpose to become a reality, a place for this being to live had to also exist. So, God created the material universe as the place where this new creature would live. Before this creative event, there was no such thing as the material reality we know. God conceived of it in His own mind and created it out of nothing.

So, within the material universe, God made a place perfectly capable of sustaining the physical life of this new creature. Earth was that place. And when the earth was ready for man, God created a paradisiacal garden for him to inhabit. It was His purpose that He and man would enjoy one another's company in this place eternally. To achieve His purpose, God manifested Himself on this physical earth in order to share fellowship with this new creature. Of course, He was still God in eternity and was not limited to His earthly manifestation, but He did accommodate Himself to the earth to fulfill His purpose.

The first man God created was Adam. Adam was soon followed by the first woman, Eve. With this creation, God was able to, and did, have fellowship with these newly created persons.

In the beginning, mankind was perfect. There was no sin and no sin nature to pollute the new material creation God had established. In those days, God and man interacted with one another on the physical earth without interference. They enjoyed intimate and unrestricted fellowship in the paradise that was Earth.

The Fall

The series of events that culminated in man committing sin against God is commonly referred to by Christian theologians as The Fall. The concept of the Fall gets to the very heart of what happened to the human condition. It helps us understand why human beings are now separated from God, and why it is so difficult for us to live a life in close personal fellowship with Him. It also gives us an understanding of our very nature. Knowing these things is essential for understanding ourselves and what is necessary to repair our separation from God.

Before going more deeply into this matter, though, an important point must be emphasized. The Fall, and the events following the Fall which God put in place to create its fix, are not mere spiritual concepts. All of this happened in actual history. The Fall and redemption from sin are actual matters with which humanity must deal—within the physical existence in which we live. We are not just addressing here internal struggles as we try to think and live rightly in daily life. An objective element is in play that must be dealt with and overcome.

Our internal tendency to sin leads to actual expressions of sin in life. This internal tendency is our sin nature inherited from Adam. The sin nature drives us to commit actual sins. It is what theologians call *original sin*. These acts can be mental (greed, lust, anger, *etc.*) or physical (stealing, sexual immorality, murder, *etc.*). The main point, though, is that all of these things are actual elements that play out in actual history, and which place genuine guilt on our lives and must be resolved.

In the beginning, as was addressed in the previous section, God created a being capable of interacting with Him in a personal relationship, and who could willfully return His love. The relationship God had with the first man and woman in the initial stages exactly fit God's purpose. It was completely intimate and unhindered. God and man enjoyed perfect fellowship as they lived together in the earthly paradise that He had created.

Unfortunately, there came a time when Adam and Eve willfully disobeyed God and did the one thing that could break fellowship with Him. When God placed them in the garden, He gave specific instructions that they could eat the fruit of any tree they found except one. Everything was fine until the day when they made the decision to disobey this one restriction.

The thought to disobey did not originate in their own minds, however. Another player had entered the scene and set up the betrayal. This fact does not take away from the guilt of Adam and Eve for their disobedience. They could have made the choice to obey God, but they didn't.

147

On that fateful day, Satan took the form of a serpent and approached Eve with the idea of eating the forbidden fruit. His deceitful portrayal of that act convinced her that doing so was not a bad thing at all. In fact, his lie convinced her that this fruit was exceedingly good—to the point that it would make them like God Himself. As it turned out, this temptation was strong enough to entice Eve, then Adam, to do the one thing God told them not to do.

The result of that act was, in one way, what Satan said it would be. It gave Adam and Eve an experiential knowledge of moral good and evil. However, Satan did not tell them the whole story. The introduction of evil created a situation where paradise, indeed all of creation, was corrupted. This evil destroyed the unrestricted fellowship that Adam and Eve had enjoyed with God. The Holy God will not have fellowship with sin.

It would have been bad enough if this separation from God had only affected the lives of Adam and Eve. But the results were far more widespread. The evil that entered the created order penetrated to the very core of humanity. As a result, the nature of mankind was infected with sin. Every person born since that time has inherited that sin nature. This nature predisposes us to express sin through our lives in the way we think and act. As a result, all human beings are separated from God because of this evil within. God simply will not allow Himself to fellowship with unholiness.

But the results of this Fall had an even wider result than the separation of man from intimate fellowship with God. As it turned out, evil was not just a spiritual concept. It had a physical manifestation that also affected the material universe God originally created as a perfect paradise. The result was the instability of the natural universe in such things as earthquakes, volcanoes, tornados, hurricanes, floods, wildfires, and the like.

At this point, it might be helpful to give a more graphic characterization of sin. In some ways it is like some kind of spiritual radiation. Much like physical radiation, it literally penetrates the entirety of the created order—only it is a spiritual element, not physical. Since the Fall, this "spiritual radiation" has permeated and corrupted everything in the physical universe. In our human existence, we are conceived in an environment where we are personally affected. As such, it plays out in every element of our existence—most prominently in our tendency to live in rebellion against God.

Life After the Fall

We already discussed the existence of the Fall and the problems it created. But to appreciate the full significance of this event, we need to address the results of this terrible tragedy in more detail.

As mentioned above, after sin entered the world, it became the primary principle that ruled the universe. The ultimate result was that it corrupted the perfect creation God had made.

First, it created a separation between mankind and God. One primary characteristic of God is that He is holy—without moral blemish. The nature of His holiness is such that He will not dwell in the presence of sin—that which is unholy. So, when the first humans opened the door and allowed sin to enter their being, God would no longer remain present with them. They not only committed a sinful act (an act of rebellion against God), but their act also created a situation where sin became part of the very fabric of their being. God would not dwell with them under those circumstances.

But sin not only became a part of the fabric of human existence, it also penetrated the entire created order. The universe, which was in perfect harmony from the time of its creation, was jolted out of kilter. The physical result of this entry of sin was to make the earth, indeed the entire physical universe, subject to decay and degradation.

From the very beginning, however, God was determined to repair it. He could have chosen simply to destroy it and start over. But He was not about to be defeated by Satan who was instrumental in initiating the Fall. So, God carried out His plan to redeem His fallen creation.

The fix, though, would not happen at the snap of a finger. The Fall had resulted from an act in history, and God designed the fix also to work through a historical process. This process would accomplish the purpose for which He had originally made the creation.

From the beginning, God intended that the first man and woman would fully populate His creation. The Fall did not prevent that from happening, but it did skew the process.

The first problem it introduced was *physical death*—that is to say, because of sin, our physical bodies are no longer immortal and will die and decay. With physical death, the fact also emerged that some of the beings who were created in God's image would not ultimately enjoy eternity with Him. At physical death, if they entered eternity in a state of separation from Him, there would be no way to restore their relationship with Him.

The second problem was *spiritual death*—that is to say, our immortal spirit would face eternal separation from God. Since God created mankind as a free-will creature with the ability to choose whether or not to enter a relationship with Himself, some people could choose not to follow Him. So, at physical death, the ultimate destination of individual human beings is settled based on the choices they make during physical life. Those who choose to follow Christ in physical life will enjoy eternity with Him, while those who choose to not follow Him will be eternally separated from Him.

Throughout history, mankind has struggled with the consequences of the Fall. We struggle with the effects of sin in the physical world such as earthquakes, tornados, hurricanes, diseases, and other occurrences in nature. We also deal with sin's effects in human life. It wreaks havoc in society in such ways as poverty, war, abortion, homosexuality, and many other problems. And finally, we face sin's effects individually as we struggle to know God and interact with Him in an environment which makes that difficult.

Satan has a powerful influence in the fallen world. He is a personal presence in the world and the father of sin. He not only got the sin ball rolling, he keeps it going using every trick he can to entice individuals to rebel against God and follow him. Mankind will struggle with sin until the time is fulfilled for God to end it.

Redemption

We have already touched on the concept of redemption—God's restoration of His fallen creation—but we need to understand how God's fix applies to our lives personally. God saw that Satan had invaded His creation and injected the sin virus in an attempt to destroy it. He could have destroyed the world and started over, as we noted. However, He proceeded on a different path. Rather than allow Satan to defeat Him, God overcame him and, in the process, fixed (redeemed) His creation. He provided mankind a means of salvation and will ultimately create a new heaven and new earth from the carcass of the old.

To do this, God began a process to reverse the effects of sin introduced at the Fall. This process began with God's plan to send a redeemer into the world who would offer Himself as a sacrifice in place of those separated from Him because of their sin. This redeemer would have to be completely without sin and, thus, worthy of this position. As no other human being was qualified, God determined that He Himself, in the Second Person of the Trinity, would be this Redeemer.

As the infection of sin had permeated the entire created order, the fix would also require removal of sin from the material universe, and at the same time accomplish the original purpose of the creation. Since the original purpose was to populate a perfect earth with creatures to fellowship with Him, God allowed the process of procreation to proceed. Only those individuals, however, who choose to spend eternity with Him are allowed the privilege of this fellowship. Those not choosing this path are destined to spend eternity outside of His presence.

As the history of the earth moved forward, God continuously revealed to mankind how to have this relationship with Him. He revealed Himself in nature, in the consciences of individual human beings, through specially called persons whom He divinely inspired

151

to write Scripture, through the incarnation of Jesus Christ, and by His Holy Spirit directly indwelling individuals who acknowledge Him. This process of revelation, though, was progressive in nature.

The initial revelation was given directly to Adam and Eve and in the moral consciences of all their descendants. Through the outworking of history, God revealed the nature of the redemptive process. He chose the nation of Israel to be keepers of this message by giving them the sacrificial system to be practiced in the temple. This system did not literally provide for the forgiveness of sin, as the animals being sacrificed were not capable of actually taking sin onto themselves. It did, however, foreshadow the actual sacrifice that would occur in the fullness of God's timing.

The actual sacrifice occurred when Jesus Christ was crucified on the cross. Jesus was not an ordinary man; He was God who stepped out of heaven and put on skin. Before ever manifesting Himself as a human being, Jesus was the Son—the Second Person of the Trinity. When He came to earth, He was born in the normal way human beings are born. His conception, however, was unique. He was not the product of the intimacy of a human man and woman. God performed a miracle, impregnating the Virgin Mary *via* the Holy Spirit (the Third Person of God in the Trinity) in order that Jesus could be conceived in her womb. This was necessary so He could be born without the sin nature that is part and parcel of natural human existence.

In order for a person to qualify as the sacrifice for the sin of mankind, it was necessary for that individual to be sinless from birth to death. Thus, Jesus, conceived and born without sin, lived a sinless life—which qualified Him to become the sacrifice for the sins of mankind.

When He was finally crucified, Jesus fulfilled God's requirements for undoing the sin problem. This process was not merely for saving mankind, it was for completely reversing *all* the effects of the Fall. In His redemptive work, Christ provided redemption for the entire sin-infected, created order—mankind as well as the physical universe. God demonstrated His power to accomplish this task with

152

Christ's resurrection. Thus, the completion of the redemptive process was sealed.

At the time of the resurrection, however, the entire redemptive process was not yet fulfilled. The full number of human beings God desired to populate His creation was not yet complete. As a result, everything is currently in place for the culmination of God's plan. We are now only waiting for the fulfillment of this last requirement. That population is being built by the continuing redemption of those who willfully enter into a personal relationship with God based on the sacrificial death and the resurrection of Jesus Christ.

In God's perfect timing, His redemptive fix will be completed.

- The beginning of this fix we have already reviewed—the eternal salvation of human beings who have entered into a personal relationship with God through Jesus Christ. This is what theologians call *justification*.

- And at the end of the process, God will fashion a new heaven and new earth out of the ruins of the fallen creation. Then, He will put His resurrected people in this recreated paradise to dwell physically and personally with Him for eternity. This is what theologians call *glorification*.

Eternity

At the beginning of this section, we noted that everything begins with an understanding of the purpose of God. Nothing in the Christian faith makes sense until we understand why God did what He did in making His creation. Once we understand that, the unfolding and culmination of God's plan is clear.

God's plan for the redemption of mankind is a process that began in His eternal and infinite mind. It was put into effect at His instigation through the creation of the world and of mankind. The ultimate outworking of His plan is expressed in the life of each individual human being based on the decisions made during life on earth.

The first necessary step for an individual is to enter into the salvation process. In theological terms, as we noted above, this first step is called *justification*. An individual makes a personal decision to repent of sin and accept God's forgiveness by inviting Jesus Christ into his or her life as Savior and Lord, Then God, in His mercy and grace:

- applies Jesus' substitutionary atonement to their sin,

- wipes out and forgets the debt it created, and

- makes the new believer an adopted part of His family.

But salvation does not end there. The second step is referred to as *sanctification*. This phase starts at the point of justification and continues for the rest of the believer's physical life. During this time, believers strive to live in an intimate relationship with God which is manifested through a process of spiritual maturation. God's plan is that the believer grows steadily more holy.

To clarify, there are people who take a legalistic approach to their understanding of salvation. They look at the Bible as a set of rules to follow in order to accomplish salvation. Certainly, the Bible does prescribe a particular approach to morality, and Christians are admonished to do what is right and avoid what is wrong. However, following God's leading in this regard is not a means for achieving salvation, rather, it is a result of the changed life one experiences at justification. This changed life causes the believer to have a great desire to obey God out of love for Him. Obedience to His moral instructions is a path to spiritual growth, not to salvation.

When an individual invites Christ into his or her life, God performs a miracle—He, in the Person of the Holy Spirit, takes up residence inside the body of the new believer. This is why Scripture calls the believer's body a "temple of the Holy Spirit." (1 Cor. 6:19-20) In that form, God enjoys fellowship with the individual believer. He also teaches him and manifests power in him to overcome the sin nature that still remains within the individual, and which works to beat the individual down. To fulfill the calling God has placed on his or her

154

life, the Christian's task is to grow in that relationship by striving for holiness. As the relationship becomes stronger, more and more sin is put aside from his life and the salvation process begun at justification becomes more complete.

This brings us to the third and final step of the salvation process. As noted above, this is the culminating aspect of God's redemptive plan and is referred to as *glorification*. This part of the salvation process begins at physical death.

As we indicated, while still alive, when the believer receives the new nature, the old sin nature is still present. This is why the tendency to sin continues after justification. The old and new natures operate in conflict with one another during the time of the sanctification process.

At physical death, however, the old nature gets scraped off. Those who invited Christ into their lives during their physical life on earth will leave the physical body with its sin nature and enter directly into the presence of God. This begins the final phase of the salvation process in which the believer dwells with Him for the rest of eternity.

This initial entry into heaven, however, is not the totality of God's redemptive plan. Redemption involves not only the salvation of the human person, but also the restoration of the created physical order that had been corrupted by the introduction of sin at the Fall. When the full number of believing human beings is accomplished according to God's plan, He will put an end to the sin-corrupted created order and recreate it as a "new heaven and new earth." This will complete the restoration of God's original plan for eternal life.

At that point, all believers brought into the presence of God at their deaths will be physically resurrected to the new earth and given resurrected glorified bodies. They will inherit glorified heavenly bodies that, like Jesus' resurrected body, will have access to the spiritual realm of the new heaven and the physical new earth.

In this new condition, God will do what He originally did with Adam and Eve—He will dwell among us. At that point, all of the resurrected human beings will have direct access to God. We will experience Him as a close friend as well as the Ruler of all creation. As was mentioned earlier when we discussed creation, this does not limit God's ability to be God in all of eternity. But as a part of His plan, He will also manifest Himself on the new earth.

In this new heaven and earth, there will be no pain, no sorrow, no death. People will do productive and purposeful work and will experience eternal life as joyful and in no way monotonous or boring. It will be fulfilling and meaningful every moment of every day. It will truly be the ultimate expression of paradise. Believers will live eternally and experience the glory of God to the full extent possible for each individual.

Few of the details about the new heaven and new earth are specifically revealed in Scripture. God has though, in the Bible, revealed to us the big picture. In the end, He will completely overcome the destructive attempt of Satan to disrupt His creation. The effects of sin will be overcome, and the created order will emerge fully developed as God originally intended it. He will have His created world and a class of eternal Kingdom citizens who will personally interact and engage Him in a mutually loving relationship throughout eternity.

So, having explained the biblical worldview to your friend, and when you are confident that they understand it, you are now ready to actually share the gospel message.

Making the Context Clear

As we have seen, the gospel message is encased in the context of the Christian faith. So, when you witness, you must clearly explain what that context is. Of course, simply clarifying the context does not typically bring a person to a point of decision as to whether or not they will follow Christ. Nonetheless, it is clear that a person can't accept something they don't understand. This explanation of the context of the Christian faith, based on a worldview paradigm, gives a non-believer a sharper picture of the Christian faith and how it differs from their own. This contrast compels a person to recognize the truth of biblical faith as opposed to the non-truth of their own beliefs.

CHAPTER 7

Sharing an Effective Witness:
The Content of the Gospel Message

What is *Gospel*?

Over the past couple of centuries, the word *gospel* has come to mean a number of different things depending on its context. For instance:

- We hear people say something is the "gospel truth." They simply mean that what they are asserting is undeniably correct.

- We hear a lot about "gospel music." This is generally applied to several traditional styles of music that usually have Christian religious themes and lyrics.

  … and …

- We know that the first four books of the New Testament, Matthew, Mark, Luke, and John, are historically called the "Four Gospels."

These popular usages are, however, not how the word was originally intended to be understood.

The English term *gospel* is actually derived from two Old English words: *god* and *spel*, which together literally mean *good story*. This eventually came to be the predominant English translation for the

New Testament Greek word *euaggelion*, meaning *good news* or *good message*.

In the New Testament, the word is most often and accurately used in the context of telling or writing about the good news of Jesus Christ.

But just what did that "good news" or "gospel" of Christ actually mean?

Let's take a look at the real content of the Christian gospel as taught by Jesus and the New Testament writers, and how, by their scriptural example, we are to convey that good news today.

The Content of the Gospel Message

All of the things dealt with up until now set the stage for sharing the message of the gospel. As we have discussed, it is essential to build a bridge of understanding that allows the person who is hearing the gospel message to understand what we are sharing. But setting the stage for them is meaningless to their salvation unless we bring them to a place where they can actually make a decision to enter into a personal relationship with God. To do this, we must explain the content of the gospel message itself.

The content of the gospel is contained in the essentials of the Christian faith. We have already discussed the concept of "the essentials" as it relates to the topic of worldview in general, and regarding the various specific belief systems. (Recall that worldview essentials define the line that one's beliefs cannot cross and remain within any given faith system. This line exists for the Christian faith, as well, and we must make this explanation clear as we share the gospel message.)

The essentials are clarified as we answer these three simple questions:

1. Who is God?

2.   What is a human being?

3.   What is salvation and how does one achieve it?

For the Christian faith, the answers to these questions are revealed in the Bible.

As such, we Christians must first know the biblical answers to these questions for ourselves, then use them as we share a witness. As we have already discussed, many practical methods have been developed to share this knowledge. These various methods use different imagery to make the explanation, and most will also use different Scripture verses. Regardless of how it is put together, however, the explanation must somehow answer these three questions for the person(s) to whom we are witnessing.

> See Appendix 5, *Verses Explaining the Gospel Message*, for specific Bible references that support the content of the following subtitled paragraphs.

Let's take a look at those answers:

Who Is God?

One of the first things we need to share is an explanation of the God of the Bible. In order to help non-believers put their decision in context, there are certain things about God that we need to make sure they understand. These include:

1.   God is a **person**,

2.   God is **holy**,

3.   God is **just**, and

4.   God is **love**.

Although the God of the Bible also has many other attributes, these points are critical because they relate specifically to how His being is connected to the salvation process.

It is important to recognize that God is a **person** because only persons are able to have self-conscious relationships. God created us as persons allowing us to fellowship with Him as a person.

God's **holiness** (moral perfection) is important because it defines why sin is such a problem. Our sin prevents us from interacting with God because He will not fellowship with sin.

God is **just.** Knowing this is critical because this expresses the consequences of our rebellion against Him. When we sin, God pronounces His judgment against it. Judgment has eternal and personal consequences when a person dies without having his or her sin forgiven.

Finally, understanding that God is **love** is critical because He cares enough for us to have provided a means of satisfying His justice regarding our sin. His love moved Him to provide us the way to enter into a personal relationship with Him. God's love is a constant, but He doesn't force it upon us. Our part is to respond to His love by repenting of our sins and by inviting Christ into our lives.

What Is a Human Being?

Two points concerning the nature of mankind must be emphasized to ensure the listener clearly understands God's purpose for humanity and humanity's problem with sin. These two are: (See Appendix 5)

1. We are created in God's image, but

2. We are fallen creatures.

The fact that we are **created in the image of God** does not mean human beings physically look like Him. Rather, we are the same quality of being as is He. This element allows us to interact with Him in a personal relationship.

Understanding that we are **fallen creatures** is also critical. This means we are not what we were created to be, but, due to our sinful nature, we have *fallen* from the holy state required for a personal relationship with God. This fallenness permeates our human nature and inclines us to rebel against Him. It does not mechanically make us rebel, but it does incline us in that direction. We are still creatures possessing a free will who can choose to rebel or not. That being the case, we are responsible for any rebellion we express. This rebellion puts us outside of the possibility of having a personal relationship with God and makes salvation necessary.

What Is Salvation?

The Bible reveals that God, as a Trinity, is One Being existing eternally in Three Persons. He does not need another being in order to have His personal need for relationship fulfilled. As Three Persons in One, He completely satisfies that need within Himself. But, for His own reasons, He wanted another personal being with whom He could further express His love. God created mankind to fulfill that purpose.

Severe Problems

We know from Genesis, Chapters 1-3, that initially things related to the creation were working out exactly as God intended. But, at a certain point, sin corrupted every element of God's creation, including the physical universe. It also created severe problems for mankind. Since God is holy and will not allow sin into His presence, the introduction of sin into the world separated the creation from God.

The first problem for us, as it relates to our fallenness, is how to live in this fallen world. Mankind was corrupted in such a way as to disrupt the personal interaction that had previously existed with God. That interaction was the purpose of mankind's creation in the first place. Before sin entered the world, man interacted with God in a personal relationship. This interaction occurred in God's perfect paradise—the Garden of Eden. But, with the entry of sin, mankind became tarnished in a way that prevents the relationship from continuing.

For God, this is not an unsolvable problem, but it is beyond the reach of human ability. Mankind does not have the power within itself to remove its sin. In this life, human beings are not able to accomplish the purpose for which we were created. People have a constant and unfilled gap in their lives which becomes filled with hatred, anger, jealousy, selfishness, and so on, as a result. Mankind is in a hopeless situation unless some power beyond itself accomplishes the fix.

The second problem we must deal with regarding our fallenness is that, besides the dissonance people experience in their personal spiritual lives, we also think and behave in ways displeasing to God—and these thoughts and actions have consequences in society. Not only is the relationship with God corrupted, but so are the relationships between human beings. This is expressed in broken homes, abused spouses and children, tension in the workplace, political upheaval, *etc.*, and even war.

These two problems are only confined to this life, and that is bad enough. But unfortunately, mankind's inability to fulfill God's purpose is not limited to life on earth, which brings us to the third, and most serious, problem. That ultimate problem is that people are in danger of being separated from God throughout *eternity*. Since humans were created to be eternal spiritual beings, their essential personhood continues even after physical death ... with two possible destinies. They will either spend eternity *in* the presence of God— or spend eternity *out of* the presence of God. If people desire to live eternally in the presence of God, the sin problem must be resolved. God will not allow sin to exist in His presence. So without some kind of fix for the sin problem, mankind is lost and without hope for eternity! (See Chapter 1, subtitle **A Christian's Motivation To Witness** for the implications of eternal separation from God.)

Problem Resolutions

So, just how are these sin problems resolved? Since sin entered the world through the disobedience of a human being, it had to be defeated by the obedience of a human being. Only this obedience can reverse what was done at the Fall. According to the biblical revelation, a fix of this nature required some human to live a perfect life (without any sin), then die as a sacrificial substitute for those who failed to live up to God's holiness.

You would expect that justice would demand that those individuals who commit sin should have to pay for their own rebellion against God. The penalty (or 'wages') for sin is death. But death, in this case, is not merely physical death, it is also spiritual death—eternal separation from God.

However, we are incapable of paying for our own sin. Only God Himself could pay this price ... and Jesus accomplished this by taking human form, living a sinless life, and dying on the cross as a substitutionary sacrifice to pay for the sins of mankind. This principle is what some Bible translations call: "propitiation" (Romans 3:25—NASB, KJV, ESV), or others (*e.g.*, NIV) call: a "sacrifice of atonement." And thus, Jesus' obedience had the effect of reversing what Adam and Eve's disobedience did at the Fall.

God created mankind for fellowship with Himself and would not allow Himself to be defeated by Satan. So, God the Father instituted the fix for Adam's and Eve's disobedience. But as we have noted, in order to effect the fix for humanity's sin, He could not use an ordinary human being. Since Adam and Eve disobeyed God in the Garden, all ordinary humans start already immersed in sin. Instead, God needed a person who did not already have this sin nature in order to satisfy His justice.

To provide the resolution for this sin problem and reunite in fellowship with those who would believe in Him, God the Son, the Second Person of the Trinity, came to earth and took upon Himself the form of a human. He was born of a human woman, but His Father was not a human father. God the Holy Spirit, the Third Person of the Trinity, miraculously came upon the Virgin Mary and caused her to become pregnant. God did this in order to incarnate as a man who was not corrupted by sin. That man was Jesus.

As Jesus lived His life on earth, He fulfilled all of the requirements necessary to qualify as the sacrifice for mankind's sins—that is, He lived a life totally free of sin. Then, having qualified to be the sacrifice, He died on the cross and actually *became* the sacrifice.

In this case, the sacrifice could not be made by the guilty persons who should have to pay for their own sins. Rather, it had to be made by a perfect, innocent, sinless person who would willingly sacrifice himself as a substitute for humanity's sin. The theological term for this process is *substitutionary atonement*. This doctrine says that sin had to be appeased by an innocent sacrifice, with the sacrificed person taking the place of the guilty party ... and that is what happened with the sacrifice of Jesus by His death on the cross. Christ's resurrection from the dead validated the entire process. It showed that He indeed had the power and authority to carry out this task.

Christ's death on the cross and resurrection from the dead accomplished the fix that God determined to carry out. The power of sin over humanity was broken, and those who accept this substitutionary atonement for their sins are forgiven without personally having to pay the penalty themselves.

This brings us to the logical companion concern ...

... and How Does One Achieve Salvation?

The substitutionary sacrifice of Christ makes God's salvation applicable to the lives of individual human beings. But just because this application is possible does not mean it is applied automatically. A requirement must be met—though not a requirement based on human effort. Based on the grace of God, it is offered to humanity as a free gift. To be applied to their sin, it must be accepted by an individual and received through the exercise of each individual's faith in Jesus Christ. That is, to receive this gift of eternal life, one must make the free-will decision to repent of their sins and accept God's offer to forgive and restore them to the relationship with God for which he or she was created. It is this act of receiving Christ that achieves salvation which God provides to those who accept it.

Lead the Person to a Decision

As we pointed out above, once we have shared with an individual how to know a personal relationship with God, the only thing left is for the person to actually make the decision to receive Christ into their life. Remember, the fact that He died for mankind's salvation does not mean that it is automatically applied to an individual's life. Each person must make a personal, free-will decision to receive it for themselves.

That being said, salvation is not merely an intellectual choice. Certainly, no one can make the choice until they understand it and its implications for them, but the choice is not merely to believe with the mind.

Making the choice will require them to act on it. It actually requires that individuals entrust the entirety of their life into God's care. This means that they must desire to live in His presence, obey His direction, and live a lifestyle reflecting God's character. It means putting aside selfish and sinful ways and willingly live according to His will.

In the process of leading a person to understand who God is, and when that person finally understands the salvation process, that individual is then in a position to make a choice whether or not to accept God's offer.

At that point be careful not to manipulate or otherwise attempt to make the choice for them—this must be *their own, informed* decision.

As much as you might desire a person to choose Christ, you can neither force them to do so—nor choose it for them. Ultimately, you are not responsible, in any way, for another person's decision. Your

167

role in their decision-making process, and your responsibility for their decision, ends when you faithfully deliver the gospel message. So as a result, while you do not get the credit when a person accepts Christ, neither do you get the blame if they don't.

And whichever choice they make, it does not mean you should no longer interact with the person. In your relationship and through your love for them, continue to try and help them in various ways regarding their spiritual walk. It is just that you are limited by the decision *they* make.

There are actually several possibilities that emerge when you bring people to a point of decision.

Of course, the first possibility is that they receive Christ into their life. This is, obviously, what we all would like to see. If they do that, then move on to helping them begin to grow in their spiritual life.

Another possibility is that they reject Christ. This is, of course, what none of us want to see, but there are those who make that choice. If that happens, it is important to do all you can to leave the door open for future witness opportunities.

A third possibility is that the person doesn't reject Christ but does let you know that they are not yet ready to make a decision. There are any number of reasons why this might be so: they may not yet fully understand the message, they may not be ready to give up a lifestyle they know is incompatible with life in Christ, or perhaps they just have not yet come to the place where they believe. Again, it is important to keep the door open for future conversations.

One other possibility is that they actually go on the attack against you. Again, there are various reasons why this outcome may occur. If that does happen, don't allow yourself to get defensive. Simply do what you can to lower the temperature and try to keep the relationship intact enough that there might be future opportunities. Whether or not this occurs should be entirely up to them. In any case, try to keep the door open for future witnessing conversations from your side.

As such, you need to view yourself as a facilitator who creates an environment that allows you to present the gospel and bring the other person to a point where they can make a decision concerning Christ. But no matter what choice your listener makes, you must continue on in an open and viable relationship.

Follow Through

Sharing your faith is not a one-step deal. It is a process, and people first have to be brought to a place where they are willing to listen. You must then give the kind of information that allows your witness to make sense.

Once these matters are taken care of (*i.e.,* you've built the necessary bridges) you are ready to actually verbalize your faith whenever the opportunities open up. This could happen at any time, so always be prepared.

Most sharing opportunities will not be one-shot presentations. One day you might talk about God, another day about morality, another day about the Bible, and so on. The opportunity to really get down to cases may happen after a tragedy or when the person feels particularly isolated and lonely. Or it could be from some other life circumstance. But when the time comes, be ready and willing.

If the Person Does Not Accept Christ

What if you share your faith with someone who decides not to accept Christ? Do you then just throw the relationship away? Of course not! If the person walks away from accepting Christ, you may not have much say regarding how your listener goes forward. But hopefully, your relationship will be such that even a rejection of Christ does not destroy the mutual trust and respect that you have developed with your friend.

It may be that this individual does not yet understand all of the implications of receiving Christ. Or possibly your listener understands but is not yet willing, for whatever reason, to alter their lifestyle to the degree they know will be necessary. It may just be a matter of time for your friend to process the whole thing.

169

People have all kinds of reasons not to accept Christ at any given moment. But if the relationship, mutual respect, and trust stay in place, other opportunities will come to share with them again down the road. Maybe, today's "No" is really a "Not yet" that will become a "Yes" in God's providence and timing.

If the Person Does Accept Christ

Suppose you present the gospel, and the person does receive Christ. Is your work done? Absolutely not! Salvation is not simply a single moment in time. It is a process that works itself out throughout the rest of one's life. A person receives Christ at a particular point in time (*justification*), but the salvation process continues and involves growing in the knowledge of Him and in God's image (*sanctification*).

The salvation process will not only involve learning what a life in Christ is like, but also changing some old lifestyle habits. Changing one's lifestyle is a particularly difficult process for someone who has lived in ways that are contrary to God's way. Both learning and changing lifestyle habits are hard work. Typically, a new Christian needs a lot of encouragement and support—especially in the early stages. Jesus referred to the entry into relationship with God as being "born again." (John 3:3 and 3:7) A new Christian is, literally, a spiritual baby, and babies cannot do much for themselves. They need a lot of help and support.

When you lead someone to Christ, be there for them once they've accepted His offer. Your relationship with them puts you in that position, so take it very seriously!

Sharing a Witness

As can be seen in this chapter, there are numerous elements you must master to be truly effective in every witnessing circumstance. The various people with whom you interact are all at different places in their understanding of the Christian message, and in their personal readiness to receive it into their lives.

Take the time to assess each person in order to figure out where they are in their spiritual journey, then share specifically the knowledge they need for their situation. If you master the principles in this chapter, you can share an effective and credible witness no matter the circumstance.

CHAPTER 8

Witnessing in Daily Life

"I just think we should let how we live our lives be our witness to unsaved people," remarked Jane as she sat in the women's Bible class. "I believe that when people see how we live they will want to know more about why Christianity is true. We can then tell them about Jesus."

"I think all we need to do is just tell the simple gospel message to everyone we can," countered Sue. "Those who are meant to get saved will, and those who aren't intended to, won't. We just have to tell them!"

"There's something to be said for both of those ideas," replied Claire, the teacher. "So how many people have you two led to the Lord using your approaches?"

Jane and Sue looked at each other. Neither answered.

Were you asked it right now, how would you respond to Claire's question? Would your response be the same as Jane's and Sue's?

But knowing what you now know … and maybe having actually practiced sharing your faith out in the real world, would you feel more comfortable about entertaining Claire's question?

We have come a long way from the beginning of this study. We have: surveyed the biblical mandate for us Christians to share a gospel witness with the lost around us,

171

- seen the situation we and other Christians now face when it comes to sharing our faith, and

- learned how to deal with it.

Based on what you have studied here, you are much better prepared to share your faith than those who only know how to share their faith with people who come from their own worldview paradigm.

Let's take one final look at what you have learned from reading this book.

Worldview Beliefs and Witness

Most Christians have a deep concern for the eternal destiny of others, but many don't make any effort to share a witness because they simply feel inadequate for the task. In some ways, that is relatively easy to fix if someone is really interested in doing so. The knowledge necessary to become confident in sharing the gospel is readily available for anyone willing to put in a bit of effort to make it a reality.

Others, though, don't have that kind of concern. They simply don't think it is their responsibility to do it. There is no doubt that modern American society contributes to that attitude. America's societal institutions are so dominated by naturalistic beliefs (and, to a lesser degree, other worldviews) that these beliefs bleed over into the thinking even of many Christians and churches.

As we have seen, Naturalism is the belief that only the natural universe exists—there is no God or any supernatural reality. Even where this belief is not overtly stated or taught, most societal institutions are operated *as if* this were true. Students are taught in school by this philosophy. Politicians operate by this philosophy. The media, businesses, the entertainment industry, and even many churches do their business based on this philosophy.

As we know, we now operate in a politically correct, mixed-worldview, secular society. Finding themselves increasingly in the minority, many Christians feel that they can't afford to offend people who hold other beliefs. That tends to cause them to talk and act in ways that hide their belief in Christ.

Sadly, this has a profound effect on many Christians' willingness to voice their faith in public. It is very difficult to express a true concern for the souls of others in an environment that sees this concern as fantasy, and Christian beliefs as wrong.

So, given this environment, we must address some very important questions:

- Is Christian Theism true?

- Does God actually exist?

- Are people headed to an eternity separated from God if they don't come to Christ?

- Are believers called to share their faith with those who do not know Him?

And we should be able to reply with a profound:

➢ "YES!" Christian Theism is true.

➢ "YES!" The actual structure of reality does include God. He does exist as an objectively real person.

➢ "YES!" People are headed to an eternity separated from God if they don't come to Christ.

➢ And "YES!" God has called believers to share their faith with people who don't know Him.

If Christians are certain these things are actually true, then they will find ways to share that message.

But keep in mind, your witness does not have to fit an old stereotype in order for you to express your faith effectively. You may, however, have to be creative. You can certainly live out your public life as God would have you do. Jane, in our opening vignette, is right in that respect. At work, you may not be able to just go up to people and start witnessing, but you can creatively let it be known that you are a believer and that you are willing to use up a break or time after work to talk about it. Then, when people ask questions, you can legitimately answer them. And if they are genuinely open to hearing about your faith, there are ways to have that conversation ... when you are not on the clock.

Your worldview beliefs definitely affect your witness. So, to be effective in your witness, you need a clear understanding of your own worldview beliefs, as well as the beliefs that dominate your environment. This gives you the tools necessary to share your faith properly within that environment.

Verbal or Silent Witness?

Whenever the topic of witness comes up, as it did in our opening vignette, it often generates a discussion about whether it needs to be verbal, or if just "living a faithful Christian life in front of people" is enough. This is a totally false dichotomy.

A faithful witness involves both living it out visibly *and* sharing it verbally. These are two sides of a single coin:

- We are not faithful witnesses if our lives don't demonstrate our faith even if we share the gospel verbally with others.

- Nor are we faithful witnesses if we do not share the gospel verbally with others, even though we may outwardly live out its precepts.

In our society,

- Many people self-identify as Christians, but do not live their lives based on the moral teachings of the Bible. They

174

approve of, or even participate in, sexual immorality, unethical business conduct, lying, cheating, stealing, promoting unbiblical doctrines, and the like. Obviously, those who do such things are not expressing a Christian witness at all.

- By contrast, there are many people who actually follow biblical moral principles but are not authentically Christian. These may be Mormons, Jehovah's Witnesses, followers of some other religion, or even some atheists.

- Conversely, and finally, many people faithfully live their lives based on biblical teachings but never verbally share their faith with others.

➢ None of these approaches meet the requirements of a faithful witness by a Christian believer.

So:

- How are those who don't know Christ to distinguish between true Christians and those who come from other belief systems?

- How are they to respond to the gospel message (which is necessary in order for them to come to Christ) if they don't actually hear the message?

➢ The answer: They can't!!! Our Christian lifestyle is an essential starting point, but by itself is insufficient.

The Great Commission in Matthew 28:18-20 is instructive at this point. It reads:

> And Jesus came up and spoke to them, saying, "All authority has been given to Me in heaven and on earth. Go therefore and make disciples of all the nations, baptizing them in the name of the Father and the Son and the Holy Spirit, teaching them to observe

175

all that I commanded you; and lo, I am with you always, even to the end of the age."

The phrase, "Go therefore and make disciples of all nations" has a nuance in the Greek language that is not clearly evident in most English translations. It literally means, *"As you are going*, make disciples of all nations." This idea of *"as you are going"* is a reference to lifestyle. It is not about traveling to some other location. Jesus was telling His followers that we are to be faithful witnesses in every part of our lives—no matter where we go or when we go.

To grasp this more fully, remember that salvation is not simply something that happens to us at a single moment in time. It is a process that begins at a particular moment but continues throughout the rest of eternity. As it relates to witnessing, though, it applies particularly to the time between our salvation's beginning point to the end of our mortal lives.

When someone invites Christ into their life, that person has stepped out of *eternal death* and into *eternal life*. That eternal life is not something picked up after we die, it begins when we receive salvation. As such, we are to live as those spiritually alive rather than those who are spiritually dead.

Of course, this does not mean we never sin again. As long as we still have the sin nature, we will struggle with that problem. Nonetheless, when Christ entered our lives, we were given a new nature—which makes it possible to overcome sin.

Our whole life after the moment of salvation is to be devoted to living for Christ. This plays out two ways as it relates to our witness. The first concerns *faithful living*. A true believer is going to live in a way that reflects Christ as their master.

The second way involves *faithful verbal sharing*. A person who truly knows Christ will not be ashamed to speak about Him. As we saw above in the Great Commission, God calls every believer to partner with Him in spreading the gospel.

The very reason we exist, and the purpose for which God created mankind in the first place, was for fellowship with Himself. As such, our lives should focus on *His* purpose. This involves being in position to fellowship with God (putting aside sin) and sharing with others how they can know Him as well (witness).

Thus, learning how to share your faith with other people is not an option. Sure, it takes work and practice to acquire the necessary knowledge and skills, but the only obstacle is found in your will. So, what is your choice: will you do it ... or not? Once you decide you will do it, you can do it. The information is available. In fact, that is what this whole book is about.

Possible Contexts for Sharing Your Witness

There are several possible approaches to physically interacting with people in order to share your witness. Each approach has its place, and it is important to be aware of them so you can be used by God appropriately.

Cold-Call Witnessing

This first approach is one we have alluded to previously—cold-call witness. Cold-call witness is the method that is assumed in most modern witness training programs. This does not necessarily mean that those programs only advocate cold calling, but they often end up promoting that approach by default. The reason is that most training programs only focus on how to share the gospel message itself, but they leave out the worldview context and the ongoing relationship elements when they present the gospel message.

As such, these programs teach their students to share the gospel message, then tell them: "Now go out and do it."

Certainly, this approach is not a bad thing. There are times when a cold-call approach is appropriate—such as in neighborhood canvassing situations or in special evangelistic events like revivals or street witnessing.

177

But cold-call approaches do not fit everyone equally. God has specifically called and gifted some people to be effective with this kind of witnessing approach, and they ought to be faithful to their calling.

Other Christians don't have the special calling of the evangelist. But even if they don't, they are not off the hook. Every believer needs to be equipped to give a witness when the opportunity presents itself. Sometimes you just come across a person who is ready to receive the gospel. For instance, when you are at work or when you are visiting a home, you may meet someone who asks: "How can I know God?" At the very least, you should be equipped to share that information.

Be careful, however, about one other thing when witnessing predominantly with the cold-call approach: It is very easy to be impersonal in this process. Witnessing is about leading people into relationship with God, not about how many people you get to "pray the prayer." The danger is that your focus can easily change from leading the individual to God, to "getting notches on your gun."

So, cold-call witnessing has its place. Every believer ought to be able to do it if the circumstances are right. But it needs to be used in a proper context to be effective. The truth is, cold-call witnessing is generally only effective for sharing with certain kinds of people—those who are ready, at that moment, to step into a life with Christ.

Relationship Witnessing

Sadly, however, the large majority of non-believers are not at a point where a cold-call approach is effective. They may not be at a place where they even understand the meaning of the message. They may still have a rebellious heart and not be open to receive the message. Because of that, in most situations, you need a way to share a witness with people over a longer period of time. Building long-term, positive, trust-based relationships is the key to this process.

Research has shown that most people who come to Christ do so by the influence of friends and family—not on the basis of a cold-call encounter. As such, it is critical for every believer to live a faithful life among all of their relationships, both by lifestyle and with words.

When witnessing in the context of such trust-based relationships, the unique calling and the special talents of successful cold-calling presenters are not necessary. Every believer is commissioned by God to be a faithful witness, even those without the specific calling and gifts of an evangelist. All Christians need to pay attention to non-believers in their web of relationships and look for opportunities to share Christ.

One important key is for *all* believers to see themselves as missionaries. God has called every believer to be a full-time minister of the gospel. While only a relatively small number of people are called to do that in a full-time capacity as a church leader or vocational evangelist, everyone is called to share a witness.

"On Mission" Witnessing

Going out on an organized mission is yet another possibility for witness where you may find opportunities to use either of the above approaches. The focus here is more on the location of the witness than the methodology used when sharing the message. The concept of doing the work of a missionary has more to do with intention than it does with location. A target individual or group is identified, a strategy for sharing with them is created, and the strategy is carried out. That is the essence of going "on mission."

Mission opportunities in our day have radically expanded because of advances in communication and transportation technology. It used to be that missionary work was pretty much left up to the "professionals." But today, there is a place for both long-term and short-term volunteer missions—in other countries, in our own country, and even in our own hometowns. And these options are available for both the professional and non-professional alike.

It is not difficult, now, to get involved in missionary work. All kinds of groups facilitate short-term mission projects, making it possible for average church members to participate in a host of mission activities. And for those led to missions as a career, numerous denominational and parachurch groups serve as sending agencies. In any case, the full range of witnessing skills is essential— including an understanding of worldview and a knowledge of the gospel message.

Missions can be conceived of in a couple of different ways—top-down and bottom-up. Neither is right nor wrong in and of themselves, but these different approaches require different strategies.

The top-down approach targets the top influencers in a group, industry, or society, with the aim of bringing them to Christ. They can then influence an entire community. In history, when Emperor Constantine legalized Christianity in the Roman Empire, his influence provided a surge in the growth of the Christian church. This same kind of dynamic has happened in many other places throughout history. This not only applies to government leaders or those in politics, but in the media, the entertainment industry, business, and in education, as well. Leaders really do influence those they lead.

The bottom-up approach focuses more on the common person. When missionaries immerse themselves in the culture of a people group (*e.g.*, groups with a common ethnicity, language, religion, or other social demographic) and seek to share their faith with them, the bottom-up strategy is usually employed. This approach is seen in church planting, disaster relief, chaplaincy, bi-vocational ministry, and the like. Again, both professional and non-professional missionaries can carry out this work.

Focus on Worldview Thinking

Rich and Donna, and Mike and Wendy, were next-door neighbors. They enjoyed some of the same things: sports, fishing, and golf. One Sunday, Rich and Donna hosted a barbeque by their pool for some of the couples on the cul-de-sac where they lived. It began at 12 noon. Mike and Wendy, however, arrived late at about 1 pm.

"Sorry we're late," said Mike. "Our church was delayed getting out today."

"No problem. Do you and Wendy go to church *every* week?" asked Rich with a tad of sarcasm in his voice.

"Just about," replied Mike.

"That's fine for you, but I just don't get all that God and Jesus stuff," said Rich as he put a burger on Wendy's plate. "When I was a kid we rarely went to church, so I guess I never made sense of it all."

Mike had been praying for an opportunity to share about Christ with Rich. "Would you mind sometime us talking about it?"

"No … when?"

"How about Tuesday at lunch?"

Rich and Mike got together that week. They talked at first about their families and jobs. Then Mike asked Rich if he could ask him several simple questions.

"Okay." *Here it comes*, Rich thought.

"First, according to your understanding, who is God?"

Rich thought a moment. "I don't believe there is a God. I think all that exists is matter and energy. None of that religion and superstition."

"Okay," said Mike. "Second question. According to your understanding, what is a human being?"

"Hmm. I guess humans are just highly evolved animals. We aren't that far removed from apes, you know."

"Next question. In your mind, what is salvation? Or, to put it another way, what is the ultimate purpose for life?"

181

Rich pondered the inquiry. "I think our purpose is just to do the best we can in the few years we have in this world."

Mike asked his last question, "So how does one achieve salvation? That is, how do we accomplish our ultimate purpose?"

"We just try to make the most out of our lives and help others when we can. We work hard to provide for our families. Actually, I've never really thought about it that much," Rich responded. Mike could see that Rich was having difficulty with the questions.

"I'll tell you what," Mike said, picking up the check for both of them, "we both have to get back to work, so how about we meet each week, same time, same place. Think about the things I asked, and we can discuss them further then."

Rich and Mike met for lunch over the next few weeks. Mike carefully showed Rich the problems with his naturalistic worldview. He then, over time, explained how the theistic worldview actually made more sense. Mike then shared the Christian worldview and why it was believable and practical.

Rich was amazed at how much Mike knew and how he answered his skeptical questions. Mike gave him a Bible and challenged him to read it, starting in the Gospel of John. Over the course of their next few lunches, Mike meticulously explained to Rich about the biblical view of God, mankind, sin, and death, who Jesus was and what He did, and how people can find salvation through Christ. Rich generally sat quietly and listened, occasionally posing questions.

Finally, the sixth time they met, Mike asked Rich if he fully understood everything he had shared with him and what he read in Scripture. "I think so," mused Rich. "I never considered any of the things you told me. I really now believe Jesus is special. It really does make sense."

So, finally, Mike looked at his friend and asked, "Rich, would you like to receive Christ as your personal Savior and Lord?"

"You know, I think I would." Together they prayed, and Rich asked God to forgive his sins and for Christ to come into his life. The two men continued to meet. Soon Rich and Donna visited Mike and Wendy's Bible Study group and church worship service. Before long they felt right at home and Donna also soon accepted Christ.

So, as the other neighbors in the cul-de-sac noticed, the next time Rich and Donna had a Sunday cook-out, it started at 3 pm.

As we have seen, effective witness involves bringing people to a place where they can make an informed decision as to whether or not they will receive Christ into their lives. But as we have also seen, this involves more than merely sharing the message of the gospel. Obviously, the gospel message must be in the mix. No one can come to God without also making a decision concerning what they will do with Christ.

Nonetheless, an effective witness necessitates more than that. It also involves putting the gospel message in a form that makes sense to the listener. We must understand what the other person believes and frame the presentation to bridge the gap between what they believe and the truth about salvation.

As Christians, it is time for us to up our game. We have to become better. We have to expand our knowledge. We have to become more skilled in every part of the witnessing process. It is not that difficult since the things we need to know are readily available. But we don't get it by sitting back and letting our faith life "just happen." We have to take some initiative. And, when we do, God will use us to touch the lives of people in profound ways to shatter their truth mirage, show them the real Truth, and lead them into an intimate relationship with Him.

Resources for Effective Witness

Glossary

Appendices

Appendix 1. Breakdown of Popular Witnessing Methods

Appendix 2. Mapping a Person's Worldview

Appendix 3. Overview of Various Belief Systems

Appendix 4. Verses Supporting the Biblical Worldview

Appendix 5. Verses Explaining the Gospel Message

Appendix 6. Study Guide for Students and Leaders

GLOSSARY

Apologetics
The art of defending one's beliefs. While most Christians associate apologetics specifically with defending the Christian faith, the word itself has more general application, as well. It can apply to attempts to justify any theory or religious doctrine using reasoned arguments.

Christian Apologetics
The art of defending the Christian faith using reasoned arguments.

Defensive Apologetics
The art of providing logical answers to questions about, and objections to, the Christian faith. This is the approach to providing logical arguments to support or defend the Christian faith that is commonly thought of when dealing with this topic.

Offensive Apologetics
The art of forcing those who are antagonistic toward the Christian faith to justify their own faith. Those who attack the Christian faith do so based on their own worldview beliefs. It is not unreasonable to require an attacker to give evidence that their faith is true before feeling obligated to justify one's own. In our material we refer to this as Incursion Apologetics.

Authority Source
Every faith system in existence has some means that it uses to justify its point of view. Whatever that is, it is its authority source. There are four authority source categories. In some way, all worldviews

(and belief systems) depend on all four, but each one has one primary authority source.

1. **Human Reason**—Naturalism's primary authority source.

2. **Human Experience**—Far Eastern Thought's primary authority source.

3. **Revelation**—Theism's primary authority source.

4. **Tradition**—Animism's primary authority source.

Belief System

A belief system is defined as a religion, cult, or philosophy. These are the beliefs that people generally hold at a conscious level. Every belief system can be identified as belonging to a particular worldview category and has the same "essential beliefs" (see definition below) as its worldview foundation.

Faith System

The term "faith system" is a broad term that includes both worldview systems and belief systems.

Reality

Reality relates to the state of things as they actually exist. Normally you would think that the concept of reality would not be that difficult to grasp. After all, anything that is not real is fantasy, and everyone knows when something is a fantasy, right? Interestingly though, for many people, it is not nearly as easy to distinguish reality from fantasy as they think it ought to be. The problem in dealing with this has to do with the definitions we use to define reality—and different worldviews define it in different ways. To be sure, there is a way reality is actually structured, and it is not structured any other way. However, human beings have an amazing ability to imagine other ways to define it, and once they do, they will live "as if" their definition is true, even though it may be contrary to the way things actually exist.

Worldview

A worldview is the assumptions people hold about the nature of reality. Every person considers that the beliefs they hold at a worldview level represent reality (the way things actually exist). They also consider that every belief that sits outside of their worldview is fantasy; that is, it couldn't possibly be true. People's worldview is their perspective on life that makes the world around them seem to make sense. It is important to recognize, though, that whatever that perspective is, it cannot be proven using empirical (scientific) means. Worldview beliefs are *assumed* by people to be true based on their faith in the validity of their perspective. Additionally, unless a person has made the effort to actually study worldview concepts, worldview beliefs are generally held unconsciously as underlying assumptions.

Biblical Worldview (or Christian Theism)

A biblical worldview consists of the set of assumptions about the nature of reality that corresponds to what the Bible teaches.

The Exclusive Nature of Worldview Beliefs

A worldview defines what a person considers to be reality. Correspondingly, everything that is outside of a person's worldview beliefs are understood to be fantasy. As such every worldview is exclusive by categorizing any contrary beliefs as false.

The Faith Nature of Worldview Beliefs

A worldview is the assumptions people make about the nature of reality. Assumptions are beliefs that seem so obvious that they are not even questioned. As such, people believe their worldview assumptions based on faith. There is no way to devise empirical proofs for them. A worldview is expressed by how it answers the three "essential worldview questions" (see below), and those questions are not subject to empirical inquiry.

Worldview Categories
There are four worldview categories. Each of these worldviews represents a unique way of understanding the structure of reality. Every religion, cult, and philosophy in existence is based on one of these four.

1. Theism.
Theism is the belief that there exists a transcendent God who is the creator and sustainer of the natural universe.

2. Naturalism
Naturalism is the belief that the natural universe, operating by natural laws, is all that exists.

3. Far Eastern Thought
Far Eastern thought is the belief that ultimate reality consists of a transcendent, impersonal, and immaterial life force. The natural universe is seen to be an illusory expression of that life force.

4. Animism
Animism is the belief that there is a single ultimate reality, but that it is divided into two parts—material and spiritual. It asserts that the two parts are dependent upon each other, and they interact in a symbiotic relationship.

Hybrids
Hybrid belief systems are an anomaly in that they are attempts to create a belief system using essential elements from two or more worldviews. Every hybrid belief system falls apart because of this, as every worldview belief contradicts the beliefs of every other worldview. As such, every hybrid belief system contains irreconcilable internal contradictions.

Non-Christian Theism
Theism is unique among the worldview categories in that it is the one that corresponds most closely to the way human beings experience reality. That said, every theistic belief system holds incompatibilities with every other theistic belief system. Each one

has its own understanding of who God is and what He is like. It is only possible for one theistic belief system to be true. Christians firmly believe that the God revealed in the Bible is the only true God. Thus, in studying this topic, it is important to distinguish between Christian Theism and non-Christian Theism. Non-Christian Theism is represented by every theistic belief system that is not Christian.

Non-Christian theistic belief systems include such beliefs as: Judaism, Islam, Mormonism, and Jehovah's Witnesses.

Worldview Essentials
Worldview essentials define the boundaries around the beliefs of a particular worldview. We are able to discern these beliefs by asking three specific questions and getting the answers to those questions based on the way a particular worldview answers them.

Note: These questions are referred to as "essential worldview questions," but they can all be answered by any belief system, and their answers define the belief system answering them.

Note: These questions are referred to as "essential worldview questions," but can also be answered by any belief system, as each one of them is based on some particular worldview platform.

Each worldview answers the three worldview questions in its own unique way. Any answer that deviates is considered outside of that worldview.

The **Three Essential Worldview Questions** are:

1. What Is the Nature of Ultimate Reality? (Belief about God)

2. What Is a Human Being? (Belief about the nature of humanity)

3. What Is the Ultimate Humans Can Achieve in Life? (Belief about salvation)

APPENDIX 1
Breakdown of Popular Witnessing Methods

E very Christian witnessing method is designed for sharing the Gospel message in a way that leads a person to a decision to either receive or reject Christ. There is a certain amount of diversity among the different methods, but all of them somehow explain the gospel by sharing the answer to the three essential worldview questions from a biblical point of view:

- Who is God?

- What is a human being?

- What is salvation and how does one receive it?

How They Answer the Essential Questions

This appendix examines how five of the most prominent witnessing methods go about answering those questions. Each of these five methods is addressed in two parts:

- Part One presents the method in overview.

- Part Two then lists the three essential worldview questions and analyzes which aspect(s) of the method's elements addresses them … and how it answers each question.

You will note that there is a certain amount of diversity in how the various methods deal with the gospel explanation, but they all essentially do nothing more than answer the three questions. By spelling these out, we hope that their gospel message content will be easy for you to grasp and share.

The Romans Road to Salvation

The Romans Road is a traditional generic witnessing technique based primarily on selected verses from Paul's letter to the Romans. The verses cited are not in their order of appearance in the book and they are used out of their immediate contexts in Paul's letter. Nonetheless, they do form a systematic outline of the basic evangelistic gospel message leading to a decision to receive (or reject) Christ as personal Savior.

The technique is scripturally sound but presupposes the witness subject already has a theistic worldview and believes the Bible is authoritative. (For the verses, please see: https://www.biblegateway.com/blog/2016/09/evangelism-the-romans-road-to-salvation/)

Part One: Overview of this Method

The Romans Road is a metaphoric, conversational gospel sharing pathway you can "walk" with your witness subject. It is a selection of Bible verses from the book of Romans in the New Testament. If you "walk a person down this road" they should end up understanding how to be saved. These are the verses and their suggested accompanying interpretative conversations to share with your subject.

1. Romans 3:23, "For all have sinned and fall short of the glory of God."

We all have sin in our hearts. We all were born with sin. We were born under the power of sin's control. Admit that you are a sinner.

2. Romans 6:23a, "The wages of sin is death ...."

Sin has an ending. It results in death. We all face physical death, which is a result of sin. But a worse death is spiritual death that alienates us from God and will last for all eternity. The Bible teaches that there is a place called the Lake of Fire where lost people will be in torment forever. It is the place where people who are spiritually dead will remain. Understand that you deserve death for your sin.

3. Romans 6:23b, "... But the gift of God is eternal life through Jesus Christ our Lord."

Salvation is a free gift from God to you! You can't earn this gift, but you must reach out and receive it. Ask God to forgive you and save you.

4. Romans 5:8, "God demonstrates His own love for us, in that while we were yet sinners Christ died for us!"

When Jesus died on the cross, He paid sin's penalty. He paid the price for all sin, and when He took all the sins of the world on Himself on the cross, He bought us out of slavery to sin and death! The only condition is that we believe in Him and what He has done for us, understanding that we are now joined with Him, and that He is our life. He did all this because He loved us and gave Himself for us! Give your life to God ... His love poured out in Jesus on the cross is your only hope to have forgiveness and change. His love bought you out of being a slave to sin. His love is what saves you—not religion, or church membership. God loves you!

5. Romans 10:13, "Whoever will call on the name of the Lord will be saved!"

Call out to God in the name of Jesus!

6. Romans 10:9,10, "... If you confess with your mouth Jesus as Lord and believe in your heart that God raised Jesus from the dead, you shall be saved; for with the heart man believes, resulting in righteousness, and with the mouth he confesses, resulting in salvation."

If you know that God is knocking on your heart's door, ask Him to come into your heart.

Jesus said in Revelation 3:20a, "Behold I stand at the door and knock, if anyone hears My voice and opens the door, I will come in to him ...."

Part Two: How this Method Answers the Essential Questions

The methodology of the Romans Road simply uses verses from Paul's letter to the Romans to address the elements of a biblical worldview, then invites people to accept Christ with the verse from Revelation.

1. Who is God?

The Romans Road has one verse that deals with an explanation of God. This verse deals specifically with the fact that God is a God of love and doesn't want human beings separated from Him.

Romans 5:8 says that God is a God of love and doesn't want us separated from Him.

2. What is a human being?

The verses used to deal with the nature of a human being point out specifically that man is a sinner separated from God, and because of that is destined for eternal death unless the sin problem is resolved.

- Romans 3: 23 says that man is a sinner, separated from God.

- Romans 6:23a says that man is a being destined for eternal death unless the sin problem is resolved.

3a. What is salvation?

In this method, the person receiving the witness is assumed to understand the biblical meaning of salvation. What is explained by this method is that eternal life is a free gift of God.

- Romans 6:23b says that eternal life is a free gift of God.

3b. ... and how does one achieve it?

The Romans Road uses two verses to lead people to receive Christ—one of which is actually not found in the book of Romans. Romans 10:9-13 shares that those who believe in Jesus and call on His name will receive salvation. Revelation 3:20 is then used as a metaphor to share the notion that in order to actually receive Christ, a person needs to 'open the door' of their life and let Him in.

- Romans 10:9-13 says to believe in Jesus and call on Him for salvation.

- Revelation 3:20 says to open the door of one's life to receive salvation.

Four Spiritual Laws

The Four Spiritual Laws is a witnessing process originally written in 1959 and copyrighted by William R. Bright (1921-2003) and the staff of Campus Crusade for Christ International (now Cru). In 1965, the text was converted into a small booklet and titled *Have You Heard of the Four Spiritual Laws?* The presentation is an outline of the basic gospel message in four points with supporting scriptures for each. Millions of its copies have been used to share Christ around the world.

The booklet, which has undergone several revisions, is designed to be read aloud without comment to the subject of the witness. The four points are followed by an invitation to receive Christ as Savior with a suggested prayer of commitment.

The technique is scripturally sound, but it presupposes the witness subject already has a theistic worldview and believes the Bible is authoritative. (See: https://crustore.org/four-laws-english.)

Part One: Overview of this Method

Just as there are physical laws that govern the physical universe, so there are spiritual laws which govern your relationship with God.

Law 1. God LOVES you and offers a wonderful PLAN for your life.

- God's Love: "God so loved the world that He gave His one and only Son, that whoever believes in Him shall not perish, but have eternal life." (John 3:16 NIV)

- God's Plan: [Christ speaking] "I came that they might have life and might have it abundantly" (*i.e.*, that it might be full and meaningful). (John 10:10)

Why is it that most people are not experiencing the abundant life?

Because ...

Law 2. Man is SINFUL and SEPARATED from God. Therefore, he cannot know and experience God's love and plan for his life.

- Man Is Sinful. "All have sinned and fall short of the glory of God." (Romans 3:23)

  Man was created to have fellowship with God; but, because of his stubborn self-will, he chose to go his own independent way, and fellowship with God was broken. This self-will, characterized by an attitude of active rebellion or passive indifference, is evidence of what the Bible calls sin.

- Man Is Separated. "The wages of sin is death" (*i.e.*, spiritual separation from God). (Romans 6:23)

  God is holy and man is sinful. A great gulf separates the two. Man is continually trying to reach God and the abundant life through his own efforts, such as a good life, philosophy, or religion—but he inevitably fails.

The third law explains the only way to bridge this gulf ...

Law 3. Jesus Christ is God's ONLY provision for man's sin. Through Him, you can know and experience God's love and plan for your life.

- He Died in Our Place. "God demonstrates His own love toward us, in that while we were yet sinners, Christ died for us." (Romans 5:8)

- He Rose From the Dead. "Christ died for our sins, ... He was buried, ... He was raised on the third day, according to the Scriptures, ... He appeared to (Peter), then to the twelve. After that He appeared to more than five hundred ...." (1 Corinthians 15:3-6)

- He Is the Only Way to God. "Jesus said to him, 'I am the way, and the truth, and the life; no one comes to the Father, but through Me.'" (John 14:6)

God has bridged the gulf which separates us from Him by sending His Son, Jesus Christ, to die on the cross in our place to pay the penalty for our sins.

It is not enough just to know these three laws ...

Law 4. We must individually RECEIVE Jesus Christ as Savior and Lord; then we can know and experience God's love and plan for our lives.

- We Must Receive Christ. "As many as received Him, to them He gave the right to become children of God, even to those who believe in His name." (John 1:12)

- We Receive Christ Through Faith. "By grace you have been saved through faith; and that not of yourselves, it is the gift of God; not as a result of works, that no one should boast." (Ephesians 2:8,9)

- When We Receive Christ, We Experience a New Birth. (Read John 3:1-8.)

- We Receive Christ by Personal Invitation. [Christ speaking] "Behold, I stand at the door and knock; if any one hears My voice and opens the door, I will come in to him." (Revelation 3:20)

- Receiving Christ involves turning to God from self (repentance) and trusting Christ to come into our lives to forgive our sins and to make us what He wants us to be. Just to agree intellectually that Jesus Christ is the Son of God and that He died on the cross for your sins is not enough. Nor is it enough to have an emotional experience. You receive Jesus Christ by faith, as an act of the will.

198

The following explains how you can receive Christ:

- You can receive Christ *right now* by faith through prayer: (Prayer is talking to God) God knows your heart and is not so concerned with your words as He is with the attitude of your heart. The following is a suggested prayer:

  "Lord Jesus, I need You. Thank You for dying on the cross for my sins. I open the door of my life and receive You as my Savior and Lord. Thank You for forgiving my sins and giving me eternal life. Take control of the throne of my life. Make me the kind of person You want me to be."

Does this prayer express the desire of your heart?

If it does, I invite you to pray this prayer right now and Christ will come into your life, as He promised.

Part Two: How this Method Answers the Essential Questions

1. Who is God?

The Four Spiritual Laws deals with the topic of God by mentioning three characteristics of God—God is love, God has a plan, and God is holy. It explains two of the three of these by simply giving a Bible verse as proof. Interestingly, there is no verse given in the booklet to back up the third point.

- God is Love: "God so loved the world that He gave His one and only Son, that whoever believes in Him shall not perish, but have eternal life." (John 3:16 NIV)

- God has a Plan: [Christ speaking] "I came that they might have life and might have it abundantly" (*i.e.*, that it might be full and meaningful). (John 10:10)

- God is Holy: (No reference given to back up this point.)

2. What is a human being?

This method's explanation of man uses the same format as for God. It specifically shares that: 1. Man is sinful, and 2. Man is separated from God. Both of these are then backed up with a Scripture verse:

- Man is sinful: "All have sinned and fall short of the glory of God." (Romans 3:23)

- Man is separated from God: "The wages of sin is death [spiritual separation from God]." (Romans 6:23)

3a. What is salvation?

The explanation of the meaning of salvation, again, uses the same approach as before—a short explanation usually backed up by Bible verses. The explanation of salvation here includes:

1. Salvation is bridging the gulf between a holy God and sinful man,

2. Christ died in our place,

3. Christ rose from the dead, and

4. Christ is the only way to God.

- Salvation is bridging the gulf between a holy God and sinful man: God has bridged the gulf which separates us from Him by sending His Son, Jesus Christ, to die on the cross in our place to pay the penalty for our sins.

- Christ Died in Our Place: "God demonstrates His own love toward us, in that while we were yet sinners, Christ died for us." (Romans 5:8)

- Christ Rose From the Dead: "Christ died for our sins, ... He was buried, ... He was raised on the third day, according to the Scriptures, ... He appeared to Peter, then to the twelve.

After that He appeared to more than five hundred ...." (1 Corinthians 15:3-6)

- Christ Is the Only Way to God: "Jesus said to him, 'I am the way, and the truth, and the life; no one comes to the Father, but through Me.'" (John 14:6)

3b. ... and how does one achieve it?

Once again, the same method is used to answer how salvation is achieved. Here, the points listed include:

- We Must Receive Christ: "As many as received Him, to them He gave the right to become children of God, even to those who believe in His name." (John 1:12)

- We Receive Christ Through Faith: "By grace you have been saved through faith; and that not of yourselves, it is the gift of God; not as a result of works, that no one should boast." (Ephesians 2:8,9)

- When We Receive Christ, We Experience a New Birth: (John 3:1-8.)

- We Receive Christ by Personal Invitation: [Christ speaking] "Behold, I stand at the door and knock; if any one hears My voice and opens the door, I will come in to him." (Revelation 3:20)

- Finally, those reading the pamphlet are invited to actually take action and pray to receive Christ.

- The personal invitation is done through praying the "sinner's prayer" (see this prayer above).

FAITH

Dr. Bobby Welch was the senior pastor of the First Baptist Church of Daytona Beach, Florida, from 1974 to 2006. While pastoring, Welch had developed a systematic memorized personal witnessing program based on an acrostic spelling of F-A-I-T-H. In 2004, he was elected President of the Southern Baptist Convention (SBC).

In 2006, the SBC adopted Welch's program and had it published by LifeWay Christian Resources, the convention's publishing arm. LifeWay then conducted events to certify leaders to train church members in a 12 week course on how to share the FAITH method (only certified leaders could order the training materials). LifeWay Christian Resources still publishes some aspects of the FAITH program, but no longer conducts certification training events.

The FAITH technique is scripturally sound but, like most other witness memorization programs, presupposes the witness subject already has a theistic worldview and believes the Bible is authoritative. (See: https://www.lifeway.com/en/product/faith-evangelism-1-journal-P005108884?intcmp=lw:recs:pdp:2&merch=rec:005108884)

Part One: Overview of this Method

Key Question: In your personal opinion, what do you understand it takes for a person to go to heaven?

Transition Statement: I'd like to share with you how the Bible answers this question if it is all right. There is a word that can be used to answer this question: FAITH (spell out on fingers).

PRESENTATION:

F is for FORGIVENESS. We cannot have eternal life and heaven without God's forgiveness. "In Him [Jesus], we have redemption through His blood, the forgiveness of sins." (Ephesians 1:7a)

A is for AVAILABLE. Forgiveness is available for all. But not automatic. "Not everyone who says to Me, "Lord, Lord," shall enter the kingdom of heaven." (Matthew 7:21a)

I is for IMPOSSIBLE. It is impossible for God to allow sin into heaven.

- God is love: "For God so loved the world that He gave His only begotten Son, that whosoever believes in Him should not perish but have everlasting life." (John 3:16)

- God is just: "For judgment is without mercy." (James 2:13a)

- Man is sinful: "For all have sinned and fall short of the glory of God." (Romans 3:23)

Question: But how can a sinful person enter heaven, where God allows no sin?

T is for TURN.

Question: If you were driving down the road and someone asked you to turn, what would s/he be asking you to do? To change direction. To turn means to repent.

- **TURN** from something—from sin and self. "But unless you repent you will all likewise perish." (Luke 13:3b)

- **TURN** to Someone—trust Christ only. The Bible tells us that "Christ died for our sins according to the Scriptures; and that He was buried and that He rose again the third day according to the Scriptures." (1 Corinthians 15:3b-4)

- "If you confess with your mouth the Lord Jesus and believe in your heart that God has raised Him from the dead, you will be saved." (Romans 10:9)

H is for HEAVEN - Heaven is eternal life:

- Here. "I have come that they have life, and that they may have it more abundantly." (John 10:10b)

- Hereafter. "And if I go and prepare a place for you, I will come again and receive you to Myself; that where I am, there you may be also." (John 14:3)

- How? How can a person have God's forgiveness, heaven and eternal life, and Jesus as personal Savior and Lord? Explain based on leaflet picture, F.A.I.T.H. (Forsaking All I Trust Him) and Romans 10:9.

Understanding what we have shared, would you like to receive this forgiveness by trusting in Christ as your personal Savior and Lord?

Part Two: How this Method Answers the Essential Questions

The FAITH method also answers the three essential worldview questions in its explanation but does so in its own unique order. Thus, to get at the three worldview questions, it is necessary to jump around a little. The point is, however, that even though the order may be different, it still shares the gospel message by answering the same three questions.

1. Who is God?

This method speaks of God by mentioning that He is *love*, and He is *just*.

- God is *love*. "For God so loved the world that He gave His only begotten Son, that whosoever believes in Him should not perish but have everlasting life." (John 3:16)

- God is *just*. "For judgment is without mercy." (James 2:13a)

2. What is a human being?

FAITH's treatment of man focuses on the point that man is sinful.

- Man is sinful. "For all have sinned and fall short of the glory of God." (Romans 3:23)

3a. What is salvation?

The FAITH method gives a good step-by-step explanation of the salvation process, also using Scripture verses to back up its points. The points it makes about salvation are:

Salvation is eternity in relationship with God:

- "I have come that they have life, and that they may have it more abundantly." (John 10:10b)

- "And if I go and prepare a place for you, I will come again and receive you to Myself; that where I am, there you may be also." (John 14:3)

But man is separated from God and must enter a relationship with him.

- "Not everyone who says to Me, 'Lord, Lord,' shall enter the kingdom of heaven." (Matthew 7:21a)

The relationship is restored by God's forgiveness of an individual's sin.

- "In Him [Jesus], we have redemption through His blood, the forgiveness of sins." (Ephesians 1:7a)

To receive the forgiveness, a person must turn from self and turn to Christ:

- "But unless you repent you will all likewise perish." (Luke 13:3b)

205

- "Christ died for our sins according to the Scriptures; and that he was buried, and that He rose again the third day according to the Scriptures." (1 Corinthians 15:3b-4)

3b. ... and how does one achieve it?

This method explains that salvation is achieved by confessing Christ as Lord using Romans 10:9.

Salvation is achieved by confessing Christ.

- "If you confess with your mouth the Lord Jesus and believe in your heart that God has raised Him from the dead, you will be saved." (Romans 10:9)

Steps to Peace with God

No evangelist in the history of Christianity preached the gospel to more people face-to-face than did Billy Graham (1918-2018). At the conclusion of each of his sermons (and those of his associate evangelists), he invited people to walk forward to publicly indicate their desire to receive Christ as Savior. When the inquirer arrived at the front of the speaker's stand, Graham would pray for them all. He then turned them over to trained volunteer counselors who would share with each individual inquirer the contents of a booklet titled *Steps to Peace with God*. That booklet, published by The Billy Graham Evangelistic Association, presents the basic gospel message in four steps followed by a prayer to receive Christ as Savior.

This method of evangelistic counseling is scripturally sound and does not necessarily require establishing a relationship with the inquirer since they have already indicated their interest in hearing the gospel. Nonetheless, the booklet can also be used as a witness tool in the same way as the previous ones discussed. In any case, as with the previously discussed methods, this one is scripturally sound and presupposes the witness subject already has a theistic worldview and believes the Bible is authoritative. (See: https://stepstopeace.org and https://www.billygrahambookstore.org/)

Part One: Overview of this Method

Step One. God's Purpose: Peace and Life

God loves you and wants you to experience peace and life—abundant and eternal. The Bible says ...

- "We have peace with God through our Lord Jesus Christ." (Romans 5:1)

- "For God so loved the world that He gave His only begotten Son, that whoever believes in Him should not perish but have everlasting life." (John 3:16)

- "I have come that they may have life, and that they may have it more abundantly." (John 10:10)

➤ Why don't most people have this peace and abundant life that God planned for us to have?

Step Two. The Problem: Our Separation.

1. God created us in His own image to have an abundant life. He did not make us as robots to automatically love and obey Him. God gave us a will and freedom of choice. We chose to disobey God and go our own willful way. We still make this choice today. This results in separation from God. The Bible says ...

- "For all have sinned and fall short of the glory of God." (Romans 3:23)

- "For the wages of sin is death, but the gift of God is eternal life in Christ Jesus our Lord." (Romans 6:23)

2. Our Attempts to Reach God: People have tried in many ways to bridge this gap between themselves and God. The Bible says ...

- "There is a way that seems right to a man, but in the end, it leads to death." (Proverbs 14:12)

- "But your iniquities have separated you from your God; your sins have hidden his face from you, so that he will not hear." (Isaiah 59:2)

➤ No bridge reaches God ... except one.

Step Three. God's Bridge: The Cross

Jesus Christ died on the Cross and rose from the grave. He paid the penalty for our sin and bridged the gap between God and people. The Bible says ...

- "For there is one God and one mediator between God and men, the man Jesus Christ." (1 Timothy 2:5)

- "For Christ died for sins once for all, the righteous for the unrighteous, to bring you to God." (1 Peter 3:18)

- "But God demonstrates his own love for us in this: While we were still sinners, Christ died for us." (Romans 5:8)

- ➢ God has provided the only way. Each person must make a choice.

Step Four. Our Response: Receive Christ.

We must trust Jesus Christ as Lord and Savior and receive Him by personal invitation. The Bible says ...

- "Here I am! I stand at the door and knock. If anyone hears My voice and opens the door, I will come in and eat with him, and he with Me." (Revelation 3:20)

- "Yet to all who received Him, to those who believed in His name, He gave the right to become children of God." (John 1:12)

- "That if you confess with your mouth, 'Jesus is Lord,' and believe in your heart that God raised Him from the dead, you will be saved." (Romans 10:9)

Where are you? Will you receive Jesus Christ right now? Here is how you can receive Christ:

1. Admit your need ("I am a sinner.").

2. Be willing to turn from your sins (repent).

3. Believe that Jesus Christ died for you on the Cross and rose from the grave.

4. Through prayer, invite Jesus Christ to come in and control your life through the Holy Spirit. (Receive Him as Lord and Savior.)

Part Two: How this Method Answers the Essential Questions

In many ways, Steps to Peace with God is similar to the Four Spiritual Laws. It expresses points about God, man, and salvation, then shares Bible verses to back up its points.

1. Who is God?

The focus of the explanation of God in this method is on God's love—particularly His love for mankind.

God loves mankind.

- "But God demonstrates His own love for us in this: While we were still sinners, Christ died for us." (Romans 5:8)

- "For God so loved the world that He gave His only begotten Son, that whoever believes in Him should not perish but have everlasting life." (John 3:16)

2. What is a human being?

The particular point made in this method about man is that he is sinful, and, because of that, is separated from God.

Human beings are sinful and separated from God.

- "For all have sinned and fall short of the glory of God." (Romans 3:23)

- "For the wages of sin is death, but the gift of God is eternal life in Christ Jesus our Lord." (Romans 6:23)

- "There is a way that seems right to a man, but in the end, it leads to death." (Proverbs 14:12)

- "But your iniquities have separated you from your God; your sins have hidden His face from you, so that He will not hear." (Isaiah 59:2)

3a. What is salvation?

Salvation is addressed with a focus on forgiveness of sin by the death and resurrection of Jesus Christ.

Salvation is forgiveness of our sin so we can enter a relationship with God.

- "For there is one God and one mediator between God and men, the man Jesus Christ." (1 Timothy 2:5)

- "For Christ died for sins once for all, the righteous for the unrighteous, to bring you to God." (1 Peter 3:18)

Salvation is forgiveness of our sin so we can enter a relationship with God.

- "For there is one God and one mediator between God and men, the man Jesus Christ." (1 Timothy 2:5)

- "For Christ died for sins once for all, the righteous for the unrighteous, to bring you to God." (1 Peter 3:18)

- "But God demonstrates His own love for us in this: While we were still sinners, Christ died for us." (Romans 5:8)

3b. ... and how does one achieve it?

The emphasis in this method related to how a person receives God's forgiveness is on human choice. That is, individuals must personally choose to enter a personal relationship with God.

Salvation is achieved by a choice to receive God's forgiveness through Jesus Christ.

- "Here I am! I stand at the door and knock. If anyone hears my voice and opens the door, I will come in and eat with him, and he with me." (Revelation 3:20)

- "Yet to all who received him, to those who believed in his name, he gave the right to become children of God." (John 1:12)

- "That if you confess with your mouth, 'Jesus is Lord,' and believe in your heart that God raised Him from the dead, you will be saved." (Romans 10:9)

Evangelism Explosion

Dr. D. James Kennedy (1930-2007) was pastor of Coral Ridge Presbyterian Church in Fort Lauderdale, Florida, from 1960 until his death. In 1962, Kennedy developed a memorized evangelism strategy he called Evangelism Explosion (EE). In 1972, he incorporated the strategy and began conducting leadership training events for teaching laypeople the methodology. The training was noted for its on-the-job training process. Evangelism Explosion International still conducts training and publishes EE materials.

As with the previously discussed methods, Evangelism Explosion is scripturally sound and presupposes the witness subject already has a theistic worldview and believes the Bible is authoritative. (See: https://evangelismexplosion.org/)

Part One: Overview of this Method

May I ask you a question?

Q #1. Have you come to the place in your spiritual life where you know for certain that if you were to die today that you would go to heaven? 1 John 5:13 tells us that you can know you have eternal life.

Let me ask you a second question ...

Q #2. Suppose you were to die today and stand before God and He were to say to you, "Why should I let you into My heaven?" What would you say?

The Gospel Message

A. Grace

1. Heaven is a free gift. "For the wages of sin is death, but the gift of God is eternal life in Christ Jesus our Lord." (Romans 6:23)

2. It is not earned or deserved. "For it is by grace you have been saved, through faith—and this not from yourselves, it is the gift of God—not by works, so that no one can boast." (Ephesians 2:8-9)

B. Man

1. Man is a sinner.
- "For all have sinned and fall short of the glory of God." (Romans 3:23)

Sin defined.
- "Be perfect, therefore, as your heavenly Father is perfect." (Matthew 5:48)

2. Man cannot save himself.
- "There is a way that seems right to a man, but in the end, it leads to death." (Proverbs 14:12)

C. God

1. God is merciful, therefore doesn't want to punish us.
- "… for God is love." (1 John 4:8b)

2. God is just, therefore must punish us.
- "Yet he does not leave the guilty unpunished; he punishes the children and their children for the sin of the fathers to the third and fourth generation." (Exodus 34:7b)

God solved this problem in the Person of Jesus Christ.

D. Christ.

Who He is: the infinite God-man:

- "In the beginning was the Word, and the Word was with God, and the Word was God." (John 1:1)

- "The Word became flesh and made His dwelling among us. We have seen His glory, the glory of the One and Only, who came from the Father, full of grace and truth." (John 1:14)

- "Thomas said to Him, 'My Lord and my God!'" (John 20:28)

2. What He did: He died on the cross and rose from the dead to pay the penalty for our sins and to purchase a place in heaven for us which He offers as a gift.

E. Faith. Key to heaven

1. What it is not: mere intellectual assent.

- "You believe that there is one God. Good! Even the demons believe that—and shudder." (James 2:19)

- "'What do you want with us, Son of God?' they shouted. 'Have You come here to torture us before the appointed time?'" (Matthew 8:29)

2. What it is: trusting in Jesus Christ alone for eternal life.

- "They replied, 'Believe in the Lord Jesus, and you will be saved—you and your household.'" (Acts 16:31)

Part Two: How this Method Answers the Essential Questions

Evangelism Explosion is another method that uses its own unique order to explain the gospel message. That said, it too answers all three essential worldview questions.

1. Who is God?

Evangelism Explosion deals with the topic of God in two parts. The first part expresses two of God's personal traits—His mercy and His justice. The idea being that He doesn't want to punish us for our sin, but that He must unless the sin problem is resolved. The second part of its treatment of God relates to Jesus and the fact that He was God who became flesh.

- God is merciful. Therefore, He doesn't want to punish us. (1 John 4:8b)

- God is just. Therefore, He must punish us. "Yet He does not leave the guilty unpunished; He punishes the children and their children for the sin of the fathers to the third and fourth generation." (Exodus 34:7b)

- He became Jesus, the infinite God-man.

  o "In the beginning was the Word, and the Word was with God, and the Word was God." (John 1:1)

  o "The Word became flesh and made his dwelling among us. We have seen His glory, the glory of the One and Only, who came from the Father, full of grace and truth." (John 1:14)

2. What is a human being?

The particular focus regarding humanity in this method is that man is a sinner. Since the matter of the consequences of sin was already addressed regarding God's mercy and justice, further explanation is not deemed necessary.

- A sinner. "For all have sinned and fall short of the glory of God." (Romans 3:23)

3a. What is salvation?

In Evangelism Explosion, the explanation of Salvation focuses on holding out heaven as a desired destination, and the fact that people are able to attain it as a free gift by faith alone in Christ.

What it is: a gift.

- Heaven is a free gift. "For the wages of sin is death, but the gift of God is eternal life in Christ Jesus our Lord." (Romans 6:23)

- It is not earned or deserved. "For it is by grace you have been saved, through faith—and this not from yourselves, it is the gift of God—not by works, so that no one can boast." (Ephesians 2:8-9)

What it is not: mere intellectual assent.

- "You believe that there is one God. Good! Even the demons believe that—and shudder." (James 2:19)

- "'What do you want with us, Son of God?' they shouted. 'Have you come here to torture us before the appointed time?'" (Matthew 8:29)

3b. ... and how does one achieve it?

Achieving salvation is expressed by emphasizing that man is unable to achieve it by his own power but can only attain it by believing (putting one's trust) in Jesus Christ.

Man cannot save himself.

- "There is a way that seems right to a man, but in the end, it leads to death." (Proverbs 14:12)

- A person must trust in Jesus Christ alone for eternal life.

- "They replied, 'Believe in the Lord Jesus, and you will be saved—you and your household.'" (Acts 16:31)

Appendix 2
Mapping a Person's Worldview

Professional missionaries have almost always needed a large skill set as they deal with people in foreign lands whose lifestyle, values, norms, and beliefs are radically different from their own.

Today, with so many mission opportunities for the non-professional, and with those radically different worldview and belief systems now here at home, lay witnesses who do short-term missions (or who simply share their faith with a friend) must also be proficient at building the bridges across these differences.

Here is an outline of what you need to know to build these bridges:

1. Learn as much as you can about the group or person you are trying to reach with your witness.

- ✓ Learn as much as you can about the background and culture of the group or person you are attempting to reach.

- ✓ Learn as much as possible about the history of their society.

- ✓ Learn the cultural expectations and taboos of their society.

- ✓ Discern the way those in their society are most willing and/or able to learn new information.

- ✓ Discover who the cultural gatekeepers are and how you can make friends with them.

- ✓ Discover the best ways to gain acceptance in order to interact with the populace.

✓ If there are language issues, figure out how to get around them.

2. Map the religious heritage of the group or person you are trying to reach.

Map how they answer the three essential worldview questions.

Map their entire religion.

✓ Learn the name of their religion.

✓ Learn what God/gods/philosophy they believe in and as much specific information as you can find about Him/them/it.

✓ Learn the ritual practices of their belief and why each is important.

✓ Learn the history of their belief.

✓ Learn any mythology that goes along with their belief.

✓ Learn the doctrines (related to essential and non-essential beliefs) of their faith.

✓ Learn the belief's hierarchical leadership structure and the roles of their leaders.

✓ Learn what their belief teaches about the consequences of not following their belief.

✓ Learn how the average believer interacts with their religion.

✓ Learn what their belief teaches about origins.

✓ Learn what their belief teaches about the afterlife.

✓ Learn what their belief teaches about morality.

✓ Learn what their belief teaches about the meaning of human life.

3. Record what you have learned on a map for each group that holds the same beliefs—or for your friend … on one page.

A handy map is provided on the next page. Simply copy it, expand it to a full-size page, and fill it in as needed.

Worldview and Belief System Map

Group or Person's Name:

Their Worldview:	Their Belief System:
What do they believe about God?	
Their Worldview Beliefs:	Their Belief System's Beliefs:
What do they believe about man?	
Their Worldview Beliefs:	Their Belief System's Beliefs:
What do they believe about Salvation and how it is achieved?	
Their Worldview Beliefs:	Their Belief System's Beliefs:

APPENDIX 3
Overview of Various Belief Systems

Descriptions of the major **Naturalistic** belief systems.
- Secular Humanism
- Modernism and Postmodernism
- Atheism, Agnosticism, and Skepticism
- Marxism

Descriptions of the major **Animistic** belief systems.
- Wicca/Neo-paganism
- Shinto
- Voodoo/Santeria
- Native American Religions
- Non-American Tribal Religions

Descriptions of the major **Far Eastern Thought** belief systems.
- Hinduism
- Buddhism
- Hare Krishna
- Sikhism

Descriptions of the major **non-Christian Theistic** belief systems.
- Islam
- Judaism
- Cultural Christianity
- Jehovah's Witnesses
- Mormonism
- Baha'i

Descriptions of the major **Hybrid** belief systems.

- New Age
- Unitarian Universalism
- Scientology
- Christian Science
- Unification Church

We describe each of these based on the following outline:

History or Background

Basic Beliefs and Practices

Essential Beliefs

God

Man

Salvation

The Essential Beliefs topics list echoes the three essential worldview questions of Chapter 3 and its later discussions of them:

1. Who is God?

2. What is a human being?

   ... and ...

3. What is salvation (*i.e.*: the ultimate one can achieve in this life) and how does one achieve it?

Naturalistic worldview belief systems:

Secular Humanism

Humanism is not necessarily bad or anti-God. It simply emphasizes the importance and value of mankind. "Secular" Humanism, on the other hand, is a coherent, dogmatic belief system asserting there is no such thing as a supernatural existence. It asserts that since man is the only known creature with personal self-awareness, only he can create values and standards. Thus, man is the ultimate standard by which all of life is measured and judged.

History

Modern Secular Humanism has its roots in the Renaissance in the fourteenth to the sixteenth centuries and developed during the "Enlightenment" of the seventeenth to the nineteenth centuries. That renewal did not exclude God as man's creator, but focused attention away from Him. Later, the development of modern science advanced humanist ideas which coalesced in the mid-1800s. One of the ways this was most prominently expressed during this time frame was in Deism. This belief system affirmed a belief in a creator God, but one who is no longer active in creation nor is He Father to mankind.

In the nineteenth century, Deism gave way to full-blown Naturalism which threw God out altogether. Elements of humanist philosophy even crept into mainline Christian churches. The trend peaked with Charles Darwin's (1809–1882) 1859 book, *On the Origin of Species*, which asserted that humanity's origin was completely and exclusively the result of natural forces at work.

In the twentieth century, scientists, philosophers, and liberal theologians promoted humanism as a non-theistic religion devoid of the supernatural. Unitarianism, once a non-Trinitarian sect of Christianity, fully adopted the concepts of humanism. In 1933, *The Humanist Manifesto I* was drafted as a creed of secular humanist thought. But Secular Humanism's optimism for perfecting human society was shattered by World War II and its aftermath. Nonetheless, many diehards continued to proclaim its tenets.

In 1973, *The Humanist Manifesto II* was released. In 2003, they updated it in *The Humanist Manifesto III*. Today, Secular Humanism dominates public education, political institutions, literature, the entertainment industry, as well as the news media.

Basic Beliefs and Practices

The Humanist Manifesto III is more of a consensus statement than its predecessors, but disavows none of what they said.

Its main points are:

- Knowledge is derived by observation, experimentation, and rational analysis.

- Humans are part of nature, the result of unguided evolutionary change.

- Ethical values derive from human experience.

- Life's fulfillment is found through serving humane ideals.

- Humans find meaning in relationships.

- Working to benefit society maximizes individual happiness.

These points attract idealistic people, but one must read the entire manifesto to understand what it entails. *Manifestos I* and *II* provided clearer perspectives than the generic points of the current manifesto.

They asserted such concepts as:

- Promises of immortal salvation or fear of eternal damnation are illusory and harmful.

- Moral values come from human experience.

- Reason and intelligence are the most effective instruments of humankind.

- The dignity of the individual is the central value.

- Intolerant attitudes unduly repress sexual conduct. The right to birth control, abortion, and divorce should be recognized.

- The individual must experience a full range of civil liberties in all societies. These include freedom of speech, a free press, democracy, opposition to government policies, fair judicial process, religion, association, artistic expression, science, culture, death with dignity, euthanasia, and suicide.

- Society should be open and democratic.

- Separation of church or ideology and state must be maintained.

- Equality must be furthered by elimination of all discrimination based upon race, religion, sex, age, or national origin.

- Mankind's division on nationalistic grounds is deplorable.

- The world community must renounce violence and force for solving international disputes.

- The world community must engage in cooperative planning for managing depleting resources.

- The problems of economic development are worldwide in scope, and the developed nations must equalize the distribution of resources.

- We resist any moves to censor scientific research on moral, political, or social grounds.

- All travel restrictions must cease, and the world be open to diverse political, ideological, and moral viewpoints.

Essential Beliefs

God

There is no type of supernatural existence at all (God, gods, angels, ghosts, or any other kind of spiritual entity). Essentially, mankind is his own god. All that exists is eternal and evolving matter.

Man

Man is a biological machine resulting from naturalistic evolution. Man has no life but what is experienced in this natural world and is responsible for his own destiny.

Salvation

For the Secular Humanist, there is no life after death. Salvation consists of promoting survival and fulfilling one's highest potential during mortal life.

Naturalistic worldview belief systems:

Modernism and Postmodernism

History

Modernism is a socially-progressive trend of thought that asserts the belief that human beings are able to create, improve and reshape their environment using practical experimentation, scientific knowledge, and technology. Its presuppositions closely resemble those of Secular Humanism. Thus, it encouraged a re-examination of every aspect of existence with the goal of finding what is holding back progress, then replacing it with something new.

While somewhat difficult to define, Postmodernism developed in the last century as a reaction against Modernism. At its core, it actually denies absolute truth and denounces Western philosophy. It also rejects universal or transcendent truth, while at the same time endorsing "political correctness." It is expressed in art, architecture, music, film, literature, mass communications, entertainment, politics, and so on. While there are various writers who have become prominent in the postmodernist movement, no single individual is identified as its father. It simply emerged as another expression of Naturalism from the Modernism it rejected.

Postmodernists maintain that there exists no objective right or wrong and dismiss the fundamental ideas of all belief systems— which they call *metanarratives*. For instance, an American metanarrative is that democracy is the best form of government. This is rejected along with all other metanarratives from every other belief system.

Postmodernism asserts that every aspect of every culture is built upon these metanarratives. This includes their understanding of science, art, architecture, music, technology, religion, *etc*. It insists that no metanarrative is any more viable than any other. Each view may be right for its own situation and context, but not necessarily for others.

Rather than operating out of metanarratives, Postmodernists work out of *mini-narratives*. These focus on individual events rather than universal principles. Judgments are made based on the circumstances of a particular situation, with no possible claim to an objective right or wrong. What is right at one point may not be right at another. What is right for one person may not be right for another. No universal truth or morality is acknowledged. Thus, knowledge has a strictly functional influence on people's lives.

Basic Beliefs and Practices

Postmodernism is difficult to define because it denies absolute truth. The easiest way to grasp postmodernist thinking is to compare it with Modernism.

Education

Modernism: Objective truth exists and can be transmitted to students.

Postmodernism: No objective truth exists. Teachers facilitate students to construct their own subjective ideas.

Health Care

Modernism: The body is studied by the scientific method. Medicine devises therapies.

Postmodernism: Alternative techniques without scientific confirmation are valid.

Science

Modernism: Universal laws of science are applied to the material world to solve problems.

Postmodernism: The universe is not based on absolute laws. The universe is interconnected but not rational.

229

Psychotherapy

Modernism: Mental health is defined objectively. Trained therapists help patients toward a healthy state of mind.

Postmodernism: The "right" mental state cannot be defined objectively. Therapists help patients construct what is right for themselves.

Religion

Modernism: Individuals can learn objective truths about God.

Postmodernism: No single religious perspective is correct. All exclusivist religious claims are denounced as "intolerant."

History

Modernism: History is an objective reality. Individuals can study events from the past.

Postmodernism: History is not objective. Studying past events is pointless except to validate oppressed people's protests of society.

Literature

Modernism: Ideas flow from an author to a reader through the written word. An author produces a text that objectively communicates propositions to the reader.

Postmodernism: Meaning flows from the *reader*, not the author. Individuals construct subjective meaning of whatever they encounter filtered through their personal cultural framework.

Biblical Interpretation

Modernism: While most Modernists don't specifically believe that the Bible contains propositional truth, they do believe in the existence of propositional truth. Thus, when dealing with Scripture, they acknowledge that if, indeed, it did come from God, then it was delivered from God through divinely inspired, but not necessarily *verbally* inspired, authors. Interpretation is, then, the process of discerning the spiritual and moral truths God wants to convey (regardless of its objective historical accuracy) using both traditional and modern critical methods of hermeneutics and literary analysis.

Postmodernism: God does not communicate truth through the Bible (if God even exists). It is simply another book with which readers construct subjective meaning filtered through their personal cultural framework.

Law and Government

Modernism: Laws are objective principles established to keep order in society. In a democratic republic, judges discern the intent of the writers and interpret based on that.

Postmodernism: All laws are political constructs designed to suppress the disenfranchised. Judges cannot objectively interpret the intent of laws. Rather, they pursue their own personal political agendas.

Morality

Modernism: Right morality can be extrapolated from objective truth.

Postmodernism: Right and wrong is "what is moral for the individual." Most Postmodernists, nonetheless, would add "... as long as it doesn't hurt anyone else."

Essential Beliefs

Modernists affirm objective truth as determined by the laws of nature and human reason.

Postmodernists incongruently deny objective truth but cannot live by that assertion. As with all worldview positions, they too are compelled to draw a line defining the parameters of reality that, in turn, define the boundaries of Postmodernism (*i.e.,* lines which cannot be crossed and still be Postmodern).

The *de facto* essential elements of Modernism and Postmodernism include:

God

For Modernists, the concept of God is based on perspectives derived primarily from human reason and science. Any claims of revealed truth (*e.g.,* the Bible or the *Qur'an*) must be weighed in light of modern science and historical research.

For Postmodernists, the concept of God is determined by each individual. No transcendent God created a meaningful world.

Man

Modernists and Postmodernists both believe human beings are animal creatures and are no different from any other except for the evolutionary development of the brain. Humans are not spiritual beings but must find their own personal meaning for life.

Salvation

For Modernists and Postmodernists, in terms of our technical use of the word, salvation (*i.e.,* "the best one can get out of life") is finding and then, living out their personal meaning in a universe that offers no transcendent meaning.

Note: Some Postmodernists, however, are self-confessed Nihilists who don't believe that there is any meaning to anything at all.

Naturalistic worldview belief systems:

Atheism, Agnosticism, and Skepticism

Background

In this section we will examine not only Atheism, but Agnosticism and Skepticism, as well. While the three positions do have distinct differences, they pretty much all land in the same place.

All three of these views are firmly in the camp of Naturalism, as they all deny any spiritual component of reality. It is often difficult to distinguish between the terms because their definitions overlap. Many people who label themselves with one of these expressions do not see the differences or how their own views fit one category or the other. We will try to make a distinction between these three belief systems, as well as stress where they intersect.

Because of the nature of these philosophical points of view, no distinctive history is identified with them. These positions have been held by people over the centuries.

Atheism

The word Atheism literally means *without god*. It derives from the Greek prefix *a*, meaning *not* or *without*, and *theos*, meaning *God*. Thus, an Atheist positively affirms that there is no god or gods. They assert that all of existence is explained naturally.

Agnosticism

The word Agnosticism also comes from the Greek. It combines the Greek *a* with the word *gnosis* (knowledge). Thus, it literally means *without knowledge*. Agnostics maintain there is not enough evidence to prove or disprove the existence of God. A true Agnostic criticizes both the Theist and the Atheist for presuming to have such knowledge. This position attempts to remain neutral on the topic of God by suspending judgment.

Agnosticism has two expressions. One asserts that there is not enough evidence to know whether or not there is a god but leaves open the possibility of obtaining that knowledge. The second type asserts that it is impossible to ever know with certainty if there is a god.

Skepticism

The word Skepticism is derived from the Greek word *skeptomai* meaning *to doubt* or *to consider*. Skeptics believe that people cannot know Truth with absolute certainty, so they should suspend judgment about it. Their skepticism applies not only to knowledge of God, but to *all* truth claims.

Basic Beliefs and Practices

Though the three approaches to denying God are semantically different, their practical consequences are the same. They all deny God, but just argue this denial differently.

These approaches include:

The Language Argument

This approach asserts that only two kinds of statements are meaningful:

1) pure definition; and

2) what can be empirically verified.

Since God cannot be defined or empirically verified, it is meaningless to talk about Him.

The Knowledge Argument

This argument denies that we can objectively know what is real because our senses are imperfect. We can only know what we experience ... albeit imperfectly.

The Moral Concepts Argument

This argument asserts that if there is a good, all-powerful God, He would not allow evil to exist. So, since evil exists, then God does not.

The Scientific Methods Argument

This argument asserts that man's belief in God is simply a psychological phenomenon to give human beings a way to deal with matters that are beyond their control. It says science must validate any belief about reality. Atheists believe that there is no transcendent God, so belief in God arises purely from man's *wish* that there be someone powerful enough to be the rescuer.

The Logic Arguments

Nay-sayers sometimes posit a couple of fallacious logical arguments to deny the existence of God.

1. One argument is that God's all-powerfulness is contradictory. This argument goes that if God is all-powerful, He could reconcile any contradiction (*e.g.*, He could make a square circle.) Since He can't do so, He must not exist.

2. A second argument proposes that God's attributes are contradictory. For instance, how can He be both love and wrath at the same time?

Essential Beliefs

God

Atheists, Agnostics, and Skeptics all assert that there is no such thing as God, or at least there is no possibility that we can know it.

235

Man

Atheists, Agnostics, and Skeptics all affirm that man is the chance result of billions of years of natural evolutionary progress.

Salvation

Atheists, Agnostics, and Skeptics all assert that there is no life after death, so survival and achieving maximum self-fulfillment in this life is mankind's highest aim. Some of them, however, acknowledge that without God, no ultimate purpose or meaning for life exists at all.

Naturalistic worldview belief systems:

Marxism

Background

Marxism is an economic and political philosophy named for its author and proponent, Karl Marx (1818–1883). It is also known as Scientific Socialism. Marxism has had a profound impact on recent history, political thought, and contemporary culture worldwide. Most modern socialist theories have originated from it.

Karl Marx was born in Trier, Germany, in 1818. His ancestors were Jewish rabbis. Prior to his birth, around 1816, his father, Heinrich, converted to Christianity in order to continue practicing law. The Prussian government had passed a law denying Jews the opportunity to serve in that profession. His mother converted when Karl was seven.

In daily life, the family did not demonstrate much interest in religion, but his parents raised Karl in an atmosphere of religious toleration. He even attended a religious school, though the purpose was to achieve a superior academic education rather than for religious training.

For his higher education, Marx attended Bonn University. He later worked on his doctorate at Berlin University. During that time, he became a committed Atheist and a political and social radical. His views were so radical, in fact, that he was unable to get a job as a professor, so he turned his focus to political activism. In order to share his ideas with a wider audience, he became the editor of a business periodical that also had a bent toward radical political viewpoints. In that position, Marx was able to develop and express his philosophy of dialectical materialism more fully (see below).

In 1843, Marx met Frederich Engles (1820–1895) who became a close friend, benefactor, and collaborator. They were very much philosophical and political soul-mates. That same year, because of Marx's radical activism, the German government closed his

237

publication and expelled him from Germany. From there he moved to Paris.

Not too long after that, Marx's radical activism got him in trouble again and he was kicked out of France. From there he moved to Brussels, Belgium where, in 1948, Marx and Engles wrote the *Communist Manifesto.*

Following its publication, he was expelled from Belgium, so he attempted to go back to Germany. The German government would not let him stay there, so he tried, once again, to move to France. But the French also would not let him return, so he moved to London.

Because of his devotion to his cause, Marx basically lived a pauper's life. He was often reduced to begging money from friends and relatives to pay his debts. He finally achieved some measure of financial success and stability after publishing his magnum opus, *Das Kapital,* in 1867. He died in 1883.

Basic Beliefs and Practices

Marxism is not just a political and economic philosophy; it is a comprehensive belief system. As such, it affirms an atheistic religious viewpoint and a contempt for philosophy. Although no single writing by Marx covers all aspects of Marxism, the *Communist Manifesto* and *Das Kapital* develop his ideas most completely.

The core of Marxism is expressed in the concept of dialectical materialism. This philosophy was based on Georg Wilhelm Friedrich Hegel's (1770–1831) view that intellectual progress results from the synthesis of a thesis and antithesis. Marx applied that theory to history and asserted that conflicting economic factors are the primary determinants of the flow of history. From this foundation, Marx developed the basic thesis that the history of society is actually the history of class struggle.

According to his assumptions, a specific class only stays in power as long as it is the best representative of the most economically productive group in society. When it can no longer maintain that status, it will be destroyed and replaced. Marx believed that through this process a classless society would eventually and inevitably emerge.

According to Marx's theory, the capitalist society of his day had destroyed the unproductive feudal nobility that went before and had replaced it with a new industrial order. In his mind, the stage was set for one final struggle between the capitalist class (*bourgeoisie*), which had completed its historic role, and the working class (proletariat) who had become the new productive class. He believed that it was these industrial workers who would complete the revolution by overturning capitalism and create a true, classless society.

Essential Beliefs

God

The Marxist god is humanity's inevitable march toward societal perfection based on dialectical materialism. This belief is built on the understanding that there is no God, but that mankind is master of his own destiny as determined by the laws of history.

Man

Marxism denies the worth and freedom of the individual. Individuals have value only as they promote the common good of society and the inevitable progress of history.

Salvation

Salvation for Marxists is achieved as these individuals deny their own personal desires and find the place where they can most effectively contribute to the collective society.

Animistic worldview belief systems:

Wicca/Neo-paganism

Background

Wicca is a particular expression of Animism out of the broader witchcraft tradition. Many different groups claim to be Wiccan with differing uses of magic, rituals, religious practice, and views of the spirit world. All encompass worship and practice that includes magic and rituals to influence the spirit world.

Witchcraft can be traced back many centuries in Africa, Europe, and the Middle East. It has no personal understanding of God. Rather, divine beings are seen to inhabit nature. In some groups, the natural order is personified as a god or goddess, but not in a personal way.

Derivatives of ancient witchcraft are still practiced throughout the world. The most common modern form was started in 1949 by an English eccentric named Gerald Gardner (1884–1964). His book, *The Craft*, Gardner used Wicca as a form of nature worship where the spirit world is present in the natural order. His inspiration was the pre-Christian pagan religions of Europe.

Gardner was fascinated with the occult. It is not clear if he intended to begin a new religious tradition, but it does seem that he invented this cult to satisfy his desire to explore occult ideas. Witchcraft has been in America since its early days. Its greatest growth, however, took place in the 1960s and 1970s during a revival of interest in the occult. Two of Gardner's followers, Raymond and Rosemary Buckland, came to America in 1962 and established a Wiccan group (or coven) in Long Island, New York.

In 1973, a convention of witches was held in Minneapolis, Minnesota, attracting 73 different groups. They attempted to write a unified statement of principles but failed because they could not agree on the wording. The following year the Council of American Witches successfully drafted the *Covenant of the Goddess*.

Basic Beliefs and Practices

The theology of Wicca varies from group to group. However, the following are a few of the doctrines common to most Wiccan covens.

Autonomy

There is no central authority or liturgy. Each tradition (*i.e.*, each coven) establishes its own rituals, philosophy, and beliefs. Individuals may also create their own.

Rituals

Individual or coven experiences are manifested through self-designed rituals. Rites acknowledge the movement of the seasons and celebrate life processes.

Experience *vs.* Dogma

The experience of the individual is of greater importance than any set of authoritarian doctrines.

Magic

Rituals in Wicca involve divination or magic. This involves contacting and manipulating people, spirits, animals, plants, or the elements (earth, air, fire, water). It is done through occult rituals, ceremonies, or the use of magic objects (amulets, talismans, charms, *etc.*).

Goddess Worship

Worship involves veneration of the *Mother Goddess* (Mother Nature). In many covens, the high priestess is seen as the embodiment of the Mother Goddess.

Feminism

Many women find Wicca compatible with feminist thought since it focuses on a goddess.

Seasonal Festivals

The worship of nature, or the natural order, is of chief importance. It is a fertility cult with festivals tied to the seasons.

Evil

Wiccans deny the existence of evil. They consider themselves practitioners of a pagan mystery religion with no embodiment of evil such as Satan or the Devil.

Horned God

Some covens worship a masculine deity along with the Goddess. This God is referred to as the Horned God, the God of the Hunt, the God of Death, or the Lord of the Forests.

Essential Beliefs

God

Wicca has no personal God who is considered to be the Creator and Sustainer of the universe. Rather, the divine life source in nature is open to contact through psychic power, mysticism, or natural magic. This life source is understood to be present in everything. Many Wiccans worship the Great Goddess and the Horned God as focus objects rather than as personal deities.

Man

Human beings are natural creatures inhabiting the material world that can interact with the nature spirits to accomplish desired ends.

Salvation

Some Wiccans and Neo-Pagans believe that at death, the spirit of an individual enters the spirit world. Others believe in reincarnation. In any case, it is all connected with the natural order of the universe. However, none believe that human beings have any need of salvation from sin (as Christians understand 'sin').

The best Wiccans or Neo-Pagans can expect from life is to live in harmony with the spiritual forces that control their lives. They accomplish this by performing certain rituals that appease the spirits.

Appendix 3

Animistic worldview belief systems:

Shinto

History

Shinto is the indigenous religion of Japan. Essentially, it is a primitive religion that centers on the worship of nature deities and deified people. It has no founder, no prophet, no savior, and little formal doctrine. Its main emphasis is the worship of the *Kami* (gods). *Kami* are everywhere and the world is *Kami*.

The origins of the ancient Shinto religion are obscure. The word itself literally means *the way of the gods*. The religion did not even have a name until the sixth century (AD) when it was named in order to distinguish it from Buddhism which had been imported from China. The early development of Shintoism is not recorded. Records only started being kept when Buddhism began to threaten Shintoism and the Japanese began writing things down as a way of preserving the old myths and oral traditions.

The Japanese usually have their wedding ceremonies in Shinto style and pronounce their wedding vows to *Kami*.

Basic Beliefs and Practices

The Creation Story

The origins of Shinto are recorded in the *Kojiki* and the *Nihongi*. According to the creation myth, after the formation of heaven and earth, two of the gods, Izanagi and Izanami, stood on the floating bridge of heaven. Izanagi was leisurely stirring the ocean brine with his spear, and when he lifted it out, the drops which fell from it coagulated to form one of the Japanese islands. Izanagi and Izanami descended to this island and produced the rest of the Japanese islands. They also produced other deities and the Japanese people.

244

One of the chief deities was the sun goddess, Amaterasu Omikami. She had a grandson named Jimmu Tenno who descended to the sacred Japanese islands to become the first historical emperor of Japan in 660 BC Japanese tradition claims an unbroken line of succession from Jimmu Tenno, and this has led to a strong emphasis on emperor worship. Since the emperors were thought to be gods, they had to be obeyed unquestioningly by all Japanese.

Nationalistic Shinto

Popular Shinto has no ethical system of its own, so ethical teachings from Confucianism and Buddhism were introduced. This is especially evident in the concepts of filial piety and the five relationships.

However, in the mid to late 1800s, a rise in Japanese nationalistic spirit led to a revival of popular Shinto at the expense of Buddhism. In 1882, Emperor Meiji officially made Shinto the state religion. State Shinto ultimately became a political force that was used to promote the superiority of the Japanese people, and to prove that the creation of the Japanese Empire was a divine event. To solidify this movement, national Shinto shrines were established.

Before and during World War II, all students were indoctrinated in the Shinto myths and taught to worship the emperor and the state. In that way, the politicians were able to use State Shinto as the basis for their war effort. At the end of the war, with Japan's defeat in 1945, Emperor Hirohito was allowed to remain as the emperor, but he was forced to deny that he was divine. This disavowal was a huge blow to the Shinto religion. Even though state Shinto was officially eliminated, there is still a core of nationalists who continue to promote it.

Essential Beliefs

God

There are many gods and even different types of gods. There are gods of nature, the ancestors, and the emperor. The emperor is a living human being while the other gods inhabit the spirit world. Even these, though, are understood to interact with humanity in a symbiotic relationship.

Man

Shinto teaches that "man is *Kami's* child." First, this means that a person was given his life by the *Kami*, so his nature is sacred. Second, it means that daily life is made possible by the *Kami*, so human personality and life are worthy of respect. Man is considered to have a divine nature, but it is seldom revealed in this life. Purification ceremonies are necessary to symbolically remove the dust and impurities that cover one's inner mind.

Salvation

The Shinto concept of salvation is deliverance from the troubles and evils of the world.

There is no Shinto concept of sin in a biblical sense. If a person appeases the gods and ancestors, follows the correct taboos, and expresses his *Kami* nature, he will ultimately find his place of immortality among the ancestral *Kami* beings.

Salvation is achieved by observing the many social and physical taboos that have become a part of Japanese life. Ritualistic purity (ceremonial washing and sweeping) is very important since this is how evil is thought to be banished.

Animistic worldview belief systems:

Voodoo (similarly, Santeria)

Background

The first thing in most people's minds when thinking of Voodoo is zombies walking around with their arms sticking out. They also think of witch doctors and sticking pins in dolls. The fact is, Voodoo is an animistic religion with origins that trace back 6000 years to West Africa. The word Voodoo is from the Nigerian word *vodu*, meaning divinity, spirit, or deity. The religion is also known as *voudou, voudoun, vodoun,* and *hoodoo.*

Voodoo's roots in the Western Hemisphere are from Haiti. Slaves from Africa were brought to the West Indies by Western Europeans. Those slaves were forced to convert to Roman Catholicism. However, they did not completely assimilate, and the result was a syncretic blend of Roman Catholic teachings with traditional African rituals.

Modern forms of Voodoo reflect this mixture. Ceremonies integrate Catholic rituals, prayers, liturgies, and reverence for the saints, with old African animistic observances. Voodoo worship places are often filled with pictures and statues of Catholic saints, and worship practices include hymns to the saints and the Virgin Mary. The saints may actually represent Voodoo gods.

Many slaves were sent from Haiti to what is now the United States. As a result, their descendants, and other adherents of Voodoo, still remain. Probably the best-known enclave is New Orleans, Louisiana. Voodoo is also practiced in parts of South America, Africa, Trinidad, Jamaica, and Cuba.

Another similar, African-originated, faith popular among many Cuban Americans is Santeria. The basics of Voodoo and Santeria are similar, though they differ in worship practices and how they identify the gods. Followers of Santeria, called Santeros, worship a number of gods including Obatalá, Oshún, Yemaya (or Yemalla),

Oyá, Changó (or Shango), Elegguá, Oggún, Ochosi, and Osun. These are also often identified with Catholic saints. The supreme god is Olofi, also called Olodumare and Olorún. Santeros believe that ritually honoring and sacrificing small animals to these gods gains magical power to influence other people.

Basic Beliefs and Practices

Voodoo's basic tenet (and Santeria's, as well) is that entities in the spirit world interact with humans on earth in symbiotic relationships. Humans provide food and other materials to help the spirits. The gods provide health, protection from evil, and good fortune to humans. These gods are mixtures of ancestral spirits and lesser gods known as *Loa*. They interact in ritual ceremonies led by Voodoo priests or priestesses.

The rituals invoke the gods' help. Various ceremonies celebrate lucky events or holidays, invoke help for escaping bad fortune, ask for healing, celebrate the birth of a child, bless a marriage, or provide a smooth transition into the afterlife at death.

Regional variations exist in Voodoo ceremonies, but they are basically similar. A priest or priestess presides with singing and dancing. Drumbeats invoke the presence of the gods as food and animal blood are offered. As the music, drink, and dance take effect, the priest (or someone else) falls into a trance as the *Loa* take possession of their body. In this state, a god may manifest itself by speaking, singing, cursing, offering advice, or healing the sick.

Essential Beliefs

God

The one supreme god is named Bondje. Beneath Bondje, are hundreds of minor gods and *Loa*, who are the spirits of departed people who led exceptional lives while on earth (much like saints in the Roman Catholic tradition). The *Loa* exercise control over nature and the health, wealth, and happiness of humans. Jesus Christ was not part of Voodoo tradition, but as Christian ideas mixed in, Jesus became one member of their pantheon of gods.

Man

Human beings are seen as material expressions of the universal life energy that all living things share. The physical body contains a soul with two parts. The *small soul* is an individual's personal essence. This part journeys out of the body during sleep (in dreams) and is possessed by the *Loa* during Voodoo ceremonies. The *large soul* is the universal life energy that enters an individual at conception and departs at death.

Salvation

Salvation, for Voodoo and Santeria practitioners does not concern forgiveness or overcoming sin. Rather, it addresses practical ways for humans to make it through life and transition to the afterlife—if they provide the gods with food and other materials and perform certain rituals and ceremonies.

Animistic worldview belief systems:

Native American Religions

Background

Explaining the worldview beliefs of Native American religions is more difficult than other belief systems because the large number of Native American tribes differ somewhat in their approaches. That being said, they all fall under the same worldview category: Animism. Our purpose here is not to explain each group's beliefs, but to analyze the worldview foundation of all traditional Native American religions.

Most Native American people groups were thought to have migrated to the Western Hemisphere from Siberia across the Bering Strait and spread throughout the Americas. Recent archeological discoveries and genetic analysis, however, indicate that there were multiple migrations, some of which may have come from other areas.

Native American worship practices evolved differently because of tribal diversity and geographical distribution. Rituals emerged in each location reflecting individual situations. Some groups were oriented toward hunting and gathering and looked to the spirits to help them find game. Others were agricultural and depended on the spirits to provide weather that allowed for good crops. All, though, were founded on an animistic worldview and held many things in common.

Modern Native American religious practices were influenced by the arrival, in the fifteenth and sixteenth centuries, of Western Europeans to the Americas. As the new arrivals from Europe spread, every element of Native American life was altered. Many died due to illness and war. In some cases, Native American spiritual practices were suppressed, and the populations were forced to convert to Christianity (mainly Roman Catholicism in South and Central America). Also, government policies forced tribes onto reservations or compelled their assimilation into Western culture.

Because of this upheaval, Native Americans now follow a variety of spiritual traditions. Some are devout Christians, while others maintain their traditional religions. It is also common to find ancient traditions syncretized with Christian or even New Age beliefs.

Basic Beliefs and Practices

While we recognize great diversity in the various Native American religious traditions, they nonetheless share several worldview similarities.

First, in every case, all of creation is seen to be interrelated, and humans are responsible to oversee and protect the material world.

Second, all life is of equal value. A sacred life force is in all humans, animals, and plants, which connects all living things. All life forms are understood to have as much right to existence as human beings and should not be damaged or destroyed. Plants and animals may be used for food, medicine, and other needs, but with limitations.

Third is a long-term concern for life. They willingly forego short-term expediency to assure long-term viability in nature.

Finally, they express gratitude to the Creator for life and all he makes possible. This gratitude is expressed in public and private worship traditions.

The Native American view of deity is dualistic, with both good and bad in the spiritual world. Most believe in a creator God who made the world. They acknowledge him in worship and prayer. They also believe in other spirits which control the weather and other circumstances affecting humans.

Since Westerners entered the picture, Christianity has greatly penetrated Native American spirituality. Some New Age teachers have also incorporated Native American concepts into their principles, and *vice versa*. One such prominent New Age author was Sun Bear (born Vincent LaDuke, 1929–1992).

Essential Beliefs

God

Most Native American groups acknowledge an all-powerful, all-knowing creator God or *Master Spirit*. They also recognize numerous lesser supernatural spirits which interact with material life from the spirit world.

Man

Mankind is one expression of the universal life force that courses through all living things. Man is to live harmoniously in the world and with all other living things, helping to maintain the web of life.

Salvation

In a broad sense, salvation does not usually concern the forgiveness of sin, rather with how to make it through this life. The spirits help people navigate the material world and move smoothly into the next. This is accomplished in various ways according to the traditions of particular tribes.

Animistic worldview belief systems:

Non-American Tribal Religions

Background

Native American religions are one category of animistic peoples. Basically, they are tribal groups that existed in what is now the United States, before Europeans colonized that area of the world. While each of them has an animistic foundation, the specific gods and religious practices vary considerably.

This type of religious practice is not limited to the Americas. Tribal religions are found, literally, all over the world. The highest concentration of people who follow tribal religions in modern times is found in Africa. In some African countries, as many as forty to forty-five percent of the people follow some form of tribal religion. There is also a very high concentration of people who follow tribal religions in Mongolia and Laos. But even developed nations tend to have measurable groups that can be characterized as believers in a tribal religion.

Categories of tribal religions include groups that are identified by their ethnicity, groups that are organized around a *shaman* (a priest or priestess who uses magic for the purpose of curing the sick, divining the hidden, and controlling events), and groups in which the animistic practices themselves are the chief identifier. In all cases, though, Animism is the approach they use for understanding the nature of reality. It is estimated that about three percent of the world's population fits into this category.

Basic Beliefs and Practices

Each tribal group tends to be unique when it comes to the specific gods worshiped and the practices used in worship. That being said, the similarities are also noticeable. Generally, there is a belief in a cosmos populated by gods. This often includes a chief god which creates other gods, the earth, the animals, and human beings.

In the practice of these religions, there will usually be sacred places that a god or sacred spirit inhabits. It is also not unusual that both males and females are considered to be part of the cosmic scheme. This element of the belief system is often associated with fertility rites. In animistic tribal groups, the religion is also generally the organizing principle for the operation of society—including its values and traditions.

The actual religious beliefs themselves tend not to have specific tenets with religious laws people are compelled to follow. The main emphasis is, rather, on making sure that the spirit world and the physical world are properly related, and that the needs of each side are taken care of. From the human side, this relationship is accomplished through prayers, offerings, and sacrifices made at the various shrines and altars of the gods and spirits.

The gods and spirits themselves tend to fall into the typical animistic categories: inanimate objects (rocks, trees, *etc.*), heavenly objects (sun, stars, *etc.*), animals, and ancestor spirits.

Essential Beliefs

God

Most animistic tribal groups believe in an all-powerful, all-knowing God who was responsible for creating the world and all in it. They also generally acknowledge numerous lesser supernatural spirits that interact with the material world from their position in the spirit world.

Man

Mankind is generally understood to be the part of the "circle of life" that has responsibilities for helping maintain the balance between the material and spiritual parts of reality. It is up to human beings to live harmoniously in the world in relationship with all other living things, and with the gods and spirits.

Salvation

The concept of salvation, in non-American tribal religions, deals primarily with the obligation to take care of human responsibilities that relate to maintaining harmony in the universe. There are things humans must do to fulfill their obligations to the gods and spirits. When these are done well, the gods and spirits also make life go well for the humans. This includes helping human beings navigate this life and move smoothly into the next.

Far Eastern Thought worldview belief systems:

Hinduism

Background

The word Hindu is derived from *Sindhu,* the Sanskrit word for the inhabitants of India's Indus River region. The English term Hinduism was introduced in the nineteenth century, and referred to India's religious, philosophical, and cultural tradition. Most of the world's billion or so Hindus are found in India, claiming ninety percent of its population. Other large groups live in Nepal, Mauritius, Fiji, Guyana, Suriname, Bangladesh, Malaysia, Trinidad and Tobago, and Bhutan.

The earliest stage of Hinduism was the Animistic pre-Vedic period. The Vedic period followed around 1500 BC when the Aryans taught their Sanskrit scriptures, called the *Vedas,* to the native population. This integrated Far Eastern Thought into the formerly animistic population.

The *Upanishad* period began around 600 BC The *Upanishads* are teachings based on the *Vedas,* but more philosophical. Vedic religion synthesized the gods into a single pantheistic principle (the absolute universal soul, impersonal life force, cosmos, or Brahman).

Hinduism has six philosophical schools. They include:

1. *Samkhya,* an atheistic and dualistic school,

2. *Yoga,* adds worship of God and physical discipline to *Samkhya,*

3. *Nyaya,* a rationalistic form of thought,

4. *Vaisheshika*, classifies all of reality into certain categories,

5. *Vedanta,* stresses the identity between god and the soul (*Brahman-atman*), and

6. *Mimamsa,* which interprets the *Vedas* literally.

Basic Beliefs and Practices

Brahman

Hinduism contains the concept of an eternal *Trimurti,* or Three-in-One God. This emphasizes impersonal manifestations of the oneness of *Brahman* consisting of Brahma, the Creator; Vishnu, the Preserver; and Shiva, the Destroyer.

Submission to Fate

Man is part of *Brahman* (the universal absolute) which determines how each person lives.

The Caste System

Individuals are born into a particular caste (social class) based on the law of *karma.* Each must remain in that station of life. Change is possible only in the next life. The major categories, in descending order (*i.e.,* furthest from merging with the life-force), are *Brahmins* (priests), *Kshatriyas* (warriors and rulers), *Vaishyas* (merchants), and *Shudras* (workers). The three higher castes fully participate in society. The *Shudras* are a class of unclean outcastes, also referred to as 'untouchables.'

The Law of *Karma*

A person's every action has consequences. Good actions create good *karma* and bad actions create bad *karma* which is carried over from one lifetime to the next. A person's present life-station was determined in previous lifetimes, and the *karma* score, created in this lifetime, determines the life-station of the next. The goal is to accumulate enough good *karma,* over as many lifetimes as it takes, to end the birth, death, and rebirth cycle and merge with the impersonal life force.

Reincarnation

Reincarnation is the chain of rebirths in which pieces of the life force move to higher or lower states through successive lives. All life progresses from lower forms up through human life—the highest level. In the human stages of reincarnation, one ascends from the lower castes to the highest caste of the *Brahmins* where the individual may shed material existence and merge with the impersonal body of life force (*moska*).

Moksha

Moksha is the final stage of the reincarnation process when an individual piece of the life force is liberated from the chain of rebirths on earth and is reunited with the transcendent impersonal body of the life force.

Yoga

Yoga consists of physical disciplines that control the body and emotions to help one accumulate good *karma*.

Dharma

Dharma consists of each person's duty (the "Law of Moral Order"), based on their caste and stage of life, necessary to attain *moksha*.

Essential Beliefs

God

Ultimate reality is an impersonal and philosophical absolute that is the ultimate manifestation of oneness (the impersonal life force). *Hindus* worship thousands of gods which are all manifestations of *Brahman*.

Man

Humans are manifestations of the impersonal life force (*Brahman*) at the upper levels of the reincarnation process. Their personal nature is an illusion, so they are ultimately without individual self or self-worth.

Salvation

Escape from the recurring cycles of life and absorption into the impersonal life force (*Brahman*) is the ultimate goal of *Hinduism*. There are three ways to achieve this:

> 1. **The Way of Knowledge.** Giving of one's life to *Brahman* by mystical identification (a philosophical approach).

> 2. **The Way of Devotion.** Commitment to the worship of a particular god who will resolve the *karma* problem (a worship approach).

> 3. **The Way of Works.** The observance of all *Hindu* laws and obligations (a works approach).

Far Eastern Thought worldview belief systems:

Buddhism

Background

Buddhism's founder was Siddhartha Gautama (the Buddha, *ca.* 560-480 BC), a Hindu prince believed to have been born in what is now Nepal. Gautama lived in luxury and was protected from the world's misery. One day he ventured beyond his compound and, for the first time, saw and realized suffering existed. At age 29, he renounced his wealth and began a quest for life's meaning.

Gautama submitted to different Hindu masters but was unsatisfied, and for six years practiced extreme self-denial. Finally, he discovered the principle of the "Middle Path," keeping himself from the extremes of either self-denial or self-gratification. Eventually, while in deep meditation, he achieved a state of *enlightenment* and gained the title of the Buddha (the Enlightened One).

Gautama proclaimed his message throughout northern India for 45 years. After his death, the religion spread incorporating divergent beliefs into his teachings. Buddhism eventually split into two major groups: *Theravada* or *Hinayana* (The Lesser Vehicle) and *Mahayana* (The Greater Vehicle).

Theravada **Buddhism**:

- Conservative tendencies

- Emphasis on Buddhist scriptures

- Concern for wisdom

- Salvation is reached by self-effort

- Monasticism and priests

- Atheism

Mahayana **Buddhism**:

- Liberal tendencies

- Emphasis on meditation

- Salvation by faith in Gautama

- Encourages laymen to practice the faith

- Polytheism and idolatry

Buddhism claims it evolved into different forms to be relevant to every culture and generation. Consequently, little "pure" Buddhism is now practiced. What is seen is a mixture of Taoism, Confucianism, and ancestor worship. An estimated 300-500 million people worldwide are Buddhists. The religion is most prominent in China, Japan, Korea, and Southeast Asia.

Basic Beliefs and Practices

The Four Noble Truths

1. **Truth of Suffering:** Life is full of pain and suffering.

2. **Truth of the Cause of Suffering:** Suffering is caused by desire.

3. **Truth of the End of Suffering:** Suffering can be overcome.

4. **Truth of the Path that Leads to the End of Suffering:** Desire is eliminated by following The Eightfold Path.

The Eightfold Path

The Eightfold Path is a guide to enlightenment that leads to *Nirvana* (see definition below). The Eightfold Path can be divided into three categories.

Issues of Wisdom

1. **Right Knowledge:** Understanding things as they really are.

2. **Right Aspirations (intentions):** Commitment to self-improvement.

Issues of Ethical Conduct

3. **Right Speech:** Abstain from false speech.

4. **Right Conduct:** Abstain from harming others, theft, and sexual misconduct.

5. **Right Livelihood:** Not dealing in weapons, living beings, meat production, or intoxicants.

Issues of Mental Development

6. **Right effort:** Maintain wholesome states (thoughts, words, and deeds) and avoid unwholesome ones.

7. **Right mindfulness (self-analysis):** Contemplate the body, feelings, and states of mind.

8. **Right Concentration:** Contemplate wholesome thoughts and actions.

Since Buddhism emerged out of Hinduism, they have several common beliefs.

Nirvana

Nirvana is Sanskrit for "extinction" or "blowing out." The ultimate goal of Buddhist spiritual practice is the end of the cycle of births and rebirths. The person ceases to exist as an individual and the life force merges with the impersonal cosmos ending all desire and suffering.

Karma

Happiness and suffering in this life result from deeds in past lives or actions in the present one, which either generate or eliminate suffering. *Bad karma* produces suffering, while *good karma* prevents suffering. The individual has free will but carries the baggage of previous lives.

Reincarnation

Every living creature (including animals) has a soul (life force) that reincarnates in a new physical expression when an old one ends. This cycle of rebirths continues until an individual reaches enlightenment, which catapults him or her into *Nirvana* where suffering ceases.

Essential Beliefs

God

In *Theravada* Buddhism: No personal God exists, only an impersonal cosmos encompassing all reality.

In *Mahayana* Buddhism: Many gods exist, one of which is Gautama. This form combines Buddhist beliefs with Taoism, Confucianism, or other religious systems. The structure of reality is still understood as the impersonal cosmos with which humanity is seeking to merge.

Man

Human beings are a manifestation of the impersonal cosmos stuck in nearly endless cycles of rebirth without individual self or self-worth.

Salvation

Salvation is reaching *Nirvana.* The key to reaching *Nirvana* is to:

- achieve enlightenment and eliminate desire by gaining wisdom (*Theravada* Buddhism)

  —or—

- place one's faith in Gautama, meditating, and repeating the names of *Bodhisattvas, i.e.,* the advanced devotees who postpone *Nirvana* to assist others (*Mahayana* Buddhism).

Far Eastern Thought worldview belief systems:

Hare Krishna

Background

Hare Krishna began in the fifteenth century (AD) when Chaitanya Mahaprabhu (regarded as an incarnation of Krishna) developed it from *Vishnu* Hinduism. Hinduism regards Krishna as the eighth incarnation of Vishnu (the Preserver, and one of the Hindu trinity of deities).

Chaitanya, however, regarded Krishna as the supreme Lord in order to make philosophical Hinduism more appealing by personalizing God. In this religion, people gain a personal relationship with Krishna by chanting his names as a mantra:

Hare Krishna, Hare Krishna, Krishna, Krishna, Hare, Hare, Hare Rama, Hare Rama, Rama, Rama, Hare, Hare.

The word *Krishna* means *the all-attractive. Hare* is *the energy of God. Rama* means *the greatest pleasure.* Hare Krishna was brought to America in 1965 when *Swami* A. C. Bhaktivedanta Prabhupada (1896–1977) founded the International Society for Krishna Consciousness (ISKCON). Prabhupada's writings (English translations, and commentaries of Hindu scriptures) included the *Bhagavad Gita*, the *Bhagavata Purana*, and the *Caitanya Caritamrita*. Before his death, he commissioned eleven commissioners to succeed him.

Hare Krishna today has an estimated 3,000 core members and about 250,000 lay constituents worldwide. ISKCON is run by two boards—one focuses on spiritual practices and the other on administration. It is organized into two sectors. Sector One is an order of monks and priests who live at a temple. The other sector consists of members living in general society.

Male monks shave their heads, except for a patch called a *sikha*, receive a Sanskrit name, and wear robes. Single monks wear saffron

265

robes, while married ones, wear white. Females wear Indian saris and do not shave their heads. Outside members wear regular clothing, follow vegetarian diets, pray and chant at home, and go to temple for 'Sunday Feast.'

Basic Beliefs and Practices

Hare Krishna doctrine has much in common with conventional Hinduism. Their sacred text is the *Bhagavad Gita* which contains conversations between Lord Krishna and a soldier named Arjuna. A number of distinctive beliefs, however, depart from traditional Hindu doctrine.

- The primary goal of life is to break from repetitive reincarnations and return to God. Body and soul are not the same, and death is a transition to the next phase of life. An individual's acts determine if karmic movement is up, down, or out of the reincarnation cycle. Breaking away is attained by chanting the mantra, which puts one in harmony with Krishna.

- Krishna is the Supreme God with whom individuals achieve a personal relationship. Jesus is understood to be a representative of Krishna.

- Hell is temporary for people who have sinned greatly while on earth. Heaven is also temporary for people who have progressed in their quest for eternity but have not achieved the full qualifications for ending the cycles of reincarnation.

- Eating food offered to Krishna is an act of communion which purifies the body. Krishna devotees reject sinful living which includes eating meat, using drugs and alcohol, illicit sex, and gambling.

- Devotees practice the Nine Processes of Devotional Service. These are:

1. Hearing about God.

2. Chanting God's names.

3. Reading and associating with devotees.

4. Serving in the temple.

5. Worshiping by preparing food and decorating God's idol.

6. Praying.

7. Encouraging others to chant.

8. Developing an intimate relationship with God.

9. Giving everything one has to God.

Essential Beliefs

God

There is one God, Krishna, who is the eternal, all-knowing, omnipresent, and all-powerful, personality of Godhead who created all. He is the seed-giving father to all living beings, and the energy of the eternal cosmic creation. Other incarnations of Godhead are expansions, or parts, of Krishna. Krishna expresses himself both personally and impersonally.

Man

Humans were originally servants of God in the spiritual world. Some turned away from Him because of a desire to experience His position. Those rebels were sent to this material world to work

267

through reincarnations in order to progress back to the spiritual world.

Salvation

Salvation for the Hare Krishna is liberation from the bonds of material reality. It is earned by chanting, hearing, singing, meditating, and worshiping. One's deeds in all reincarnated lives are judged positively or negatively based on *karma*. When good deeds have atoned for bad, a person can realize oneness with Krishna, cease the cycles of rebirth, and return to the eternal spiritual world.

Far Eastern Thought worldview belief systems:

Sikhism

Background

Sikhism was founded in the Punjab region of India in the fifteenth century (AD) by *Guru* Nanak (1469–1539). It was a combination of Hinduism and Islam. Nanak taught devotion, brotherhood, charity, obedience, patience, humility, and piety. One of his most essential sayings was, "Realization of Truth is higher than all else. Higher still is truthful living."

Followers are called Sikhs, meaning disciples. Throughout the centuries, Sikhs have endured wars and conflicts with both Hindus and Muslims in India. Nanak was followed by nine other *gurus* until 1708.

The holy book of Sikhism is called the *Adi Granth* and was written by various *gurus* between 1469 and 1708. The other *gurus* included *Guru* Amar Das (1479–1574), *Guru* Angad Dev (1504–1552), *Guru* Har Krishan (1556–1564), *Guru* Ram Das (1534–1581), *Guru* Arjan Dev (1563–1606), *Guru* Hargobind (1599–1644), *Guru* Har Rai (1630–1661), *Guru* Tegh Bahadur (1621–1675), and *Guru* Gobind Singh (1666–1708).

Sikhs first came to North America in 1897 when Sikh British soldiers from India served in western Canada. In 1908, several thousand Sikhs from India immigrated to California. In 1969, they built the largest Sikh temple in the world in Yuba City, California. The chief American Sikh organization is the Sikh Council of North America. There are about 25 million Sikhs in the world, with an estimated 500,000 living in North America.

Basic Beliefs and Practices

Sikh practices revolve around several key principles established by *Guru* Nanak and his successors. They include the following:

- *Māyā* is the illusion or 'unreality' of the values of the world including ego, anger, greed, attachment, and lust—known as the Five Evils.

- *Nśabad* (the divine Word) is the totality of the divine revelation. Gurus (teachers) are the voice of God for knowledge and salvation.

- *Nām* is repetition of the name of God with inward, personal devotion.

- *Kirat karō* is a balance of work, worship, charity, and defending the rights of all people.

- *Cha dī kalā* is an optimistic view of life.

- *Va chakkō* is the concept of the sharing of material needs.

Sikhs assert that all people of all races are equal in God's eyes. Men and women are equal and share the same rights, and women are even allowed to lead in prayers.

Sikhs have a number of strict prohibitions:

1. *Cutting hair*: Sikhs are forbidden to cut their beards or hair.

2. *Intoxication*: Consumption of alcohol, drugs, tobacco, and other intoxicants is not allowed.

3. *Adultery*: Spouses must be physically and mentally faithful to one another.

4. *Blind spirituality*: Superstitions and rituals should not be observed or followed—including pilgrimages, fasting, ritual purification, or circumcision.

5. *Material obsession*: Obsession with material wealth is not encouraged.

6. ***Sacrifice of creatures***: The practice of widows throwing themselves on the funeral fires of their husbands, ritual animal sacrifice, *etc.* are forbidden.

7. ***Non-family-oriented living***: A Sikh is encouraged NOT to live as a recluse, beggar, *yogi*, monastic (monk/nun), or celibate. *Sikhs* are to live as saint-soldiers.

8. ***Worthless talk***: Bragging, lying, slander, back-stabbing, *etc.* are not permitted.

9. ***Priestly class***: Sikhism does not have priests.

10. ***Eating***: Eating meat killed in a ritualistic manner is not allowed.

11. ***Sexual relations***: Premarital or extramarital sexual relations are not permitted.

Essential Beliefs

God

As is taught in Islam, Sikhs believe God is one (*i.e.*, not trinitarian), and is the eternal, sovereign, all-powerful, all-knowing Creator. At the same time, the Hindu concepts of *karma* and reincarnation are taught.

God both transcends and indwells the universe. He is the abstract principle of truth and has never known an incarnation. Neither can He be defined. However, God is personal in that He can be loved and honored. Nanak, the first *guru*, called God the 'true name' (*Sat Nam*) because he wanted to avoid any term implying God could be limited. The Christian doctrine of the Trinity is rejected.

Man

Humans are separated from God because of self-centeredness and willful ignorance. Consequently, people are bound up in the process known as transmigration of the soul—continual birth, death, and rebirth (reincarnation). The next life is dependent on the law of *karma*, a notion that one's thoughts, words, and deeds have a direct impact on future reincarnations. The goal of Sikhism is to break this cycle.

Salvation

The endless cycles of reincarnation are caused by selfish desire and ignorance of God. It is believed that these cycles may be ended by full devotion to God. Life's ultimate goals are liberation from continual birth and rebirth, and union with God. Salvation is achieved by obedience to the above principles and devotion to God who reveals Himself and allows humans to meditate on His name and nature.

Non-Christian Theistic worldview belief systems:

Islam

Background

Islam means *submission*. A Muslim is "one who submits" to the will of God (Allah). Islam has a strict unitarian understanding of God that combines elements of Judaism and Christianity. Its founder, Mohammed (*ca.* AD 570–632), considered the last and greatest of the prophets, was born in Mecca, Arabia, in 570 His father died before his birth, and his mother died when he was six. His grandfather kept him for a short time, but he was raised primarily by his uncle. He did a lot of traveling with his uncle and encountered people of different religions who influenced his thinking.

When he was twenty-five years old, Mohammed married Khadija, a wealthy widow fifteen years his elder. None of their children survived except a daughter.

In that era, Arabians were polytheistic, and "Allah" was one of their gods. Mohammed, disturbed by this idolatry, concluded that Allah was the only true God. Starting in 610, Mohammed supposedly received revelations from the angel Gabriel. After his death in 632, his followers collected his revelations into the *Qur'an*. At first, Mohammed and his few followers were persecuted. In fact, on July 16, 622, he escaped assassination and fled to the city of Yathrib (Medina). This escape, called the *Hegira* (flight), marked the official beginning of Islam.

Mohammed established a theocracy in Medina combining politics with his new religion. He replenished Medina's treasury by plundering caravans going to Mecca. This led to a war in which Mohammed prevailed. Most Arab tribes, along with those in Mecca, were then forced to adopt Islam. After Mohammed's death, his successors conquered Syria, Jerusalem, Egypt, Persia, and Mesopotamia. War was the primary way Islam spread.

Main Islamic Groups

Islam consists of several denominations with similar beliefs, but with some differences. The largest denominations are the Sunni and the Shia. Eighty-five percent of the world's Muslims are Sunni and fourteen percent are Shia. The other one percent consists of small sects. This division has caused numerous wars.

Sunni

The divine revelations to Mohammed recorded in the *Qur'an*, and the *Hadith* (a record of the verbal explanations attributed to Mohammed and others in the early Islamic community), are the foundations of Sunni doctrine. Caliphs were considered Mohammed's rightful successors to rule the Muslim world. Controversy over the fourth *caliph* split Islam into the two branches. Sunnis argued that later *caliphs* had to be elected. The largest caliphates had generally dissipated by the fifteenth century (AD) being replaced by more secular states.

Shia

Shia, conversely, asserts that Islam's leaders (*Imams*) must descend from the fourth *caliph*, Mohammed's cousin and son-in-law Ali ibn Abi Talib (husband of his youngest daughter Fatimah). A total of twelve such *Imams* ruled until the last one disappeared in 874 Many Shia Muslims believe he is still alive and will reappear in the last days. Today, Shia mullahs (clerics) rule by divine appointment with absolute authority on matters of theology and politics in Iran.

Basic Beliefs and Practices

The Five Doctrines:

1. Allah is the one true God.

2. Allah has sent many prophets to guide men. The *Qur'an* mentions twenty-eight (most from the Old and New

Testaments). Jesus was a sinless prophet, but Mohammed was the last and greatest.

3. The *Qur'an* is the greatest of four inspired books. The other three are the *Tawret* (the Pentateuch), the *Zabur* (Psalms), and the *Injil* (Evangel of Jesus).

4. Angels are Allah's intermediaries to man. Fallen angels are demons.

5. At the Day of Judgment, everyone's deeds will be weighed to determine their eternal destiny in Heaven or Hell.

The Five Pillars:

1. Recitation of Islam's creed (the *Shahadah*): "There is no God but Allah, and Mohammed is his prophet."

2. Prayer five times a day facing Mecca (*Salat*).

3. Almsgiving *(Zakat)*.

4. Fasting during daylight hours in the month of Ramadan (*Sawm*).

5. The pilgrimage to Mecca at least once in a lifetime, if able (*Hajj*).

Essential Beliefs

God

Allah is the only God. He is totally transcendent and human beings cannot know him personally—they can only know about Him by His revelation. The Trinity is rejected as polytheism. Believing Jesus is the Son of God is blasphemy. Islam teaches a rigid doctrine of predestination and says evil and good come from Allah. Whatever Allah chooses is right in all situations.

Man

Human beings are special creations of God and are not sinful by nature, only by act. They have no need to be saved from sin, only to act correctly.

Salvation

For a Muslim, correct actions are defined by the *Qur'an*. God keeps track of a person's right and wrong acts. At death, a person's good and bad deeds are weighed. Those with greater good than bad may enter Heaven. Even so, there is no guarantee of salvation. It is only "as Allah wills."

Non-Christian Theistic worldview belief systems:

Judaism

Background

The story of the Jewish faith begins when God chose Abraham to form the basis of a special people who would represent Him to the rest of the world. Abraham's descendants eventually conquered what became the land of Israel and set up a kingdom. A key element of the Hebrew (Jewish) religion was the sacrificial system practiced first in the tabernacle and then in the Jerusalem temple. This kingdom ultimately divided into two kingdoms, Judah and Israel, which were both later conquered, and the people disbursed and taken into exile.

In due time the Jewish people returned to Israel, but were successively ruled by Babylon, Persia, Greece, and finally Rome. After a rebellion against the Romans, in AD 70, Jerusalem and the temple were destroyed, and the Jewish people dispersed throughout the world. At that point, the sacrificial system ceased functioning. Nonetheless, local synagogues (congregations) continued on as the places observant Jews met, and still meet, for worship and study.

Over the centuries, the Jews have somehow maintained their identity, even though they have been repeatedly scattered around the world. They did not have their own nation again until 1948, but the sacrificial system has not been revived.

It is important to note that many people who identify as Jewish see it as an ethnic, heritage, or cultural designation but do not necessarily believe or practice Judaism as their religion. In fact, many Jewish people regard themselves as Atheists, Agnostics, or Secular Humanists. And even some are "Messianic Jews" who regard Jesus as their Messiah.

There are four primary religious Jewish groups today:

- **Orthodox**: This group observes most of the traditional dietary and ceremonial laws. They also affirm the inspiration of the Old Testament with the *Torah* (the first five books) being most important.

- **Reform**: The Reform branch began in the early nineteenth century AD and is the home of liberal Judaism where *Talmudic* practices and precepts have been put aside for an ethical system based on a monotheistic philosophy.

- **Conservative**: Between the Orthodox and Reform groups lie the Conservatives. This group began in the late nineteenth century AD as a reaction to the Reform movement. It retains the feasts and many traditional customs but reinterprets the Law to make it relevant to modern thought and culture.

- **Hasidic**: The Hasidic branch of Judaism began in the eighteenth century AD as an ultra-orthodox and mystical group.

Basic Beliefs and Practices

While there is a lot of variety within the Jewish community, two basic elements establish their identity as a people.

Worship

Ritual and ceremony are important to consecrate life with God in a calendar of daily, weekly, and yearly celebrations. The best-known festivals include Passover, the Festival of Weeks, the Feast of Tabernacles, *Yom Kippur* (Day of Atonement), and *Rosh Hashanah* (Jewish New Year). The purpose of the celebrations is to remember their sacred history. Stories, both biblical and non-biblical, relating God's deliverance are told over and over.

Since the first destruction (in 586 BC) of the temple Solomon built in the mid-tenth century BC in Jerusalem, Jews have also gathered for worship in local synagogues. Ritual, prayer, and the study of the Law serve as the replacement for the sacrifices held in the temple in Jerusalem until it was finally destroyed in AD 70.

Morality

Judaism has a strong emphasis on morality and ethics. The traditional idea behind the Jewish ethic is that God has ordained in Scripture a certain way to live, the observance of which has been passed down through the generations.

This ethical emphasis is primarily based on the teachings of the law God gave Moses as contained in the *Torah*. Sins are understood to be specific acts, so Jews have developed rules of behavior and codes of conduct to avoid them. From time to time, movements have emerged to get back to the original meaning of the *Torah*. But because of their understanding of sin, this legalistic approach is difficult to replace.

Morality is heavily tilted toward the "good of the community" and contains a strong sense of social and economic justice.

Essential Beliefs

God

Judaism is solidly monotheistic. God is viewed as a complete unity, powerful, just, merciful, and loving. He is a personal being who has a relationship with mankind. He continually works in the world and offers humans the opportunity to fulfill their obligations to Him. The Holy Spirit is recognized simply to be the expression of God's interaction with humanity in this world.

Man

Mankind is viewed as a special creation of God who was created in His image. Man has a great responsibility to live rightly before God.

In Jewish theology, the distinguishing mark of humans is their ability to make ethical choices. Mankind also has a responsibility to help order the world in accordance with God's purposes.

Salvation

For most Jews, the most they expect to gain from practicing their faith is to have a full and meaningful earthly life. Having a good family, a stable and successful occupation, and doing what they can to contribute to society, are important values for Jewish people. The fact is, most Jews do not have a clear belief about life after death. Ideas about heaven and hell are rarely discussed.

Some religious Jews, however, do anticipate a resurrection from the dead and final judgment based on how a person has lived and obeyed the Torah. Other Jews have adopted ideas from other religions and worldviews, such as reincarnation or spiritualism. There simply is no standard perspective among Jews on what salvation is or how it is attained.

Sin, in Jewish theology, is not a state, it is simply an act. This is why the law is so important. The foundational belief is that if individuals obey the Jewish law, they avoid sin. When they fail, they only need to come to God in repentance.

There is, therefore, no need for a Savior. Forgiveness for sin is accomplished by penitence, good deeds, and a little of God's grace. External things like obedience to the *Torah*, *kosher* food preparation and dietary rules, and observance of the weekly Sabbath and the holy days are the means by which people are able to please God.

Non-Christian Theistic worldview belief systems:

Cultural Christianity

Background

Up until the last two to three generations, the primary worldview foundation in America was Theism—and mostly, Christian Theism. This has been described in various ways. Sometimes America has simply been called a "Christian nation," or it is not uncommon to hear a reference to the *Judeo-Christian ethic*—especially since the 1930s' rise of Nazism in Germany. The point is that the nation was founded by Christians who built its foundational institutions on Christian ideas. Of course, America is a prime example of a country that is considered Christian, but is certainly not the only one which fits that category. A great deal of Europe is also said to fit that mold.

One of the most important principles of *biblical* Christianity is that every individual must come to Christ based on a personal decision to do so. Thus, a person is not a Christian by virtue of having been born in a country or a family with a Christian heritage, nor by having been baptized and raised in a Christian church.

In spite of the true nature of the Christian faith, there are masses of people who define Christianity based on their national or family origin or their affiliation with a Christian church. These people know the rituals and church forms, and simply self-identify as "Christian" because they do not follow some other religion.

Basic Beliefs and Practices

One thing that makes Cultural Christianity so difficult to deal with is that from the outside it may look like the real thing. Typically, Cultural Christians: will self-identify as Christians, are a member of some Christian church, and usually were baptized in one mode or another at some point in their lives.

Participation in the Christian faith by Cultural Christians can be quite varied and is expressed in several ways. Some Cultural Christians have not set foot in a church in years. These people believe the only requirement for being a Christian is saying they are one. Participation in church (or other aspects of the Christian faith) is not necessary to their identity as a "Christian."

Others participate on special occasions—for instance, at Easter and Christmas. These people, also, generally believe they are Christians based purely on self-identification, but also feel a need to occasionally participate in something.

Still others are very active in their churches and may even be church leaders. Many believe participation in church activities proves they are Christians. This situation is not at all uncommon in churches calling themselves Christian, but which have theological positions that do not require a personal relationship with God through Jesus Christ as the means of salvation or church membership.

The main thing that identifies Cultural Christians is internal—the fact that they have never repented of sin and invited Christ into their lives. This sometimes makes Cultural Christians hard to identify, and even more difficult as witnessing subjects. They generally hold to a Christian worldview (which often has been hybridized by Naturalism or various other non-Christian beliefs), identify with some recognized Christian church, and agree with a Christian understanding of morality (even if they don't completely follow it).

Essential Beliefs

God

Cultural Christians usually, though not always, hold a theistic worldview and believe in the God of the Bible as the Creator. That being said, almost always, beliefs from other worldviews have been allowed to creep in. Some of the more common aberrations may include a belief in the Darwinian Theory of Evolution or a belief that God is willing to overlook a non-biblical lifestyle. It is also not at all unusual for these people to claim belief in the God of the Bible yet make up their own concepts of God because they have no idea what the Bible actually teaches.

Man

Cultural Christians often hold a view of mankind in line with the culture at large. This frequently includes the notion that human beings are basically good and that they are capable of living a life good enough to please God.

Salvation

Most Cultural Christians believe they will go to heaven because they self-identify with the Christian faith, or because they try to live "good lives." They tend to have no concept of the biblical requirements for salvation by grace through faith in Christ, or they misunderstand what the Bible teaches about the subject.

Non-Christian Theistic worldview belief systems:

Jehovah's Witnesses

Background

In 1870, Charles Taze Russell (1852–1916) began an independent Bible study focusing on the second coming of Christ and prophetic biblical chronology. In 1879, he founded the monthly publication *Zion's Watch Tower and Herald of Christ's Presence,* which was used by study groups he established.

Zion's Watchtower and Tract Society (later renamed the Watchtower Bible and Tract Society (WBTS) was incorporated in 1884 with Russell as president. From 1886 until his death in 1916, Russell wrote a series of books called *Studies in the Scriptures.* Their contents formed the basis of Jehovah's Witnesses' unchristian theology.

Russell was succeeded as president in 1917 by his legal assistant, Joseph Franklin Rutherford (1869–1942). Rutherford continued Russell's authoritarian leadership style. He was imprisoned briefly in 1918 for preaching against military service. He was a charismatic speaker who often railed against Christian churches and biblical scholars. Rutherford died in 1942.

Other Jehovah's Witnesses presidents included Nathan H. Knorr (1942–1977), Fredrick W. Franz (1977–1992), Milton G. Henschel (1992–2000), and Don Adams (2000–2014). The current corporate presidents are Robert Ciranko and Leon Weaver, Jr. The organization expanded worldwide under these men's leadership, from about 113,000 in 1942 to almost nine million in 2020.

Basic Beliefs and Practices

Several distinctive beliefs characterize the theology and practice of Jehovah's Witnesses.

- The official name of the Jehovah's Witnesses organization is the Watchtower Bible and Tract Society (WBTS). The WBTS is regarded as Jehovah God's sole channel for the flow of biblical truth to men on earth. Members attend local congregations called Kingdom Halls and regularly do door-to-door visitation and distribute WBTS literature.

- Jehovah's Witnesses claim the Bible is their only authority. Their official version is *The New World Translation of the Holy Scriptures* (NWT). They claim it is the best translation ever made, but most Greek and Hebrew scholars agree that it is poorly done and extremely biased against the deity of Christ.

- Jehovah's Witnesses deny the Trinity, the divinity of Christ, His bodily resurrection, salvation by grace through faith, and eternal punishment of the wicked.

- There is no hell as a place of everlasting punishment for the wicked in Jehovah's Witnesses' theology. They claim that it is: 1) wholly unscriptural, 2) unreasonable, 3) contrary to God's love, and 4) repugnant to justice.

- Over the years, Jehovah's Witnesses have made many prophesies concerning the end of the world which did not come true. Those prophecies were later reinterpreted, or conveniently expunged, from Watchtower literature.

Essential Beliefs

God

The true God's name is Jehovah. His principal attributes are love, wisdom, justice, and power. God is a spirit being, invisible and eternal, but has a spiritual body and is not omnipresent. The historic Christian doctrine of the Trinity is denied.

In His pre-human existence, Jesus was called "God's only begotten Son" because Jehovah created Him directly. As the "firstborn of all

285

creation," Jesus was used by God to create all other things. Jesus became the Messiah at His baptism, was executed on a torture stake, and rose again spiritually. The personality and deity of the Holy Spirit are denied.

Man

God created man in His own image, but Adam and Eve willfully disobeyed God. Thus, humanity lost immortality and must experience physical death. There is no conscious existence at death. The dead go to the common grave of mankind where they are not conscious of anything as they await the final resurrection.

Salvation

Jehovah's Witnesses believe that due to Adam's sin, atonement was required to restore what was lost. Only a perfect human, Jesus Christ, could offer up the equivalent of what Adam lost. He was nailed to a wooden pole and hung there upright. After that, He slept in death for parts of three days, then Jehovah God resurrected Him to life as a mighty spirit being (not physically).

Requirements for salvation, in addition to faith, include baptism by immersion, active association with the WBTS, righteous conduct, and absolute loyalty to Jehovah (*i.e.,* the WBTS). There is no assurance of salvation, only hope for a resurrection. Those who fail to live up to the requirements, or who are disfellowshipped (excommunicated) by the WBTS, have no hope of salvation.

Only 144,000 faithful elect Jehovah's Witnesses, known as the *Anointed Class*, will go to heaven to rule with Jesus. Most Jehovah's Witnesses, past and present, feel that they will be numbered beyond these 144,000 but hope to be among the *other sheep* or *great crowd* who will be resurrected and live physically forever in Paradise on earth.

Non-Christian Theistic worldview belief systems:

The Church of Jesus Christ of Latter-day Saints
(traditionally known as the LDS, or the Mormon Church)

Background

Joseph Smith, Jr. was born December 23, 1805, in Vermont, and grew up in Palmyra, New York. According to his own story, in the fall of 1820, as a teenager, Smith wanted to know which church to join. One day he went into the woods near his home to pray about the question. While he was praying, he claimed that the Heavenly Father (God) and His Son, Jesus, appeared to him. Jesus told him to join none of the churches because they were all in error and corrupt. Jesus told him that in time He would use Smith to restore His true church to the world.

In September of 1823, Joseph said he had a second vision, this time of an angel named Moroni. Moroni showed him a set of golden plates buried near his home that were supposedly a record of ancient Jewish peoples who lived in America. In 1829, Smith translated the plates, and in 1830 published them as *The Book of Mormon*.

Under God's direction, said Smith, on April 6, 1830, he and five other men established the restored "Church of Christ" in Fayette, NY. Later, the church's name was changed to the current Church of Jesus Christ of Latter-day Saints (LDS). Because of opposition in New York, in 1831, the church migrated to Kirtland, Ohio, and later to Independence, Missouri. There they also faced conflict due to rumors that the Mormons (as they came to be known) were practicing polygamy.

Because of that conflict, Smith's followers moved on to Nauvoo, Illinois, in 1840. There, in 1844, Smith was arrested and on June 27, 1844, was assassinated by a mob in nearby Carthage, Illinois. Beginning in 1846, Smith's successor, Brigham Young, led most of the remnant membership westward where they settled in what is now Utah.

Today the Church claims almost seventeen million members (traditionally known as Mormons) worldwide, with nearly seven million of those in the United States.

Basic Beliefs and Practices

The LDS has the following requirements for all faithful members:

1. Faith and repentance toward the Mormon God (called Heavenly Father).

2. Baptism by immersion in the LDS Church and the laying on of hands to receive the Holy Ghost.

3. Ordination as Aaronic Priests and Melchizedek Priests for all worthy men.

4. Young men are expected to serve a two-year mission for the church. Single young women are also encouraged to do so.

5. Receiving endowments. These are secret ceremonies in LDS temples necessary to prepare them for life after death.

6. Celestial (Temple) Marriage for time and eternity.

7. Participating in baptisms and ordinances for the salvation of the dead.

8. Observing the "Word of Wisdom." This means abstaining from all alcohol, tobacco, and caffeine products.

9. Tithing ten percent of one's income and attending weekly congregational worship called Sacrament Meetings.

10. Faithfully following the teachings of The Four Standard Works (LDS Scriptures):

- *The King James Bible,*

- *The Book of Mormon, Another Testament of Jesus Christ,*
- *The Doctrine and Covenants,* and

- *The Pearl of Great Price.*

11. Faithfully following the teachings of the LDS Presidents (the 'Living Prophets') and General Authorities (official church leaders).

Essential Beliefs

God

God, called Elohim or Heavenly Father, was once a man, as we now are, who was exalted by his god to godhood (exaltation) after living a faithful life on his planet. in his exalted life, he lives with his wife (or wives), and they produce spirit children. In addition to this earth's god, there are also countless other gods in the universe.

God did not create the world from nothing (*ex nihilo*), but organized earth out of pre-existent matter.

Jesus (known as Jehovah in his preexistence) was the firstborn pre-existent spirit son of the heavenly parents. He eventually attained godhood and was later sent to earth as the "only-begotten" Son of God (Heavenly Father) in the flesh. The Holy Ghost is another god but does not have a body of flesh and bones.

Man

God and his wife procreate spirit children in a preexistent world who are later born on earth in physical bodies. Physical birth is the first necessary step in the Church of Jesus Christ of Latter-day Saints' understanding of the plan of salvation for Heavenly Father's children to attain exaltation. *All* people, however, are mortal because of the fall of Adam. Thus, Jesus suffered, died, and was raised from the dead to restore immortality to everyone regardless of their faith.

Salvation

All people will be raised to immortality because of Jesus' redemption. After judgment, however, everyone will be sent to one of three levels of heavenly glory based on their works while living on earth:

1. The Celestial Kingdom is the destination for worthy members. Only faithful members, who obey all of the church's requirements (listed above) will go to the Celestial Kingdom where they may be exalted to godhood.

2. All other honorable people will spend eternity in the Terrestrial Kingdom.

3. The Telestial Kingdom will be the home of the ungodly, wicked, and filthy.

Non-Christian Theistic worldview belief systems:

Baha'i Faith

Background

Baha'i originated in Iran (formerly known as Persia) in the nineteenth century AD. Some Muslims in that country believed Allah was going to raise up a new, divinely-inspired prophet like Mohammed in their land. In 1844, Mirza Ali Mohammed (1819–1850) took upon himself the title 'The Bab' (the Gate) and proclaimed the imminent coming of this prophet.

Large numbers of people followed him and became known as Babists. The Persian (Iranian) government and the Islamic clergy partnered together to kill Mirza Ali when he was thirty years of age, declaring him an apostate from Islam. They also massacred more than twenty thousand of his followers.

In 1863, another Persian, named Baha'u'llah (1817–1892), claimed to be the prophet that Mirza Ali had predicted. Many followers of the Bab became disciples of the new prophet and changed their movement's name to Baha'i to honor him. Baha'u'llah called upon all people to unite in one common faith to establish abiding peace.

Baha'u'llah was also persecuted. After forty years of imprisonment and exile, he died in 1892 at the age of seventy-five. His son, Abbas Effendi, also known as Abdul-Baha (1844–1921), succeeded him.

In 1893, the Baha'i religion came to the United States. After Abdul's death in 1921, his grandson, Shoghi Effendi (1897–1957), became the new leader.

Effendi died before he was able to appoint a successor. As a result, a new system of leadership was established called the Baha'i Universal House of Justice. It consists of a nine-person board that interprets and applies the laws of Baha'u'llah.

Basic Beliefs and Practices

Baha'i believes in one God who at various times in history sends messengers, who they refer to as "manifestations of God." Through these messengers, God restates His purpose and will in every age. These manifestations provided revelations from God. Abraham, Moses, Krishna, Buddha, Zoroaster, Christ, and Muhammad were manifestations for their times. The current generation's manifestation is Baha'u'llah to whom followers of all religions should now turn for spiritual guidance.

Baha'i's Ten Basic Principles Include:

1. The oneness of mankind.

2. Independent investigation of truth.

3. The common foundation of all religions.

4. The harmony of science and religion.

5. Equality of men and women.

6. Elimination of all prejudice.

7. Universal education.

8. A solution to the economic problem.

9. A universal language.

10. Universal peace by a world government.

Today, in order to be considered a Baha'i, one must be a formal member of the mainstream Baha'i religious organization and pledge obedience to the Baha'i administrative order. Baha'i seeks universal systems of education, human rights, currency, weights, measures, and language, and are very active in United Nations organizations.

Essential Beliefs

God

Baha'i teaches that there is only one expression of God who is absolutely indivisible. In concert with Islamic beliefs, He is considered to be transcendent to the point of total inaccessibility and could never incarnate as a human. God is the creator of all things, but not the cause of all things. Rather, all that exists flows eternally out of Him. God is the changeless One who is separated from interactive relationship with His created order.

The way God is known is by divine-human manifestations who are pure mirrors of His attributes. There have been nine manifestations in the half-million-year cycle of human history including Abraham, Krishna, Moses, Zoroaster, Buddha, Christ, Mohammed, the Bab, and Baha'u'llah. Baha'u'llah is the supreme manifestation for the current cycle of human history.

Man

Humanity is a creation of God, and men and women of all races are equal in His sight. People of different races should have equal educational and economic opportunity, access to decent living conditions, and equal responsibilities. Man is not inherently evil but has the capacity for doing evil deeds. Each man decides whether to follow God, thus determining his eternal destiny.

Salvation

To the Baha'i, salvation means drawing nearer to God and progressing-on the path to deep and satisfying happiness. Salvation is deliverance from the captivity of people's own lower nature.

This captivity breeds private despair and threatens social destruction. Humans can realize their true potential and unite with God because He has sent His manifestations to show them the path to spiritual growth.

Salvation is obtained by believing in the manifestation of God in the age in which one lives, and by following his teachings.

In our current time, this means following the teachings of Baha'u'llah.

Hybrid worldview belief systems:

The New Age Movement

Background

The history of the New Age Movement is difficult, if not impossible, to completely trace. Many various religious and spiritual movements and diverse writers and leaders contributed to what became a multi-faceted and broadly defined spiritual movement beginning in the 1970s and continuing into the twenty-first century. Perhaps its earliest roots go back to the Far Eastern Thought traditions of Hinduism and Buddhism along with pre-Christian European paganism. Many ideas from these sources have been introduced or revived in the West over the past century.

Some major teachers whose ideas influenced New Age thinking included: Emanuel Swedenborg (1688–1772), a Swedish scientist and mystic; German Franz Mesmer (1734–1815), who taught a form of healing he called, "animal magnetism;" and Russian mystics Helena Blavatsky (1831–1891, the founder of Theosophy); and George Gurdjieff (1872–1949).

Other movements that coalesced to form the New Age Movement were nineteenth century Spiritualism (which taught communication with the dead), the New Thought Movement of Phineas Quimby, and Edgar Cayce (a twentieth century mystic called the 'Sleeping Prophet').

Today a bevy of New Age teachers, writers, and entrepreneurs still promote their latest spiritual discoveries. New Age concepts have quietly intruded into various avenues of society including medicine, business, education, art, entertainment, and even science. A number of celebrities have attached their names to New Age concepts of one kind or another including Oprah Winfrey and Shirley MacLaine. Some of the most popular New Age teachers in recent years include Deepak Chopra, James Redfield, Eckhart Tolle, Barbara Marx Hubbard, Christopher Hills, and Marianne Williamson.

295

Basic Beliefs and Practices

It is impossible to fully summarize the diverse Basic Beliefs and Practices of the New Age Movement in any coherent systematic way. Nonetheless, researchers have found several common strains running through many of them including the following:

Monism

All reality is one—including God, humankind, the universe, time, and space. All is a unitary whole.

Pantheism

Everything is God. All (god) is impersonal energy, force, or consciousness.

You Are God

The goal of life is to awaken to the god who sleeps at the root of one's being.

The Human Problem

New Agers basically deny the existence of sin. Mankind's problem is that the great majority of humans are unaware of their true divinity.

Reincarnation

Many New Agers teach that humans go through many lifetimes which will eventually culminate in oneness with the universe. This also includes the Far Eastern Thought concept of positive and negative *karma*.

Enlightenment

Human ignorance is overcome through enlightenment which can be realized through various techniques including meditation, yoga, past-life regression, trance channeling, crystals, or other occult practices.

Essential Beliefs

God

In New Age belief, the concept of God is rather nebulous. In fact, differing views depend on the particular elements that are incorporated into the various New Age expressions. In some cases, the concept of God draws from Far Eastern Thought and uses a pantheistic approach. In those cases, ultimate reality is some form of spiritual life force. Other New Age approaches incorporate animistic ideas. In those, the life energy is usually expressed in nature, with man being a part of the "circle of life."

Man

Again, the view of humanity in New Age belief depends on the particulars of a given expression. Those who follow a Far Eastern Thought approach will see man as an expression of the impersonal life force. This is often expressed by individuals, themselves, being referred to as gods. Some incorporate elements of reincarnation, *karma*, and/or evolution of man to a higher form (culminating in a utopian Age of Aquarius). Forms based on animistic leanings tend to see humanity as an element of nature with the ability to connect, somehow, with the earth.

Salvation

As indicated, salvation, in New Age belief, is, influenced by the particular approach taken by specific expressions of the movement. Far Eastern Thought based approaches tend to look to some kind of progression to a higher level of existence—sometimes in a reincarnated life and sometimes in some kind of afterlife. Animistic expressions tend toward an afterlife with some vague connection with nature.

Hybrid worldview belief systems:

Unitarian Universalism

Background

The concept of God as a single unitary being—contrary to historic Christian Trinitarianism—can be traced to the teachings of Arius (AD 256–336), a pastor in Alexandria, Egypt. He argued that the Scriptures do not, and the early church fathers did not, teach a Trinitarian concept of God, and that Jesus made no claims to deity. His unitarian view was rebuked by the Council of Nicaea in AD 325 but Unitarianism revived it again later—after the Protestant Reformation with Michael Servetus (1511–1553) in Spain, and Faustus Socinus (1539–1604) in Poland. Later, a Hungarian named Frances David (1510–1579) led the first movement to be labeled Unitarian.

The first American Unitarian church was King's Chapel in Boston, Massachusetts. In 1786, the previously Episcopalian congregation embraced the Unitarian view. Soon afterward, Harvard University followed suit.

The American Unitarian Association (AUA) was established in 1825 and was led by William Ellery Channing (1780–1842), pastor of Federal Street Congregational Church in Boston. Most Unitarian ministers of that time, despite their rejection of Trinitarianism, still relied on the Bible for their theological formulations.

In the twentieth century, Unitarianism abandoned all biblical authority. In fact, the movement internally debated the very existence of God. Eventually, it came to be dominated by Secular Humanism. This culminated in 1933 with the publishing of the Humanist Manifesto. Half of its signers were Unitarian ministers.

Universalism also emerged at various times throughout the history of the Christian church. It is the theological doctrine that all souls will ultimately be saved, and that there is no eternal hell.

Universalists often deny miracles exist and reject any reference to them in Scripture.

American Universalism developed from the influence of Pietists and Anabaptists in Europe. The first known Universalist church in America was probably the Freedonia Meeting Hall in Newberry County South Carolina. The first General Society was held in 1778, and annual conventions began in 1785. In 1804, the convention changed its name to The General Convention of Universalists. In 1866, it was known as the Universalist General Convention. In 1942, they changed the name to the Universalist Church of America.

In 1961, the Unitarian churches merged with the Universalist Church of America to form the Unitarian Universalist Association (UUA). The UUA developed into a society focusing on liberal social, political, environmental, and gender-related issues. One surprising modern trend is the growth of neo-paganism and witchcraft in some UUA congregations. The influence of Secular Humanism also has declined with the rise of Postmodernism.

Basic Beliefs and Practices

No specific doctrinal perspective is required for membership in a Unitarian Universalist church, and members are not bound by any statement of belief or creed. Most Unitarian Universalists maintain that human reason, intuition, and scientific research are the only reliable sources for discovering all truth. Generally, they reject supernatural sources of knowledge—especially divine sources of revelation such as the Bible or other religious texts. That being said, neo-pagan Unitarian Universalists do accept supernatural beliefs that defy naturalistic presuppositions.

Essential Beliefs

God

No particular belief about God is taught, nor is any doctrinal belief stated, concerning the existence or nature of a god. It is each individual's choice what, if any, concept of deity they wish to accept. Historically, Unitarians had a theistic worldview, but rejected the Christian doctrine of the Trinity as polytheistic. Currently, some Unitarian Universalists profess belief in gods and goddesses of various numbers and kinds.

Unitarian Universalists who believe that Jesus actually lived (and many of them do not) regard Him as a moral teacher or religious reformer. They reject the claim that He was the unique incarnation of God.

Man

Unitarian Universalists reject the biblical doctrine of original sin. They teach that all people are basically good and have no need for spiritual redemption from the effects of sin.

Salvation

Salvation, in Unitarian Universalist belief, is finding one's own self-fulfillment and truth. There is no essential need for the traditional concepts of Christian redemption and salvation. People are not sinners; they do not need forgiveness from sin.

Most Unitarian Universalists do not concern themselves very much with the question of life after death. Those who do believe in some concept of existence after this life describe it in vague terms. Heaven and hell are seen only as states of mind in this life that may or may not extend beyond death.

Some who follow a neo-pagan approach in the UUA probably have adopted Eastern or New Age concepts of reincarnation or spiritualism. Nearly all Unitarian Universalists reject any concept of an eternal hell for punishment of sin.

Hybrid worldview belief systems:

Scientology

Background

Scientologists believe L. Ron Hubbard (1911–1986) was a modern genius who discovered the answers to life's questions and unraveled the secrets of our past, present, and future existences. His writings and speeches are considered absolutely authoritative, especially his book *Dianetics: The Modern Science of Mental Health.*

Lafayette Ronald Hubbard was born in Nebraska in 1911. He spent most of his childhood on his grandfather's Montana ranch while his parents served overseas in the U.S. Navy. Hubbard later stated that visits with parents to Asia in the 1920s introduced him to Eastern philosophies and religions.

As a young man, Hubbard developed a career as a science fiction writer and claimed to have explored the world. He also claimed that he received near-fatal wounds in World War II. While recovering, he formulated his novel psychological theories that were revealed in his 1950 book *Dianetics: The Modern Science of Mental Health.*

In 1954, Hubbard incorporated the Church of Scientology in order to promote his ideas using a religious facade. The official name of the church is Church of Scientology International, Inc. His books and church spread worldwide, but Hubbard became a recluse. He spent most of his last years aboard his yacht being waited on hand-and-foot. He died inauspiciously in 1986.

Researchers not associated with the Church of Scientology have documented numerous inaccuracies in Hubbard's account of his life. They allege he fabricated and exaggerated many of his personal claims and plagiarized many ideas he used in his writings.

The name Scientology comes from the Latin *scio,* which means: to know, and the Greek word *logos,* meaning: the word or outward form by which the inward thought is expressed and made known. Thus, Scientology means "knowing about knowing."

Basic Beliefs and Practices

In his writings and lectures, L. Ron Hubbard taught the following key concepts.

The universe is composed of "the Eight Dynamics." These are eight levels of existence that have Dynamic urges to survive:

1. **Self**: Surviving as an individual.

2. **Creativity**: Survival of the family unit by bearing children.

3. **Group**: Surviving as a group (a company, state, nation, race, or any group).

4. **Mankind**: Survival of all mankind.

5. **Life Forms**: Survival of life forms (animals, birds, insects, fish, and vegetation).

6. **Physical Universe**: Survival of the physical universe itself.

7. **Spiritual Dynamic**: Survival as spiritual beings.

8. **Infinity**: The "allness of all."

Hubbard asserted that the human mind consists of two dimensions:

1. the **Analytical mind** (the conscious, rational, and problem-solving part of one's mind), and

2. the **Reactive mind** (the part of the mind not under a person's rational, conscious control or awareness).

As a person goes through life, he or she accumulates *engrams.* These are unconscious mental images recorded in the **Reactive mind** that have negative effects on a person's mental and physical life.

Using a method developed by Hubbard, called Dianetics, a person can systematically remove engrams and their negative effects from the mind. The word *Dianetics* comes from the Greek words *dia,* meaning *through* and *nous,* meaning *soul.* A specially trained Scientology counselor, called an Auditor, conducts intense Dianetic sessions called auditing.

The Auditor uses an electronic instrument called an E-Meter (Electropsychometer) in the auditing process. The Preclear (person being audited) holds a metal tube in each hand The tube is wired to the E-meter which emits a slight electric current. The auditor watches a gauge to detect engrams as the person answers questions. Supposedly, the Preclear will eventually reach a state of mind called Clear. Clear supposedly eliminates all engrams and their ill effects on the mind and body.

Essential Beliefs

God

The Church of Scientology International has no clear definition of the nature or person of God. References to a Supreme Being are rare in Scientology literature. When there is a reference to it, it is called "the Eight Dynamic" or "Infinity." The Supreme Being is defined in vague, pantheistic terms as embracing the "allness of all."

Man

Human beings are considered to be eternal spirits (Thetans) migrating from one body to another over time. Engrams are stored in one's Reactive mind and acquired from one's past lives, prenatal experience, and early childhood. These engrams prevent individuals from realizing their innate divinity and experiencing a happy and fulfilled life using their Analytical minds.

Salvation

Scientology teaches that engrams are removed from the mind only by an expensive process of Dianetic counseling. A person who has attained Clear may need further auditing to remove engrams held over from previous lives. Auditing sessions may cost as much as $1,000 per hour.

A person will experience many Thetans (reincarnations) in many lives over thousands of years. Eventually, however, Thetans can:

- liberate themselves completely from the material world,

- attain total spiritual awareness, and

- become one with infinity.

Hybrid worldview belief systems:

Christian Science

Background

Mary Ann Morse Baker (1821–1910) was a frail young woman who suffered many illnesses. However, in 1866, she claimed she discovered the secret of *Divine Science* after being healed miraculously from a crippling fall. In 1875, she founded the Christian Science Association in Lynn, Massachusetts, and published her book, *Science and Health with Key to the Scriptures (Science & Health)*. She taught her principles of divine healing, and her book became a best-seller.

After two earlier failed marriages, Mary married Asa Albert Eddy (d. 1882) in 1877 and together they established The Church of Christ, Scientist (Christian Science) with its headquarters in Boston, Massachusetts. Christian Science interprets the Bible in light of Mrs. Eddy's writings, particularly *Science & Health*, in which she interprets it according to her metaphysical presuppositions.

Basic Beliefs and Practices

The Bible, claimed to be the church's primary authority, must be interpreted according to the principles related in *Science & Health*. Mrs. Eddy ascribed arbitrary spiritual meanings to common biblical terms. For example, *Jerusalem* is defined as "Mortal belief and knowledge obtained from the five corporeal senses" (*Science & Health*, p. 589). *Holy Ghost* is defined as "Divine Science; the development of eternal Life, Truth, and Love" (*Science & Health*, p. 588). Her allegorical Bible reading leaves it open to whatever interpretation she chose.

Jesus Christ is the means by which individuals achieve physical healing. Healing also involves character transformation, harmony in relationships, schooling, career, marriage, mental health, and every other aspect of life, all accomplished through prayer.

For practitioners, physical healing confirms the primary mission of Christian Science—to heal "the sins of the world" through understanding the power of Christ, or divine Truth.

Understanding the nature of God and His laws is necessary to heal systematically and consistently. When a person prays with understanding, healing occurs. Jesus' healing work provides the foremost example of how his followers also can turn to God's omnipotent love for healing.

An important Christian Science practice is studying the weekly Lesson-Sermon outlined in *The Christian Science Quarterly*. It includes excerpts from the Bible and *Science & Health*. It also contains a sermon read in Sunday services throughout the world.

Sunday School is provided for children and teenagers. Wednesday evening meetings include readings from the Bible and *Science & Health* on current topics. Member's testimonies of healing through prayer are also commonly shared.

Essential Beliefs

God

God is not a person but is "incorporeal, divine, supreme, infinite Mind, Spirit, Soul, Principle, Life, Truth, Love." (*Science & Health*, p. 465) These synonymous terms refer to one absolute God. They express the nature, essence, and wholeness of Deity. The attributes of God are justice, mercy, wisdom, goodness, and so on. (*Science & Health*, p. 465)

The Trinity is redefined as life, truth, and love. God's essential essence is spirit or mind, and only that which reflects His nature is real. Thus, matter does not really exist. Jesus was a discoverer of the Christ-Ideal but there is an essential difference between Jesus the man and the *Christ Principle* which came upon Him as He comprehended it.

Man

People are Divine Spirits. Since matter does not exist and humanity reflects God's nature, human beings are not really made of matter. "Spirit is God, and man is His image and likeness. Therefore, man is not material; he is spiritual." (*Science & Health*, p. 468) Since only those ideas that reflect God's nature are actually real, then sin, death, disease, and pain are not real, but only illusions.

Salvation

Since matter, sin, disease, and death are illusions and unreal, people are not subject to them. Thus, when individuals fully realize this principle, disease should disappear. Since God and man are *immortal spirit* or *mind*, then death is also only an illusion. It is a transition from the illusion of the material to the ultimate reality of immortal spirit.

Christian Science believes that salvation involves an individual overcoming the "false" idea that he or she exists—based on a realization of their divine spirit and mind.

We acknowledge that the crucifixion of Jesus and His resurrection served to uplift faith to understand eternal life, even the allness of Soul, Spirit, and the nothingness of matter.

—*Science & Health*, p. 497

Hybrid worldview belief systems:

The Unification Church

Background

On January 6, 1920, Yong Myung Moon was born in northern Korea. Moon claimed that at age sixteen (1936) he saw Jesus Christ who changed his name to Sun *Myung* Moon (Sun *Shining* Moon). Moon was imprisoned during the Japanese military occupation of Korea. After World War II, he began preaching a set of unusual new doctrines.

In 1948, North Korean communists arrested Moon again. However, he was liberated in 1950 during the Korean War and went to Seoul. In 1952, Moon released *The Divine Principle*, a compilation of his doctrines. On May 1, 1954, he established The Holy Spirit Association for the Unification of World Christianity, or the Unification Church (UC). The official name of the church is now the Family Federation for World Peace and Unification. Its members are sometimes referred to as Moonies, though they do not particularly like that designation.

On April 11, 1960, Moon married Hak Ja Han (b. 1943), in what the UC calls the "Marriage of the Lamb" which, the UC asserts, established "The True Family." During the 1960s, the movement gained converts in Korea.

Moon toured the United States in the 1970s and, during that time, several thousand Americans converted. Many family members of those converts complained that their loved ones were manipulated by UC indoctrination. Many UC defectors shared stories of psychological, spiritual, and labor abuse by UC leaders.

In 1982, Moon founded The Washington Times newspaper which became a conservative alternative to The Washington Post. However, that same year he was sent to US federal prison for tax evasion. Ultimately, on March 23, 2004, Moon and his wife were crowned by the UC as the world's "Savior, Messiah, Returning

Lord, and True Parents" in the U.S. Senate building in Washington DC. This supposedly ushered in the "Completed Testament Age" of history which will bring a period of world peace and prosperity. In 2008, Moon appointed his youngest son, Hyung Jin Moon (an American citizen born in 1979), to be the new leader of the church. Moon died in South Korea on September 3, 2012.

In North America, at its peak, the UC never had more than about ten thousand members. Nonetheless, the church exerted a level of public influence of greater proportion than its numbers would indicate. Moon's church accumulated millions of dollars as a result of various fundraising campaigns by UC members. The church also acquired controlling interest in a wide-ranging number of business ventures worldwide. For instance, in the education field, the UC appoints a majority of the board of trustees of the University of Bridgeport (Connecticut).

Basic Beliefs and Practices

The beliefs of the Unification Church are a complicated mixture of Eastern philosophy, Christian and biblical terminology, and the many bizarre notions of Rev. Moon. The primary tenets were contained in several books, the most important being *The Divine Principle*. They included the following points.

- Rev. Moon is regarded as the "Lord of the Second Advent." He was the equivalent of Christ who has come to finish the work Jesus failed to complete.

- All reality is understood as a sort of cosmic dualism of universal polar opposites: positive/negative, active/passive, direct/indirect, objective/subjective, masculine/feminine.

- Because of its corruption, God sent a redeemer to restore the human race to its proper state. Jesus was to "pay indemnity" (suffer) to redeem mankind from spiritual death, and to restore humanity's godly bloodline. Jesus accomplished only the first phase (spiritual redemption) of this mission. He failed in the second phase (physical redemption) because he was crucified before he could marry and produce children. Therefore, another redeemer, Rev. Moon, came about two thousand years later to finish the divine mission.

- Like Jesus, Moon suffered for mankind (paid indemnity). However, he did not die violently, but lived a long life, married a perfect mate, and produced "perfect children." Together, they completed the "Four Fold Foundation" and formed the "Perfect Family" or "True Family."

Essential Beliefs

God

God is the "Universal Prime Energy" who (or that) constantly interacts with the universe in what is called the "Four Fold Foundation" (also called the "Four Position Foundation: Origin, Subject, Object, and Union") of human history.

Man

God divided His creation by making Adam (masculine) and Eve (feminine) from which would come a union producing a divine bloodline of pure perfect children. Thus, the God-Adam-Eve-child union would complete the "Four Fold Foundation" which would thereafter be reproduced through all humanity.

Before Adam and Eve could produce perfect offspring, however, the serpent (symbolic for Satan) sexually seduced Eve and produced an evil Satanic human bloodline through Cain. Later, Eve had Abel with Adam, who represents a godly line.

Salvation

The best they can get out of life is to faithfully serve the church, produce offspring, and live a long life. At death, they expect to transition to the spirit world where they will enjoy fellowship with Rev. Moon and Jesus. Eventually they will be resurrected from the dead to be part of the eternal kingdom of God.

People receive the benefits of Moon's Messiahship by joining the UC, pledging obedience to him, and entering into a marriage relationship blessed by Moon's family.

APPENDIX 4
Verses Supporting the Biblical Worldview

These verses support the paragraphs that comprise the Gospel message in **Chapter 6, Sharing an Effective Witness: The Context of the Gospel Message**, specifically **Activity 3. Explain the Scope of the Christian Worldview**, of **The Gospel Process** section of that chapter.

Creation

There Is Only One God
Deuteronomy 4:35, 39; 6:4, 32:39; 2 Samuel 7:22; 1 Kings 8:60; Isaiah 43:10–11; 44:6, 8; John 17:3; 1 Corinthians 8:4–6; 1 Timothy 2:5.

God Is Eternal
Deuteronomy 33:27, Psalm 103:17, Proverbs 8:23, Isaiah 40:28, Habakkuk 1:12, Romans 1:20, Revelation 1:8.

God Is Purposeful
Exodus 9:16, Proverbs 19:21, Isaiah 46:10, Jeremiah 29:11, Romans 8:28, Ephesians 2:10, 2 Timothy 1:8–9.

God Is a Unity and Diversity (Trinity)
Matthew 3:16–17, 28:18–20; John 14:16–17; 2 Corinthians 13:14; Galatians 4:6; Ephesians 2:18–22; Hebrews 9:14; 1 Peter 1:2.

The Father Is Deity
Genesis 1:1; 2:7; Exodus 3:14, 6:2–3, 15:11ff., 20:1ff.; Leviticus 22:2; Deuteronomy 6:4; 32:6; 1 Chronicles 29:10; Psalm 19:1–3; Isaiah 43:3,15, 64:8; Jeremiah 10:10, 17:13; Matthew 6:9ff.,

7:11, 23:9, 28:19; Mark 1:9–11; John 4:24, 5:26, 14:6–13, 17:1–8; Acts 1:7; Romans 8:14–15; 1 Corinthians 8:6; Galatians 4:6; Ephesians 4:6; Colossians 1:15; 1 Timothy 1:17; Hebrews 11:6; 12:9; 1 Peter 1:17; 1 John 5:7.

The Son Is Deity
Genesis 18:1ff.; Psalms 2:7ff.; 110:1ff.; Isaiah 7:14; Isaiah 53:1–12; Matthew 1:18–23, 3:17, 8:29, 11:27, 14:33, 16:16,27, 17:5, 27, 28:1–6,19; Mark 1:1, 3:11; Luke 1:35; 4:41, 22:70, 24:46; John 1:1–18, 29, 10:30, 38, 11:25–27, 12:44–50, 14:7–11, 16:15–16, 28, 17:1–5, 21–22, 20:1–20, 28; Acts 1:9; 2:22–24, 7:55–56, 9:4–5, 20; Romans 1:3–4, 3:23–26, 5:6–21, 8:1–3, 34; 10:4; 1 Corinthians 1:30, 2:2, 8:6, 15:1–8, 24–28; 2 Corinthians 5:19–21, 8:9; Galatians 4:4–5; Ephesians 1:20, 3:11, 4:7–10; Philippians 2:5–11; Colossians 1:13–22, 2:9; 1 Thessalonians 4:14–18; 1 Timothy 2:5–6, 3:16; Titus 2:13–14; Hebrews 1:1–3, 4:14–15, 7:14–28, 9:12–15, 24–28, 12:2, 13:8; 1 Peter 2:21–25, 3:22; 1 John 1:7–9, 3:2, 4:14–15, 5:9; 2 John 7–9; Revelation 1:13–16, 5:9–14, 12:10–11, 13:8, 19:16.

The Holy Spirit Is Deity
Genesis 1:2; Judges 14:6; Job 26:13; Psalms 51:11, 139:7ff.; Isaiah 61:1–3; Joel 2:28–32; Matthew 1:18, 3:16, 4:1, 12:28–32, 28:19; Mark 1:10, 12; Luke 1:35, 4:1, 18–19, 11:13, 12:12, 24:49; John 4:24, 14:16–17, 26, 15:26, 16:7–14, Acts 1:8, 2:1–4, 38, 4:31, 5:3, 6:3, 7:55, 8:17, 39, 10:44, 13:2, 15:28, 16:6, 19:1–6; Romans 8:9–11, 14–16, 26–27; 1 Corinthians 2:10–14, 3:16, 12:3–11, 13, Galatians 4:6; Ephesians 1:13–14, 4:30, 5:18; 1 Thessalonians 5:19; 1 Timothy 3:16; 4:1; 2 Timothy 1:14, 3:16; Hebrews 9:8, 14; 2 Peter 1:21; 1 John 4:13, 5:6–7; Revelation 1:10, 22:17.

Man Created in the Image of God
Genesis 1:26–27, 8:3–8.

Creation of the World
Genesis 1:26–27, 9:6.

Creation of Man
Genesis 2:7, 18; 21–31, 3:8–9.

Man in the Garden of Eden
Genesis 2:8–28, 3:8.

The Fall

The Fall Event
Genesis 3.

Life After the Fall
Genesis 1:28.

Consequences of the Fall
Genesis 3:16–24, Isaiah 59:2, Ezekiel 18:20, Matthew 25:31–46, Romans 5:12; 6:23, 8:18–22, Galatians 5:19–21,6:7–8; Revelation 21:8.

Redemption
Luke 1:26–38.

Justification.
Exodus 6:2–8; Matthew 1:21, 16:21–26; 27:22–28:6; Luke 1:67–69; John 1:29, 3:3–21, 36; 5:24, 10:7–9, 25–28; Acts 2:21, 4:12, 15:7–11, 16:30–31, 17:29–31; Romans 1:16–18, 3:21–24, 5:8–10, 10:9–13, 6:19–20, 15:10; 2 Corinthians 5:18–20; Galatians 2:20, 3:13; Ephesians 1:7, 2:8–22.

Sanctification
John 15:1–16, 6:1–23, 8:1–18, 13:11–14; 1 Corinthians 1:18; 2 Corinthians 5:17; Galatians 5:22–25; Ephesians 4:11–16; Philippians 2:12–13; Colossians 1:9–22, 3:1–24; 1 Thessalonians 5:23–24; Titus 2:11–14; 1 John 1:6–2:11.

Eternity

Glorification

John 3:16, Romans 8:8:17, 23, 30; 1 Corinthians 4:17, 15:42–44; Philippians 3:20–21; Colossians 3:4, 1 John 3:2, Jude 1:24–25.

Appendix 5

Verses Explaining the Gospel Message

These verses support the paragraphs that comprise the Gospel message in **Chapter 7, Sharing an Effective Witness**, subtitle: **The Content of the Gospel Message**, specifically the three essential questions in that chapter.

Who is God?

God Is a Person
Genesis 1:26–30, Exodus 3:14, 1 Samuel 17:26, Jeremiah 31:3, James 5:11.

God Is Holy
Exodus 15:11, Leviticus 19:2, 1 Samuel 2:2, Isaiah 6:3, Matthew 5:48, 1 Peter 1:14–16, 1 John 2:29, Revelation 4:8.

God Is Just
Deuteronomy 10:17–18, Psalm 50:6, Isaiah 30:18, 61:8, Colossians 3:25, Hebrews 10:30, 1 Peter 1:17–22, Revelation 19:11.

God Is Love
Deuteronomy 7:9; Psalm 86:15; John 3:16, 4:7–21; Romans 5:8, 8:37–39; Galatians 2:20, Ephesians 2:4–5, 1 John 4:7–21.

What is a Human Being?

We Are Made in God's Image
Genesis 1:26–27, 8:3–8.

We Are Fallen Creatures
Genesis 3, 9:6; Psalms 51:5; Isaiah 6:5; Romans 1:19–32, 3:3:10–18, 23, 5:12, 7:14–25; 1 Corinthians 15:21–22; Ephesians 2:1–12; Colossians 1:21.

What is Salvation?

Justification
Exodus 6:2–8; Matthew 1:21, 16:21–26, 27:22–28:6; Luke 1:26–38, 1:67–69; John 1:29, 3:3–21, 36, 5:24, 10:7–9, 25–28; Acts 2:21, 4:12, 15:7–11, 16:30–31, 17:29–31; Romans 1:16–18, 3:21–24, 5:8–10, 10:9–13, 6:19–20, 15:10; 2 Corinthians 5:18–20, Galatians 2:20, 3:13; Ephesians 1:7, 2:8–22; Philippians 2:5–8.

Sanctification
John 15:1–16, 6:1–23, 8:1–18, 13:11–14; 1 Corinthians 1:18; 2 Corinthians 5:17; Galatians 5:22–25; Ephesians 4:11–16; Philippians 2:12–13; Colossians 1:9–22, 3:1–24; 1 Thessalonians 5:23–24; Titus 2:11–14; 1 John 1:6–2:11.

Glorification
John 3:16; Romans 8:8:17, 23, 30; 1 Corinthians 4:17, 15:42–44; Philippians 3:20–21; Colossians 3:4; 1 John 3:2; Jude 1:24–25.

How does one achieve salvation?
Ephesians 2:4–10, John 1:12, Acts 2:36–39.

APPENDIX 6
Study Guide for Students and Leaders

There is no single *right* formula for group study. Each group has its own purpose, goals, time constraints, background knowledge, and study situation. Because of that, we have chosen to create a two-part Group Study Guide which includes both a Student's Guide and a Leader's Guide that is flexible enough to be used in any situation. For those who want to do a relatively short study, it is possible to gain a solid overview of the material that does not have a tremendous amount of depth. On the other hand, those who want to go deep and truly master the knowledge and skills shared in this book can take a longer approach and do that.

This eight part guide parallels the chapter divisions in the book. Using this format, participants are able to get a big-picture overview of the witnessing process based on a worldview perspective and delve as deeply into the particulars as fits their need.

If you intend to make your study as short as eight weeks for your group, you can simply follow the outline as it is presented here, addressing one Chapter per study session. As was mentioned above, it will take you through the material in the entire book and get quite a good overview, but you will probably not have the time necessary to go into any of it in depth.

If, on the other hand, your group's desire is to master the knowledge and skills in the book more fully, you will probably want to have more than one session on each chapter. So, we have annotated the study *Discussion Questions* to the subtitles of the chapters for easy reference and for the convenience of managing more than one study session per part.

Helps for the Group Leader

Regardless of the particular approach you take, we recommend that as you lead this study of *Shattering The Truth Mirage*, do all you can to make it an informal and relaxing time. All the while, particularly keep in mind that this is designed to be imminently practical. In fact, there is nothing more practical in the Christian faith than sharing the gospel message.

Obviously, there is a knowledge base that must be mastered in order for one to effectively share the faith, but there are skills that are equally important. Grasping both the knowledge and skills contained in the book will help group members to become more competent in addressing matters of the Christian faith. Furthermore, it will make them more confident in their ability to stand strong and share their faith out in the world.

Below are some ideas that can aid you as you lead the class discussions. Please feel free to use these as a jumping-off point to help group participants get the most out of this study.

Leader Preparation Before Each Session

1. Each week, read the corresponding chapter of *Shattering The Truth Mirage* once all the way through and take some observation notes.

2. Read through the corresponding session in the Leader Guide and answer each question yourself. Add to your observation notes.

3. Read the Group Leaders Notes and add further to your observation notes.

4. Use your compiled observation notes as a prompt for class discussion. Don't be concerned about getting through the entirety of your personal observations. Your job is to be a facilitator in order to encourage participants to speak what's on their hearts. By personally being well prepared, you will

be in a position to move the discussion forward in case some people get stuck. Your main job is to encourage discussion. Listen to understand, not to respond—but be ready to respond as needed.

5. Be yourself in leading the group session. Do it your way, as the Holy Spirit guides you, and allow others the same latitude as they seek God's leading in their lives.

6. Bathe everything and everyone in prayer. Pray throughout the week for every family, every group member, every session, and whatever else the Holy Spirit puts on your heart to share with the group.

Understanding the Leader Guide

It is certainly possible for the group leader to simply study each week's material and present it to the group during class. However, it is a fact that the greater the participation by the class members, the more fully they will master the material.

We recommend that each participant actually read the material that will be covered in the book BEFORE class so that they can actively participate in a discussion with the leader and the other class members.

This leader guide for *Shattering The Truth Mirage* will provide you with suggestions for leading a small group through the study. The features for each session include:

Opening

Of course, it is best to open the study session with prayer. Focus on achieving the goals of the group for this session ... to the glory of God in their application in the lives of the members and those they witness to.

Review

Each session begins with a quick recap of the previous session to help maintain continuity in the study.

Introduction

For groups that wish to cover the entire book in eight sessions, the suggested introduction can be used. However, for groups that wish to make this a longer study, it will be necessary for group leaders to create their own introductions based on the amount of material they plan to cover in a given session. The idea is to give an illustration about using the material to be studied in real life.

Discussion Questions

Each session has questions corresponding session-by-session to the material in *Shattering the Truth Mirage*. These questions are designed to encourage a vigorous discussion and dialog in order to help members not only understand the witnessing concepts more fully based on a worldview paradigm, but to also help them more deeply grasp the implications of those concepts for their faith life. To help the discussion along, the parts of the book that correspond to the questions are listed.

What Have You Learned?

Each session should end with an opportunity for participants to express what they have learned from the session, and to share how they believe this will be helpful in becoming more faithful in their witness in the world.

Advanced Witness Skills

The basic knowledge and skills necessary to share an effective witness in virtually any circumstance are explained in *Shattering the Truth Mirage*, and this study guide will walk you through that step by step. However, as with virtually any other skill, in order to become proficient, one must move beyond mere knowledge and into

321

mastery. This will, no doubt, require individuals to continue learning and growing beyond merely going through this training course.

At the end of each unit, there will be a category called, **Advanced Witness Skills**, that will specifically list what should be the focus of your mastery efforts. This is knowledge that is found in the book, but which must be studied and practiced in order for it to become second nature for use in everyday life. If you have time in the class, having individuals wrestle with these matters on a personal level with each other can be useful in helping individual members grasp a deeper understanding of the personal implications of witnessing for their lives. As was done with the discussion questions, In order to help this process along, the parts of the book that correspond to the questions are listed.

Closing

Bring the session to a close with appropriate prayers for living out the lessons of the study and any personal issues the members may have.

Group Study and Discussion Topics
Chapter by Chapter

Group Study Guide: Session Outline for

Chapter 1:
Starting with the Basics

Opening

Open with prayer. Ask God to give participants wisdom and understanding to use this material to become more knowledgeable about their own faith, and more effective in their witness to those they know who are not believers.

Review

In this first session, spend the review time having each person introduce themselves to the group. As a means of getting to know one another better, have each person share one thing others probably know about them, and one thing they likely don't know.

Sample Introduction

The first thing people do when they decide to enter a new profession is embark upon some kind of training. That opportunity may involve schooling, on-the-job training, or even self-study. The reason for the training is that it is impossible to become proficient with the necessary skills to do a given job without learning the things related to that specific task. This principle applies to virtually every area of life.

It also applies to your ability to share your faith in Christ with people who don't know Him. Anyone can share their own testimony, and in some cases that might be enough. However, in our current societal environment, a lot of people will not consider that a valid consideration as it relates to what they believe. With the massive pluralism that now exists in our society, believers who are serious

323

about sharing their faith need to intentionally prepare by using knowledge and skills that cover a broad spectrum.

Discussion Questions

1. Define the noun and verb forms of the word *witness* and distinguish between them. See subtitles:
   Starting with the Basics
   What Is Witness?
   Witness: As a Noun and as a Verb

2. Does it make a difference whether Christians conceive of their witness as an event or a process? If so, what difference does it make? See subtitle:
   Witness: Event or Process?

3. Does the Bible mandate that Christians are to share a witness for Christ? If so, in what way? See subtitle:
   The Biblical Mandate

4. What should be the motivating factors for Christians to share their faith? See subtitle:
   A Christian's Motivation To Witness

5. What is God's part in the witnessing process? See subtitle:
   God's Part of the Process

6. What is a believer's part in the witnessing process? See subtitle:
   A Believer's Part in the Process

7. What part does a non-believer play in the witnessing process? See subtitle:
   The Recipient's Part of the Process

8. How do the three actors in the witnessing process interact with each other? See subtitle:
   How These Players Fit Together

What Have You Learned?

What have you learned from the session that will help you be more effective in your witness out in the world?

Advanced Witness Skills

- Clearly understand the definition of a witness, as well as how God has mandated Christians to share their faith. Consciously spell out how God has specifically called *you* to step into that role. See subtitles:
  What is Witness
  The Biblical Mandate

- Identify what motivates you, on a personal level, to share your faith. If you struggle with being motivated to witness, figure out what specifically is causing that lack of motivation. See subtitle:
  A Christian's Motivation to Witness

- Specifically distinguish God's calling on your life regarding how and to whom you should focus your witnessing efforts. Particularly identify how event and process evangelistic efforts fit into the picture. See subtitle:
  Witness: Event or Process?

- Develop a clear and conscious understanding of your role in the witnessing process and identify what it means for you to stay within the boundaries of your role. See subtitle:
  Who are the Ones Involved In A Witness?

Closing

Close with prayer that God will motivate the participants to actively seek out opportunities to use this material as they seek to witness in their daily lives—plus any personal issues of the group's members needing prayer.

Group Study Guide: Session Outline for

Chapter 2:
Why a Knowledge of Worldview is Important for Witness

Opening

Open with prayer. Ask God to give participants wisdom and understanding to use this material to become more knowledgeable about their own faith, and more effective in their witness to those they know who are not believers.

Review

Take a few moments to allow the participants to share what they learned in last week's session that they did not know before. Have them share how they applied, or could have applied, any of the new knowledge in their life. Also, discuss its impact on their daily lives since the last session.

Sample Introduction

In 1997, thirty-nine members of a cult called Heaven's Gate committed suicide in their San Diego headquarters. These people believed alien spaceships were following behind the Hale-Bopp comet, which was visibly passing by the earth at that time. They believed that by committing ritual suicide, their consciousness would exit the human body and be captured by the alien ships. The spaceships would then take them to another world in our universe where they would live in pure bliss.

This kind of belief seems, to most people, to be a bizarre fantasy. The majority of people in our society consider people who would believe such a thing as living in "la-la land." But obviously, these people *did* believe it. They believed it to such an extent that they willingly committed suicide to make it happen.

As we look at the many different belief systems now in the world, virtually everyone looks at their own beliefs as true, and at other beliefs as fantasies. But the fact is, all of these beliefs contradict each other. It is impossible for more than one to actually be true—yet each and every one has ardent adherents.

So how do we differentiate between actual reality and fantasy? How do we analyze for truth when it comes to faith matters? The study of worldview concepts allows us to make those distinctions.

Discussion Questions

1. What is the definition of a worldview? See the chapter opening following its title:
   Why a Knowledge of Worldview is Important for Witness
   ... and the subtitle:
   What is Worldview?

2. What implications emerge from the fact that:

   - A worldview is a set of assumptions? See subtitle:
     A Worldview is a Set of Assumptions

   - A worldview is exclusive? See subtitle:
     A Worldview is Exclusive

3. What does it mean that a worldview defines reality? See subtitle:
   What is *Nature of Reality*?

4. What are the three possible origins of a worldview? See subtitle:
   Where a Worldview Comes From

5. Why does *change* make accepting a different worldview so difficult? See subtitle:
   What Makes Witnessing So Difficult?

Appendix 6

6. What are the five reasons a worldview paradigm is helpful in the witnessing process? See subtitle:
    Reasons for Using a Worldview Paradigm

What Have You Learned?

What have you learned from the session that will help you be more effective in your witness out in the world? See subtitle:
Reasons for Using a Worldview Paradigm

Advanced Witness Skills

• Make sure that you know the definition of a worldview. Clearly understand the significance of the fact that it involves deep personal assumptions about the nature of reality. See subtitle:
    What is Worldview?

• Make sure you can identify other people's worldview foundations, and how they came to hold their worldview beliefs. See subtitle:
    Where a Worldview Comes From

• When you determine to share your faith with someone, make sure you understand how to identify what kind of change that person will have to make if they invite Christ into their life. See subtitle:
    What Makes Witnessing So Difficult?

• Make sure you clearly understand the five reasons worldview concepts are important: to the point of being able to explain them. See subtitle:
    The Importance of Worldview In Witness

Closing

Close with prayer that God will motivate the participants to actively seek out opportunities to use this material as they seek to witness in their daily lives—plus any personal issues of the group's members needing prayer.

328

Group Study Guide: Session Outline for

Chapter 3:
Preparing for Witness

Opening

Open with prayer. Ask God to give participants wisdom and understanding to use this material to become more knowledgeable about their own faith, and more effective in their witness to those they know who are not believers.

Review

Take a few moments to allow the participants to share what they learned in last week's session that they did not know before. Have them share how they applied, or could have applied, any of the new knowledge in their life. Also, discuss its impact on their daily lives since the last session.

Sample Introduction

Even though it has been many years since I played football, I still vividly remember the two-a-day practices that took place every summer—beginning a couple of weeks before the beginning of school. I remember what it was like when we began hitting each other in pads after not having done so since spring training. I remember the deep muscle soreness that it brought on. I remember the days out in the hot Florida sun where the temperature reached the mid-90s on the field, and much hotter than that inside our pads. I remember my lungs burning from the wind sprints and the practice repetitions where I had to run as hard as I could down the field, then come back and do it again.

Yes, the beginning of summer practice was tough. But I also remember that after a couple of weeks of doing that every day, the muscle soreness, the sensitivity to the heat, and the burning lungs diminished as I got into great physical shape. Soon, I was not really bothered by all of those things but was ready to go against opposing teams and really play football.

What is true in football is also true when it comes to getting to where sharing an effective witness for Christ becomes second nature. In order to get to that place, it is necessary to put in effort to become proficient. But once you get there, you are in a position to share your faith at any time, and under any circumstance.

Discussion Questions

1. What is the knowledge base that a Christian must master to effectively share the gospel message? See subtitle:
   Master the Knowledge Base

2. What personal preparation must a Christian make to effectively share the gospel message? See subtitle:
   Master Yourself

3. What place does intentionality play in effectively sharing the gospel message? See subtitle:
   Witness Intentionally

4. What things must be accounted for when building a relationship for the purpose of sharing a witness? See subtitle:
   Prepare for Building a Relationship

5. Why is it important to discern a person's worldview beliefs before attempting to share the gospel with them? See subtitle:
   Gather the Person's Worldview Information

6. What specific information must a Christian gather to discern another person's worldview beliefs? See subtitle:
   Map and Analyze the Person's Worldview Beliefs

7. Why is it important to discern a person's commitment level to their beliefs before sharing a witness with them? See subtitle:
   Understand the Person's Commitment Level

What Have You Learned?

What have you learned from the session that will help you be more effective in your witness out in the world?

Advanced Witness Skills

- Be able to explain to someone else the concept of worldview. See subtitle:
    A Basic Understanding of Worldview

- Identify the resources you need to consult to learn the basic beliefs of any belief systems you might encounter. See subtitle:
    The Specific Belief Background of the Person with Whom You Want to Witness

- Be able to explain the entire scope of a Christian worldview: Creation, the Fall, Life after the Fall, Redemption, Eternity. See subtitle:
    The Scope of the Christian Worldview

- Be able to explain in detail the essentials of the Christian faith (Be able to explain the answers to the 3 essential worldview questions based on the teachings of the Bible). See subtitle:
    The Essentials of the Christian Faith

- Specifically identify people with whom you would ultimately like to share a witness. Then develop a plan to insert yourself into their life. See subtitle:
    Witness Intentionally

- Identify specific questions you need answered from an individual to understand their worldview beliefs. See subtitle:
    Map and Analyze the Person's Worldview Beliefs

- Become proficient at mapping a person's worldview beliefs. (See Appendix 2.) See subtitle:
    Mapping a Person's Worldview and Belief System

- Learn the specific weaknesses of every worldview system. See subtitle:
  ### *Analyze Worldview Weaknesses*

- Specifically learn to identify the bridge points between the Christian faith and every belief system you will encounter in your witnessing efforts. See subtitle:
  ### *Worldview Bridge Points*

Closing

Close with prayer that God will motivate the participants to actively seek out opportunities to use this material as they seek to witness in their daily lives—plus any personal issues of the group's members needing prayer.

Group Study Guide: Session Outline for

Chapter 4:
Building Bridges for Witness

Opening

Open with prayer. Ask God to give participants wisdom and understanding to use this material to become more knowledgeable about their own faith, and more effective in their witness to those they know who are not believers.

Review

Take a few moments to allow the participants to share what they learned in last week's session that they did not know before. Have them share how they applied, or could have applied, any of the new knowledge in their life. Also, discuss its impact on their daily lives since the last session.

Sample Introduction

If I want to drive my car from Tallahassee to Marianna, Florida, I have to cross the Apalachicola River. This is actually a pretty wide river, and even the land on either side of the river can be fairly swampy. In addition, when there is a lot of rain, the river overflows its banks and becomes even wider.

A lot of traffic needs to cross that river, so to solve the problem, the government built a bridge—a very long bridge. That way, cars can enter the area around the river on dry land, go over it, and get off on the other side without being stopped by the water. Without the bridge, the cars could not travel from one side of the river to the other.

A similar problem presents itself when it comes to people's beliefs. A worldview is a way to deal with reality by differentiating what is real from what is fantasy through a descriptive construct of reality. So if a person holding one worldview wants to share about their faith with someone holding a different worldview, the communication will necessarily begin in an environment where the person hearing the message considers the beliefs of the one speaking the message to be a fantasy. In order to cross that conceptual barrier, a conceptual bridge must be built.

Discussion Questions

1. What does it mean to build a worldview bridge? See subtitle:
    Worldview Bridge

2. What does it mean to build a gospel bridge? See subtitle:
    Gospel Bridge

3. Explain the starting point for a witness to a Naturalist. See subtitle:
    Naturalism

4. Explain the starting point for a witness to an Animist. See subtitle:
    Animism

5. Explain the starting point for a witness to a Far Eastern Thought believer. See subtitle:
    Far Eastern Thought

6. Explain the starting point for a witness to a Non-Christian Theist. See subtitle:
    Non-Christian Theism

7. Explain the starting point for a witness to someone who believes in a hybrid belief system. See subtitle:
    Hybrid Belief Systems

What Have You Learned?

What have you learned from the session that will help you be more effective in your witness out in the world?

Advanced Witness Skills

- Be able to define and explain the concept of a worldview bridge and a gospel bridge. See subtitle:
  Bridge Building from One Worldview to Another

- Be able to explain the weaknesses of Naturalism. See subtitle:
  Weakness of Naturalism

- Be completely conversant with the starting points for witness to a Naturalist. See subtitle:
  Starting Point for Witness to Naturalists

- Be able to explain the weaknesses of Animism. See subtitle:
  Weakness of Animism

- Be completely conversant with the starting points for witness to an Animist. See subtitle:
  Starting Point for Witness to Animists

- Be able to explain the weaknesses of the Far Eastern Thought worldview. See subtitle:
  Weakness of Far Eastern Thought

- Be completely conversant with the starting points for witness to a Far Eastern Thought believer. See subtitle:
  Starting Point for Witness to Far Eastern Thought Believers

- Be able to explain the weaknesses of Non-Christian Theism. See subtitle:
  Weakness of Non-Christian Theism

- Be completely conversant with the starting points for witness to a Non-Christian Theist. See subtitle:
  Starting Point for Witness to Non-Christian Theists

- Be able to explain the weaknesses of hybrid belief systems. See subtitle:
  Weakness of Hybrids

- Be completely conversant with the starting points for witness to a believer in a hybrid belief system. See subtitle:
  Starting Point for Witness to Hybrid Believers

Closing

Close with prayer that God will motivate the participants to actively seek out opportunities to use this material as they seek witness in their daily lives—plus any personal issues of the group's members needing prayer.

Group Study Guide: Session Outline for

Chapter 5:
The Art of Argument

Opening

Open with prayer. Ask God to give participants wisdom and understanding to use this material to become more knowledgeable about their own faith, and more effective in their witness to those they know who are not believers.

Review

Take a few moments to allow the participants to share what they learned in last week's session that they did not know before. Have them share how they applied, or could have applied, any of the new knowledge in their life. Also, discuss its impact on their daily lives since the last session.

Sample Introduction

When two armies face each other to do battle, they each go to the fight with a strategy to defeat their enemy. There are actually two different approaches an army can take as they face off. If they believe they are more powerful than the other side, they can take an offensive posture and go on the attack. If they don't believe they have enough firepower to attack, they can take a defensive posture and try to hold off the enemy. Neither one of these strategies is necessarily better than the other. There are times and situations when an offensive approach is better, and others when a defensive approach is best.

The same dichotomy is true when sharing the gospel. Both approaches have their place. But in order to be truly effective, it is necessary to be proficient in discerning which approach is most likely to succeed in actually engaging—then convincing—other people.

Appendix 6

Discussion Questions

1. What does it mean to argue offensively? See subtitle:
   Arguing on the Offensive

2. What role does relationship play in arguing offensively? See subtitle:
   Dealing with Relationships

3. What must Christians do to keep from being on the defensive in discussions about faith? See subtitle:
   How People Try to Put Christians on the Defensive

4. Why is it important to know the weaknesses of non-biblical belief systems? See subtitle:
   Problems in Non-Christian Belief Systems

5. What does human experience tell us about the truth of worldview beliefs? See subtitle:
   Problems Matching Human Experiences with Worldview Doctrines
   Table 1. Evaluating the Truth of Worldview Categories.

6. What are the five steps Christians must keep in mind when interacting with people who are antagonistic to the Christian message? See subtitle:
   Do Your Due Diligence

7. What does it mean to argue defensively? See subtitle:
   Arguing Defensively

8. What are the ten types of defensive evidence Christians need to know when sharing the gospel? See subtitle:
   Arguing Defensively

9. Why is it important to discuss the truth about reality in a witnessing situation? See subtitle:
   The Value of Argument

What Have You Learned?

What have you learned from the session that will help you be more effective in your witness out in the world?

Advanced Witness Skills

- Learn to immediately recognize when someone is attempting to put you on the defensive because of your Christian faith. See subtitle:
  How People Try to Put Christians on the Defensive

- Be proficient in turning around the arguments of those who attack the Christian faith and making them defend their own faith. See subtitle:
  How People Try to Put Christians on the Defensive

- Be conversant with every type of evidence that supports the validity of the Christian faith. See subtitle:
  Arguing Defensively

Closing

Close with prayer that God will motivate the participants to actively seek out opportunities to use this material as they seek to witness in their daily lives—plus any personal issues of the group's members needing prayer.

Group Study Guide: Session Outline for

Chapter 6:

The Context of the Gospel Message

Opening

Open with prayer. Ask God to give participants wisdom and understanding to use this material to become more knowledgeable about their own faith, and more effective in their witness to those they know who are not believers.

Review

Take a few moments to allow the participants to share what they learned in last week's session that they did not know before. Have them share how they applied, or could have applied, any of the new knowledge in their life. Also, discuss its impact on their daily lives since the last session.

Sample Introduction

I have often had opportunities to debate matters of faith with Atheists. In those discussions, it is quite usual for them to attack the Christian faith as being "unscientific." The problem is, they define unscientific as any belief that doesn't correspond to naturalistic philosophy. Based on their Atheism, they paradoxically try to make Christians prove the Christian faith using *only* the beliefs of Atheism. One way they do this is to pick out certain Bible verses and claim they contradict science.

This kind of attack has serious problems on several fronts. One of the biggest is that they pull Bible verses out of their context. In almost every case, the Bible doesn't actually say what they claim it says. Context is everything to understand Scripture.

This same principle applies when explaining the gospel to someone who is not a Christian. They need to understand the gospel message in *its* context. As such, it is essential that when sharing your faith, make sure that the listener understands the message in full.

Discussion Questions

1. What are some important matters that need to be considered when entering into a witnessing situation? See subtitle:
   Get People into the Presentation

2. What three steps must be taken to distinguish between non-Christian and Christian beliefs, and how should these be handled? See subtitle:
   Distinguish Non-Christian Belief from Christian Belief

3. Explain the five elements of the scope of the Christian worldview: Creation, The Fall, Life after the Fall, Redemption, and Eternity. See subtitle:
   Explain the Scope of the Christian Worldview

4. Why is it so important to make sure a non-believer understands the context of the Christian message? See subtitle:
   Making the Context Clear

What Have You Learned?

What have you learned from the session that will help you be more effective in your witness out in the world?

Advanced Witness Skills

Become proficient in your ability to fully explain the scope of the Christian worldview. See subtitle:
Explain the Scope of the Christian Worldview

Closing

Close with prayer that God will motivate the participants to actively seek out opportunities to use this material as they seek to witness in their daily lives—plus any personal issues of the group's members needing prayer.

Group Study Guide: Session Outline for

Chapter 7:
The Content of the Gospel Message

Opening

Open with prayer. Ask God to give participants wisdom and understanding to use this material to become more knowledgeable about their own faith, and more effective in their witness to those they know who are not believers.

Review

Take a few moments to allow the participants to share what they learned in last week's session that they did not know before. Have them share how they applied, or could have applied, any of the new knowledge in their life. Also, discuss its impact on their daily lives since the last session.

Sample Introduction

When sharing the gospel message, it is critical that what you share *is* the actual gospel message. For example, how many times have you watched a televangelist on TV preach a gospel of prosperity? Their entire message is that if you send them money, God will bless you with a financial windfall—and, if He doesn't, you just didn't have enough faith (or send enough money). Well, that is not the gospel message.

The message of the gospel is very specific. It identifies man's problem as sin and that sin separates people from God. It then explains that God provided a means for this sin problem to be resolved and tells how to obtain it. It is in receiving this message by faith that God's provision for salvation actually gets applied to an individual's life. As such, the content of the message is critical, and Christians must be able to share this information if an effective witness is ever to take place.

Discussion Questions

1. What exactly is the content of the gospel message? Discuss the three worldview questions that must be answered, along with their answers. See subtitle:
   The Content of the Gospel Message

2. How important is it to lead a person to make a decision to receive Christ? Why? Why now? See subtitle:
   Lead the Person to a Decision

3. What should the Christian do at the end of a witnessing opportunity? See subtitle:
   Follow Through

What Have You Learned?

What have you learned from the session that will help you be more effective in your witness out in the world?

Advanced Witness Skills

- Be proficient in explaining the content of the gospel message to the point of being able to lead a person to invite Christ into their life. See subtitle:
  The Content of the Gospel Message

Closing

Close with prayer that God will motivate the participants to actively seek out opportunities to use this material as they seek to witness in their daily lives—plus any personal issues of the group's members needing prayer.

Group Study Guide: Session Outline for

Chapter 8:
Witnessing in Daily Life

Opening

Open with prayer. Ask God to give participants wisdom and understanding to use this material to become more knowledgeable about their own faith, and more effective in their witness to those they know who are not believers.

Take a few moments to allow the participants to share what they learned in last week's session that they did not know before. Have them share how they applied, or could have applied, any of the new knowledge in their life. Also, discuss its impact on their daily lives since the last session.

Sample Introduction

I once had a college professor who thought he was an expert on any topic that anyone could possibly bring up. His academic specialty was sociology, but that didn't matter. If you wanted to talk about fishing, he was an expert. If you mentioned you were a plumber, he was an expert. If you told him you built a rocket, he would probably claim to be an expert on that, too. The only problem is, he was all talk and no action. By claiming to be an expert at everything, he was acknowledging the importance of these things. Yet by not actually being able to do them, he made himself out to be a hypocrite. All of his students got tired of him very quickly.

The vast majority of Christians will acknowledge that sharing a witness is an important part of the Christian faith. Sadly, most of that majority never do it—in fact, most don't even know-how.

In truth, the focus of a Christian witness should not be, "I need to witness." Rather, it should be, "I *am* a witness—how can I witness better?" When sharing one's faith is part of a believer's identity, then witness in daily life becomes an actual reality.

Discussion Questions

1. How do a society's prominent worldview beliefs affect a Christian's ability to share an effective witness? See subtitle:
   Worldview Beliefs and Witness

2. Which kind of witness is more important: verbal or visible? Why? See subtitle:
   Verbal or Silent Witness?

3. What are the pros and cons of cold call witnessing? When is it be appropriate? See subtitle:
   Cold Call Witnessing

4. What part do relationships play in sharing a witness? See subtitle:
   Relationship Witnessing

5. In what ways can Christians share a witness in a missions situation? See subtitle:
   "On Mission" Witnessing

6. Summarize the importance of understanding worldview concepts when sharing a witness. See subtitle:
   Focus on Worldview Thinking

What Have You Learned?

What have you learned from the session that will help you be more effective in your witness out in the world?

Advanced Witness Skills

- Identify specific people with whom you wish to share a witness and develop a plan for actually doing it. See Chapter 3:
   Witness Intentionally

Closing

Close with prayer that God will motivate the participants to actively seek out opportunities to use this material as they seek to witness in their daily lives—plus any personal issues of the group's members needing prayer.

Leader's Teaching Notes
Chapter by Chapter

Group Study Guide: Group Leader Notes for

Chapter 1:
Starting with the Basics

Use the **Group Study Guide: Session Outline** for this session, supplementing the *Discussion Questions* portion with these teaching points:

Discussion Questions

1. Explain the noun and verb forms of the word *witness* and distinguish between them. See subtitles:
   Starting with the Basics
   What Is Witness?
   Witness: As a Noun and as a Verb

   • The noun form refers to the person who shares the knowledge they have of some event. As it relates to Christian witness, it is a person who knows Christ and shares that knowledge.

   • The verb form refers to the act of sharing the knowledge one has of some event. In Christian parlance, it relates to the act of sharing the gospel message.

2. Does the Bible mandate that Christians are to share a witness for Christ? See subtitle:
   Witness: Event or Process?

   In what way?

   • Note the Bible verses dealing with this topic.

3. What should be the motivating factors for Christians to share their faith? See subtitle:
   The Biblical Mandate

   - The biblical mandate.

4. Does it make a difference whether Christians conceive of their witness as an event or a process? See subtitle:
   A Christian's Motivation To Witness

   If so, what difference does it make?

   - Those who conceive of their witness as an event will tend to see their witness opportunity as something that happens in a particular instance in time.

   - Those who conceive of their witness as a process will tend to focus on developing relationships and use them to express their faith over a longer time period.

5. What is God's part in the witnessing process? See subtitle:
   God's Part of the Process

   - God's part of the witnessing process is to actually change a person's life after they make a decision to receive him.

6. What is a believer's part in the witnessing process? See subtitle:
   A Believer's Part in the Process

   - The part of Christian believers in the witnessing process is to share the gospel message.

7. What part does a non-believer play in the witnessing process? See subtitle:
   The Recipient's Part of the Process

   - The part of the non-believer in the witnessing process is to make a decision about whether or not to receive Christ into their life.

8. How do the three actors in the witnessing process interact with each other? See subtitle:
   How These Players Fit Together

- God creates the life change when a person is saved.

- The believer is the messenger to share the message.

- The non-believer must personally decide to follow Christ.

Group Study Guide: Group Leader Notes for

Chapter 2:
Why a Knowledge of Worldview is Important for Witness

Use the **Group Study Guide: Session Outline** for this session, supplementing the *Discussion Questions* portion with these teaching points:

Discussion Questions

1. What is the definition of a worldview? See the chapter opening following its title:
    Why a Knowledge of Worldview is Important for Witnessing
   ... and the subtitles:
    What is Worldview?

   - A worldview is a set of assumptions people hold about the nature of reality.

2. What implications emerge from the fact that a worldview is a set of assumptions? See subtitles:
    A Worldview is a Set of Assumptions
    A worldview is Exclusive

   - As assumptions, a person's worldview is a set of beliefs. They are held by faith with no empirical proof to back them up.

3. What implications emerge from the fact that a worldview defines reality? See subtitle:
    What is *Nature of Reality*?

   - As an individual's personal definition of how reality is structured, their worldview defines for them what they accept as real and fantasy. Everyone lives life based on what they consider to be real and rejects what they consider fantasy.

4. What are the three possible origins of a worldview? See subtitle:
    Where a Worldview Comes From

    •   Circumstances: People's first worldview is derived from the beliefs of those who raised them.

    •   Crisis: Sometimes people confront different worldview beliefs that seem to make more sense than those they were raised with and this conflict provokes a change of beliefs.

    •   Choice: It is possible to study the worldview possibilities and make a conscious decision as to which one is the most reasonable.

5. Why does *change* make accepting a different worldview so difficult? See subtitle:
    What Makes Witnessing So Difficult?

    •   When a person changes their worldview, it affects every part of their personhood: mental, physiological, emotional, and spiritual. It takes effort to go against one's already established life direction in all four of these areas, which makes it difficult to change and maintain the change.

6. What are the five reasons a worldview paradigm is helpful in the witnessing process? See subtitles:
    Reasons for Using a Worldview Paradigm
    Reason #1. It Helps Us Understand Faith
    Reason #2. It Helps Us See the Objective Truth of the Gospel
    Reason #3. It Gives Us Confidence in the Truth of the Gospel
    Reason #4. It Provides an Understanding of the Beliefs of Others
    Reason #5. It Provides an Understanding of the Weaknesses of Other Faiths

Group Study Guide: Group Leader Notes for

Chapter 3:
Preparing for Witness

Use the **Group Study Guide: Session Outline** for this session, supplementing the *Discussion Questions* portion with these teaching points:

Discussion Questions

1. What is the knowledge base that a Christian must master to effectively share the gospel message? See subtitle:
    Master the Knowledge Base

    *   The essential knowledge base Christians need to master in order to effectively share the gospel message consists of: 1) a basic understanding of worldview concepts, 2) the specific belief background of the person with whom one wishes to witness, 3) the scope of the Christian worldview, and 4) the essentials of the Christian faith.

2. What personal preparation must a Christian make to effectively share the gospel message? See subtitle:
    Master Yourself

    *   Acquire a perspective that is first and foremost God centered.

    *   Create a mindset of intentionality.

    *   Make sure one's personal relationship and fellowship with God is strong.

3. What place does intentionality play in effectively sharing the gospel message? See subtitle:
    Witness Intentionally

- Intentionality provides motivation and direction for sharing a witness.

4. What things must be accounted for when building a relationship for the purpose of sharing a witness? See subtitles:
   Prepare for Building a Relationship
   Learn Their Language
   Learn Their Culture
   Learn Their Religion
   Learn Their Lifestyle

5. Why is it important to discern a person's worldview beliefs before attempting to share the gospel with them? See subtitle:
   Gather the Person's Worldview Information

   - A person's worldview expresses their beliefs about what is real and what is fantasy. Without this understanding, it is very difficult to know how to engage a person at the belief level.

6. What specific information must a Christian gather to discern another person's worldview beliefs? See subtitle:
   Map and Analyze the Person's Worldview Beliefs

   - In order to discern a person's worldview beliefs, it is important to know:

     1) what they believe about God, man, and salvation,

     2) the weaknesses associated with their belief system, and

     3) the points where it is possible to bridge the gap between your beliefs and theirs.

7. Why is it important to discern a person's commitment level to their beliefs before sharing a witness with them? See subtitle:
   Understand the Person's Commitment Level

354

- A person's commitment level will generally determine the amount of explanation that will be needed to show a person his belief's weaknesses, and the validity of the Christian faith.

Group Study Guide: Group Leader Notes for

Chapter 4:
Building Bridges for Witness

Use the **Group Study Guide: Session Outline** for this session, supplementing the *Discussion Questions* portion with these teaching points:

Discussion Questions

1. What does it mean to build a worldview bridge? See subtitle:
    Worldview Bridge

    - A worldview bridge is an explanation of the biblical worldview that is done in such a way as to make sense to a person who holds a different worldview. Building a worldview bridge is the act of making that explanation.

2. What does it mean to build a gospel bridge? See subtitle:
    Gospel Bridge

    - Building a gospel bridge involves sharing the particular elements of the gospel message that are necessary for a non-believer to understand the message.

3. Explain the starting point for a witness to a Naturalist. See subtitle:
    Naturalism

    - The starting point for a witness to a Naturalist involves two worldview bridge elements and three belief system bridge elements.

    a. Worldview Bridge Element #1: Naturalism itself is a faith position that completely lacks objective support.

    b. Worldview Bridge #2: God is an objective person.

   c. Belief System Bridge #1: The truth about God can only be known from the Bible.

   d. Belief System Bridge #2: Explain the scope of the Christian Worldview - See Chapter 6 subtitles: **Creation, the Fall, Life After the Fall, Redemption, Eternity**

   e. Belief System Bridge #3: Explain the Gospel Message - See Chapter 7 subtitles: **Who is God, What is Man, What is Salvation**

4. Explain the starting point for a witness to an Animist. See subtitle:
   Animism

- The starting point for a witness to an Animist involves two worldview bridge elements and three belief system bridge elements.

   a. Worldview Bridge #1: The Animistic position has nothing to support it.

   b. Worldview Bridge #2: There is only one God.

   c. Belief System Bridge #1: The truth about God can only be known from the Bible.

   d. Belief System Bridge #2: Explain the Christian Worldview - See Chapter 6 subtitles: **Creation, the Fall, Life After the Fall, Redemption, Eternity**

   e. Belief System Bridge #3: Explain the Gospel Message - See Chapter 7 subtitles: **Who is God, What is Man, What is Salvation**

5. Explain the starting point for a witness to a Far Eastern Thought believer. See subtitle:
   Far Eastern Thought

   - The starting point for a witness to a Far Eastern Thought believer involves two worldview bridge elements and three belief system bridge elements.

     a. Worldview Bridge #1: The Far Eastern Thought position has nothing to support it.

     b. Worldview Bridge #2: God is a personal, objective person.

     c. Belief System Bridge #1: The truth about God can only be known from the Bible.

     d. Belief System Bridge #2: Explain the Christian Worldview - See Chapter 6 subtitles:
        Creation, the Fall, Life After the Fall, Redemption, Eternity

     e. Belief System Bridge #3: Explain the Gospel Message - See Chapter 7 subtitles:
        Who is God, What is Man, What is Salvation

6. Explain the starting point for a witness to a Non-Christian Theist. See subtitle:
   Non-Christian Theism

   - The starting point for a witness to a Non-Christian Theist involves one worldview bridge element and three belief system bridge elements.

     a. Worldview Bridge #1: The truth about God can only be known from the Bible.

b. Belief System Bridge #1: The truth about God can only be known from the Bible and it is a reliable authority source.

c. Belief System Bridge #2: Explain the Christian Worldview - See Chapter 6 subtitles:
Creation, the Fall, Life After the Fall, Redemption, Eternity

d. Belief System Bridge #3: Explain the Gospel Message - See Chapter 7 subtitles:
Who is God, What is Man, What is Salvation

7. Explain the starting point for a witness to someone who believes in a hybrid belief system. See subtitle:
Hybrid Belief Systems

-   The starting point for a witness to a Non-Christian Theist involves two worldview bridge elements and three belief system bridge elements.

a. Worldview Bridge #1: Hybrid belief systems have serious problems with their authority source.

b. Worldview Bridge #2: There exists an objective, personal God who can be known.

c. Belief System Bridge #1: The truth about God can only be known from the Bible.

d. Belief System Bridge #2: Explain the Christian Worldview - See Chapter 6 subtitles:
Creation, the Fall, Life After the Fall, Redemption, Eternity

e. Belief System Bridge #3: Explain the Gospel Message - See Chapter 7 subtitles:
Who is God, What is Man, What is Salvation

Group Study Guide: Group Leader Notes for

Chapter 5:
The Art of Argument

Use the **Group Study Guide: Session Outline** for this session, supplementing the *Discussion Questions* portion with these teaching points:

Discussion Questions

1. What does it mean to argue offensively? See subtitle:
    Arguing on the Offensive

    *   Arguing offensively is the act of forcing an antagonist to justify their own worldview beliefs before being willing to accept their criticism of the Christian faith.

2. What role does relationship play in arguing offensively? See subtitle:
    Dealing with Relationships

    *   Developing a mutually respectful relationship when talking about faith matters is very important as this topic can be very sensitive. Without that kind of relationship, it is unlikely that a person will stay engaged in the conversation very long.

3. What must Christians do to keep from being on the defensive in discussions of faith? See subtitle:
    How People Try to Put Christians on the Defensive

    *   There is no reason any Christian should have to be on the defensive in faith discussions because the Christian faith represents the actual structure of reality. To avoid this, however, believers must take the time and make the effort to understand the weaknesses of the arguments of any attacker, as well as the strengths of the Christian faith.

4. Why is it important to know the weaknesses of non-biblical belief systems? See subtitle:
    Problems in Non-Christian Belief Systems

   • The weaknesses of non-biblical belief systems are places where Christians can gain an opening to share the gospel message.

5. What does human experience tell us about the truth of worldview beliefs? See subtitle:
    Problems Matching Human Experiences with Worldview Doctrines
    Table 1. Evaluating the Truth of Worldview Categories

   • When the beliefs of a particular worldview don't match up with the way human beings experience life, it is an indication that the beliefs are not true.

6. What are the five steps Christians must keep in mind when interacting with people who are antagonistic to the Christian message? See subtitle:
    Do Your Due Diligence

   • The five steps Christians should keep in mind when interacting with antagonists include:

     1. We must be able to deconstruct opposing belief systems.

     2. We must never allow people to evaluate the Christian faith based on assumptions from other worldview systems.

     3. We must learn how to hold people accountable for their attacks on our faith.

     4. We must always argue to the end, to the highest degree possible.

     5. We must never make personal attacks on our opponents.

7.   What does it mean to argue defensively? See subtitle:
     Arguing Defensively

   - Arguing defensively is the act of giving reasons why the Christian faith is true. It often involves answering the questions or objections of non-believers.

8.   What are the ten types of defensive evidence Christians need to know when sharing the gospel? See subtitle:
     Arguing Defensively

   - The ten types of defensive evidence Christians need to know when sharing the gospel include (Note: Each type represents a category of evidence, not a specific piece of evidence):

     1. Evidence for the Validity of the Bible

     2. Identity Evidence

     3. Eyewitness Evidence

     4. Corroborating Evidence

     5. Rebuttal Evidence

     6. Medical Evidence

     7. Evidence of the Missing Body

     8. The Evidence of Jesus' Post-resurrection Appearances

     9. Circumstantial Evidence

     10. Experiential Evidence

9. Why is it important to discuss the truth about reality in a witnessing situation? See subtitle:
The Value of Argument

- Discussing the truth about reality allows a person to share the gospel message: which is the Christian's understanding of the very nature of reality. See subtitle:
What is *Nature of Reality*?

Group Study Guide: Group Leader Notes for

Chapter 6:
The Context of the Gospel Message

Use the **Group Study Guide: Session Outline** for this session, supplementing the *Discussion Questions* portion with these teaching points:

Discussion Questions

1. What are some important matters that need to be considered when entering into a witnessing situation? See subtitle:
    Get People into the Presentation

    *   Matters that need to be considered when entering into a witnessing situation include: 1) discerning how to best engage the conversation, 2) distinguishing non-Christian belief from Christian belief, and 3) explaining the scope of the Christian worldview.

2. What three steps must be taken to distinguish between non-Christian and Christian beliefs, and how should these be handled? See subtitle:
    Distinguish Non-Christian Belief from Christian Belief

    *   The three steps must be taken to distinguish between Non-Christian and Christian beliefs include: 1) eliciting the other person's beliefs, 2) sharing the problems inherent in the other person's belief system, and 3) contrasting the Christian faith with their belief system.

3. Explain the five elements of the scope of the Christian worldview: Creation, The Fall, Life after the Fall, Redemption, and Eternity. See subtitle:
    Explain the Scope of the Christian Worldview

- The five elements of the scope of the Christian worldview include: (See subtitles: **Creation, the Fall, Life After the Fall, Redemption, Eternity**)

  1. Creation: The key concept in God's creation of man relates to his purpose for doing so: relationship.

  2. The Fall: The Fall represents how man became separated from God, and what that separation has caused.

  3. Life after the Fall: Life after the Fall is characterized by sin and death.

  4. Redemption: Redemption represents God's plan for restoring the brokenness that was caused by the Fall.

  5. Eternity: Eternity explains man's eternal destiny.

4. Why is it so important to make sure a non-believer understands the context of the Christian message? See subtitle:
   Making the Context Clear

- An explanation of the context of the Christian message is an account of the Christian faith based on a worldview paradigm. This explanation gives a non-believer a clear picture of what the Christian faith is all about, and how it is different from their own faith. It is this contrast that helps a person recognize the truth of biblical faith as opposed to the non-truth of their own beliefs.

Group Study Guide: Group Leader Notes for

Chapter 7:
The Content of the Gospel Message

Use the **Group Study Guide: Session Outline** for this session, supplementing the *Discussion Questions* portion with these teaching points:

Discussion Questions

1. What exactly is the content of the gospel message? Discuss the three questions that must be answered, along with their answers. See subtitle:
    Lead the Person to a Decision

*   The content of the gospel message includes:

    1. Who is God? God is the person who has revealed Himself in the Bible.

    2. What is a human being? A human being is a person created in the image of God ... but is fallen.

    3a. What is salvation? Salvation involves the redemption of sinful man and was accomplished by Jesus Christ as he became man's substitutionary atonement by his death on the cross.

    3b. How does one achieve salvation? A person achieves salvation by entering into a personal relationship with God through the finished work of Jesus Christ on the cross.

2. How important is it to lead a person to make a decision to receive Christ? See subtitle:
    Lead the Person to a Decision

Why?

- Leading a person to a decision is essential, as deciding to follow Christ is the only way a person can gain eternal life.

3. What should the Christian do at the end of a witnessing opportunity? See subtitle:
   Follow Through

- At the end of a witnessing opportunity, a Christian should continue to engage the person to help them move forward in their spiritual walk.

Group Study Guide: Group Leader Notes for

Chapter 8:
Witnessing in Daily Life

Use the **Group Study Guide: Session Outline** for this session, supplementing the *Discussion Questions* portion with these teaching points:

Discussion Questions

1. How do a society's prominent worldview beliefs affect a Christian's ability to share an effective witness? See subtitle:
    Worldview Beliefs and Witness

    *   The worldview beliefs that dominate a society set the environment within which Christians must express their faith life. A society that is receptive to the Christian faith makes it easier to share one's faith, while one that is hostile makes it more difficult.

2. Which kind of witness is more important: verbal or visible? See subtitle:
    Verbal or Silent Witness?

    Why?

    *   Each kind of witness has its place, but it must be kept in mind that at some point a person must actually hear the gospel message in order to respond to it.

3. What are the pros and cons of cold call witnessing? When is it be appropriate? See subtitle:
    Cold Call Witnessing

    *   Cold call witnessing is appropriate in situations where there is limited access to individuals.

- Cold call witnessing is less appropriate in situations where there is an opportunity for a relationship with a non-believer, as it limits the opportunity for future sharing.

4. What part do relationships play in sharing a witness? See subtitle:
   Relationship Witnessing

   - There are various reasons why a non-believer may not receive Christ quickly. Having a relationship with a non-believer provides for continued interaction about faith matters over an extended period of time.

5. In what ways can Christians share a witness in a missions situation? See subtitle:
   "On Mission" Witnessing

   - Christians should always be ready to share their faith, regardless of the situation. This preparation involves knowing a non-believer's worldview and belief system beliefs in order to know how to bridge the gap between their beliefs and the Christian faith. It also involves knowing specifically how to share the gospel message.

6. Summarize the importance of understanding worldview concepts when sharing a witness. See subtitle:
   Focus on Worldview Thinking

   - Understanding worldview concepts allows a believer to understand the beliefs of those who are not Christians, as well as the beliefs of the Christian faith. This indicates how to bridge the gap to share a faithful witness for Christ.

Authors Bios

Dr. Tal Davis is the executive vice president of MarketFaith Ministries. He spent many years in denominational work as an interfaith witness specialist. He has also served as a senior pastor and church staff member. Tal lives in Flowery Branch, GA with his wife Barbara.

Dr. Freddy Davis is the president of MarketFaith Ministries. He brings to the table many years of experience in ministry as a pastor, international missionary, church planter, teacher, radio host, and church growth consultant. Freddy lives in Tallahassee, FL with is wife Deborah.

CPSIA information can be obtained
at www.ICGtesting.com
Printed in the USA
JSHW010436160723
44694JS00001B/2